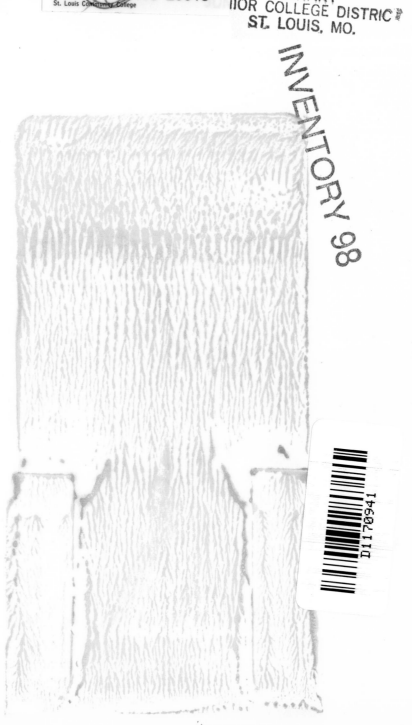

Patriotism Limited 1862-1865

Provost Marshal General James Barnet Fry
Director of the Civil War Drafts

Patriotism Limited
•1862-1865•

THE CIVIL WAR DRAFT
AND THE BOUNTY SYSTEM.

By Eugene Converse Murdock.
Marietta College

THE KENT STATE UNIVERSITY PRESS

Frontispiece from National Selective Service Headquarters,
Washington.
Library of Congress Card Catalog Number 67-64665.
Copyright © 1967 by Eugene Converse Murdock.
All rights reserved.
Manufactured in the United States of America
at the press of The Oberlin Printing Company.
Designed by Merald E. Wrolstad.
First Edition.

To the memory of the one who was my greatest inspiration,
my mother.

Preface.

When George W. Peck wrote in 1887 that he had enlisted in the Civil War not for glory but for the bounty, he was not joking.* Of course, Peck had no intention of deserting as so many bounty soldiers did, but he does remind us that many patriots did go to the war chiefly for the money. What is surprising, however, is that no historian has really shown much interest in the Civil War bounty system, when in fact it is one of the more fascinating features of that period of crisis. With the spotlight directed at so many relatively inconspicuous corners of the conflict it is not easy to understand why the drafts and the bounty system have been overlooked. But they have been overlooked, and this volume is an attempt to bring them back from oblivion.

My interest in the subject was first aroused when, as a member of the Advisory Committee of Historians of the Ohio Civil War Centennial Commission (a group created in 1960 to organize and promote a research program on Ohio Civil War history), I suggested that someone ought to dig into the problem of bounties and desertions. The idea was approved, but no one was available to undertake the job. A casual offer of my own services was accepted. The result was a sixty-page pamphlet, *Ohio's Civil War Bounty System*, published in 1963. That rather sketchy introduction only whetted my appetite.

* George W. Peck, *How Private Geo. W. Peck Put Down the Rebellion* (Chicago 1890) P.13.

vii

The bounty system flourished in all states roughly in proportion to their population: the larger the state the more complex the problem, the smaller the state the less we hear about it. Although a survey of all northern states would have been desirable, my first thought was to examine the largest state, where all aspects of the bounty system should logically appear. This assumption proved correct. Consequently, this work focuses chiefly on New York state—center of the most elaborate broker and jumper operations. But we need only change the names of a few people and places and this book could well be a review of bounty affairs in Massachusetts, Pennsylvania, or Illinois. The pattern set forth here was repeated throughout the North.

There are two lessons to be learned from this story. First, draft officials always carry heavy burdens. By the nature of things, they are unpopular, continuing targets for abuse and ridicule. It is high time a word of thanks was offered to them for their unselfish and impartial service. Second, we should recognize that a general draft, hedged with careful exclusions, is the only fair and equitable system for raising an army in wartime in a democratic state. In a moment when some young people contemptuously burn draft cards, and others seek refuge from the draft inside college walls, we need to be reminded of this simple truth.

Visits to the various public libraries in New York and in the State Library in Albany took care of the newspaper research necessary for this study. Then, in a search of the National Archives, I found the unpublished draft records which no one seems to have inspected since the days of Provost Marshal General James B. Fry. Grants from the Shell Assists Fund and Marietta College greatly facilitated this work. Also, I wish to thank Ruth Kent of the Kent State University Press for her editorial assistance and my wife, Peg, for her contributions: keeping the youngsters out of the way, and helping with galley proofs and index.

Eugene C. Murdock

Williamstown, W. Va.
May, 1967

Contents.

· 1 ·

Armies Are Hard to Raise.

I T WAS A MUGGY July morning in 1863 as Charles E. Jenkins, Provost Marshal of New York's Ninth Congressional District, resumed the draft lottery in his Manhattan headquarters at Forty-Sixth Street and Third Avenue. A sullen mob was gathering outside the building, when suddenly a shot rang out, quickly followed by a barrage of paving bricks through the windows. In a moment Jenkins and his staff were assaulted by the men inside who had been watching the drawing. Luckily, the provost marshal escaped through the rear of the building just as the mob set it afire. For an hour a frenzied crowd fought the firefighters who tried in vain to save private residences. Police Superintendent John Kennedy finally worked his way into the center of the disorders, only to be set upon and nearly beaten to death.

It was not long before New York City was out of control. Inflamed by agitators, liquor, and mob psychology, rioters took over a one hundred and twenty block area in the central and east-side districts of Manhattan. The small police force was no match for the vengeful horde of 50,000. And army units normally garrisoned in the city had been summoned two weeks before to protect the farms and fields of southern Pennsylvania from Lee's invading forces. For nearly three days the looting, lynching, and burning ran on unchecked.

Recent writers are inclined to scale down the number of people killed and the cost of the destruction, but the Draft Riots of 1863 stand out as the worst in the nation's history. The unprovoked burning of a Negro orphanage, sending 233 youngsters into the streets, is a prime example of the senseless deeds during the riots.[1]

1

What caused thousands of New Yorkers to go berserk during those July days of 1863? Did not the mass of citizens of the North fully support Lincoln's Administration and its conduct of the war effort? Were not the nation's young men willing to volunteer for army duty so freely that the War Department could not absorb them all? How then does one explain this breakdown in civil government and the triumph of anarchy?

Contrary to the generally held notion, the record shows that the Lincoln Administration did *not* have the loyal support of everyone and that a great many citizens would not serve in the army under any circumstances. By the summer of 1863 additional troops were badly needed and volunteers simply were not signing up fast enough to meet the needs. Consequently, a draft law was adopted which compelled military service from all qualified young men whose names happened to be picked in a lottery. What triggered the debacle in New York was the drawing of draftees' names, most of whom were low-income, working-class Irish. As recent immigrants, these people had little interest in the "War for the Union." Moreover, they hated Negroes as possible job competitors. One feature of the new draft law, the so-called "commutation clause," added fuel to the mounting discontent. This provision, apparently favoring the rich, permitted any draftee to exempt himself from service by paying three hundred dollars. The Draft Riots thus became a crusade against the wealthy, as well as against the Negro and the military authorities.

Yet many others besides the Irish had little use for the draft, the war, or the government. Among their number were men who were willing to volunteer, but only for the bounty money. They had no intention of serving with the army. Thomas Mahany was a typical case in point. On January 20, 1864 Mahany appeared at a recruiting office in Albany and offered to enlist, but was rejected for defective eyesight. Undeterred, he traveled on down the Hudson to Poughkeepsie, went to another recruiting office and again volunteered his services. This time the local physician was less squeamish and Mahany was accepted. That same night, with his bounty money in his pocket, Mahany escaped from the barracks and returned to Albany. Like others before him, he expected to enlist again, pocket another bounty, go to still another town and repeat the maneuver. Unfortunately for Mahany, he got drunk, was jailed, found to be a bounty-jumper from Pough- keepsie, and was consequently packed off to that town and detained as a deserter.[2]

Another type of scoundrel, little troubled by the nation's ordeal and quite anxious to improve his own financial situation, was the bounty broker. Brokers were middlemen who capitalized on the ignorance and gullibility of young volunteers by arranging for their enlistment and then exacting a large fee for the favor. Threats, deception, kid- napping and even murder were not infrequently employed by the broker in his mad thirst to "put men in." Poor Daniel Lawrence was an example. Lawrence was a seaman on shore leave in New York late in February 1865. One night he entered a Hester Street saloon only to be accosted by a gang of brokers who wanted to enlist him. When Lawrence refused, the brokers assailed him with fists, feet, and knives and finally dumped him, semi-conscious and carved to the bone, into the street. Lawrence was eventually taken to a hospital, where he died. The examining surgeon found seventeen stab wounds in the vic- tim's head, chest, and arms.[3]

It is customary to assert that the Civil War sparked a spirited up- surge in patriotic sentiment, both North and South. It was a moment when each section, certain its fundamental beliefs were in jeopardy, called upon its people for help. But they did not need to call; citizens by the thousands rallied to the colors, while thousands more minded the store at home and supplied the wherewithal for war. Admittedly there were those who volunteered only for money, or paid to avoid service, or evaded the draft, or deserted, but they are seldom dis- cussed at length in the many books about the Civil War. According to popular legend, the vast majority of people poured out their blood, time, and money, without hesitation or any thought of reward when the two great causes clashed.

This description is by no means inaccurate, but the Civil War years were, nonetheless, an era of very limited patriotism. The organized disloyalty of the Copperheads was a problem, of course, but equally troublesome was the unorganized, non-political opposition of the indi- vidual who was either unconcerned with the war, or who exploited

the abnormal times and circumstances for his own advantage. The
many histories of the period have played down or ignored the Thomas
Mahanys, the rioters, and the men who murdered the David Law-
rences.

In 1863, 20 per cent of the population of the North was concentrated in New York State. New York supplied more men for the Army,
accounted for more bounty money, and was the center of operations
for more bounty-jumpers and bounty brokers than the other Union
states combined. The limited patriotism of the Civil War was not
confined to any one state, but it was particularly apparent in New
York because of its size. For that reason a study of the bounty system
in New York State will afford a useful insight into the system's general
workings.

But why was conscription necessary in the Civil War? A quick survey of earlier recruitment systems will show why. In the days of absolute monarchy prior to the American Revolution the soldier had
been a professional, a mercenary. He was hired by the king to help
the latter acquire territory and spoils, and he fought against other
mercenaries. In the War for Independence, however, this changed
because now the masses of the people—American people—were ar-
rayed against "the King's men." All citizens had a stake in the fortunes
of the new democratic state whose army necessarily had to be raised
from among the people themselves. The permanent standing army
idea was rejected because it smacked too much of King George III's
mercenaries, and was viewed as an instrument of tyranny. Consequently, the Americans in their early years of independence, came to
rely upon a citizens army of militia, which would be called to the
colors only when danger threatened.[4]

But shortcomings in the militia system were soon apparent and it
had to be abandoned. The selection of officers by popular election
was not conducive to good discipline, the short terms of service did
not permit proper training, and the refusal of the troops in several
states to serve outside their own borders were the major weaknesses.
Hence in the first half of the nineteenth century the militia method
of recruitment was supplanted by the volunteer system.[5] The change
in emphasis over the years becomes obvious by comparing the War

of 1812, when 88% of the military force was militia, to the Mexican War when the balance had shifted heavily to the side of volunteers. But just as the drawbacks of the militia were too many for its survival, so too, the volunteer system developed its own set of flaws.[6] Not the least of these was the relatively small number of men who would volunteer.

Lincoln's calls for volunteers throughout 1861 resulted in a mammoth enlistment of 700,000 men. This was such an impressive showing that by early spring, 1862, Secretary of War Stanton actually ordered all recruiting offices closed! Yet within two months, another call for troops went out when it became apparent, following General McClellan's failures, that no easy victory was in sight. It was now recognized that the previous year's enlistment of 700,000 represented the full, hard core of patriotic citizenry. Response to Lincoln's July 2, 1862 call was so feeble that in two weeks' time Congress was compelled to pass a new law drafting men for military service.[7]

Not only had the limits of patriotism been reached within the volunteer system, but other factors inhibited further recruitment. It began to look like a long, wearying war. The summer and fall crops had to be tended. Forthcoming fall elections brought anti-Administration feelings into the open. Arbitrary arrests and the preliminary Emancipation Proclamation further strengthened opposition. And finally, a growing war boom gave pause to the potential volunteer who asked himself why he should go to war and be killed when he could stay home and be rich?[8]

Conscription, unpopular as it might be, was the answer. Attracting little attention in the Federal Period, conscription was seriously considered for the first time—though not adopted—in the last year of the War of 1812. It was bitterly attacked then as "Napoleonic," a symbol of dictatorial rule. When it finally reached the form of law in 1862, Washington hedged on the necessary controls for fear of this inherited antagonism. Fred Albert Shannon, in his *Organization and Administration of the Union Army, 1861-1865*, makes clear that the states rights feelings were so strong in the North that the federal government was reluctant to assert any initiative in the raising of troops.[9]

In addition to the notion that the draft was "Napoleonic" was the related belief that a citizen had no constitutional obligation to defend his country in time of need. If he wanted to defend it that was fine and praiseworthy, but he should not be compelled to do so. State loyalties were strong (in the North as well as the South), and nationalism, as Americans understand it today, was not a fully-developed concept. Long years of myth-making about the wickedness of conscription left little room for discussion; it was merely assumed to be undemocratic and therefore un-American.

—The first draft act in American history was signed by Lincoln on July 17, 1862. It was by no means a comprehensive draft law, for out of deference to the various local sensibilities it permitted state control and sought to revive, for one final time, the antiquated militia machinery. By its terms the President might call the militia—all able-bodied males between 18 and 45—into service for a period of up to nine months, and assign quotas to all the states. If the militia structure in a particular state was in good working order, which was rarely the case, the governor probably could raise his quota by calling for volunteers under the existing state law. But where the state system was defunct the President was empowered to prescribe rules and regulations for the enrolment and raising of the required troops. On August 4, 1862 Lincoln issued a call for 300,000 nine-month militiamen and five days later the War Department published detailed orders on how the enrolment and draft should be handled.[10]

— Although the militia draft was first set for August 15, so many delays developed that some states were still drafting in late November. Enrolment resistance, exemption hearings, and the desire of many governors for more time to fill their quotas with volunteers—by which they might avoid the "dreaded draft"—caused an avalanche of appeals to descend on Washington. The War Department usually acceded to such requests, as long as the governor guaranteed that the quota would be met by a certain date. Several states got their drafts underway by mid-September, but it was not until November 10 that it was finally ordered in Wisconsin. Violent resistance to the enrolment and the draft occurred in Maryland, Pennsylvania, Illinois, Indiana, Ohio and Wisconsin, and was an important reason for the delay in those states. On September 24, 1862, Lincoln was compelled to suspend the privilege of the writ of habeas corpus in cases involving draft re-sisters.[11]

The results of militia drafting left much to be desired. Shannon called it "a failure" as a direct means of raising an army. By rough estimates the draft raised from 60,000 to 70,000 men out of quotas of 335,000. As a stimulus to recruiting, however, the draft worked well, because for the July 2 and August 4 calls, 300,000 three-year volunteers, and 300,000 nine-month militiamen were eventually raised, and only 12 states, mostly in the East, were compelled to draft.[12]

But by the winter of 1862-63 it was recognized that a general conscription plan, under federal authority, was the only method left to furnish the troops needed to carry on the war. The defeats of the summer, winter, and spring—Second Bull Run, Fredericksburg, Vicksburg, and Chancellorsville—focussed attention on this need and caused Congress, the Administration, and the military leaders to think more in terms of general conscription. And since the state governors had administered the militia draft badly, the new law had to be firmly under the control of the federal government. Upton noted that the militia draft had at least instructed the government what should not be done and re-directed its thinking into more appropriate channels.[13]

On February 9, 1863, Senator Henry Wilson, Republican of Massachusetts and Chairman of the Committee on Military Affairs, introduced into the upper house a measure for "enrolling and calling out the national forces." Debate on the bill occupied only one day, February 16, as the Republicans, in full command, pushed it through with little interference. More opposition developed in the House of Representatives, where the bill was considered from February 23 through February 25, but the Republican leadership was in control there, too, and by a party vote the measure was approved with amendments, 115-49. On February 28 the Senate accepted the House changes, and Lincoln signed the bill on March 3, 1863.[14]

For administrative convenience the Enrolment Act subdivided each state into districts, which were coterminous with congressional districts and sometimes labeled "provost marshal districts." Each provost marshal district was to be governed by a three-man "enrolment board" appointed by the Federal Government, and chairmaned by a "provost

marshal" with "rank, pay, and emoluments of a captain of cavalry."
Provost marshals were generally army officers, although occasionally
they were recruited from civilian ranks. A second member of the
board must be a "licensed and practicing physician and surgeon,"
while the third member, the "commissioner," needed no particular
qualifications. This board was responsible for enrolment, conducting
the draft, determining exemptions, mustering draftees into service,
and tracking down draft evaders. The provost marshal was also empowered to enlist volunteers in advance of a draft. Their total number
was to be credited against a district's quota. In addition to these
duties the provost marshal was responsible for the apprehension and
arrest of deserters and spies in his district. This provision was strongly
criticized later because it had the effect of confusing draftees and
deserters in the public mind.[15]

At the apex of the draft structure was the Provost Marshal General,
who ruled a separate bureau in the War Department. It was the duty
of the Provost Marshal General to prepare and issue regulations for
the conduct of the draft, keep a close watch on its progress, advise
the President and Secretary of War on matters related to it, maintain
a complete record of draft statistics, and keep an account of all financial income and outgo. On March 17, 1863, Colonel James Barnet Fry,[16]
who had served under McDowell at First Bull Run and then in the
West in 1862, was appointed Provost Marshal General, a post he held
until the office was abolished after the war. Although the Provost
Marshal General was the frequent target of mayors, governors, and
local recruiting committees for alleged quota discriminations, Fry
proved an able, honest, and hard-working administrator, who has
never received proper recognition.

The Enrolment Act made no provisions for any state provost marshals; hence the chain of command went directly from the Provost
Marshal General to the 178 district provost marshals. Readily grasping
the inconvenience of this arrangement, Fry in April, named a provost
marshal for each state, designating such person as an Acting Assistant
Provost Marshal General (hereafter abbreviated to AAPMG). Because
of its size, New York was split into three divisions, with headquarters
in New York City, Albany, and Elmira, and one AAPMG was assigned

to each office. The functions of these officials were "to superintend the operations of the district provost marshals and other subordinates of the bureau and conduct the intercourse necessary with the state authorities."[17]

The law stated that all males between 20 and 45 were to be enrolled in two classes. Class One included single men from 20 to 45 and married men from 20 to 35, while Class Two included married men from 35 to 45. Class Two was not to be called out until the list of names in Class One was exhausted. A draftee might claim exemption for a number of reasons, but the principal source of exemption was physical disability. Considerable confusion arose over the question of what precisely constituted "physical disability." Mental disability was easier to establish than physical disability, so there was not much of a problem there, but alienage and financial stringency—the other main causes for exemption—were both conducive to fraud. People may have lived in their communities as patriotic Americans for twenty years, when suddenly, it came to light that they had been "German citizens all the time." Also, draftees who were the principal financial support for their parents were eligible for exemption, but here too deception was widely practiced.

In its desire for public approval, the Congress inserted many provisions in the law to soften the harsh fact of conscription, but invariably these provisions only led to abuse. The two most notorious features of the act provided that a draftee might avoid service by either furnishing a substitute or, as previously stated, by paying a three hundred dollar commutation fee. Substitution was not condemned as much as commutation, although there were many critics who argued that every draftee who was physically able should serve. But the central object of laboring class scorn was the opportunity afforded a draftee to pay $300 and exempt himself from service. Since three hundred dollars was close to a year's wages for the average workingman, it was claimed that this provision practically excluded that class from buying its way out, while wealthy people could pay the amount without blinking.[18]

The purpose of substitution was to allow those who were in essential industrial or agricultural employment to remain at their jobs and thus

promote the war effort. But in fact, the law made a farce of the theory
of substitution. Anyone who had the resources and desire to furnish a
substitute could do so without reference to the importance of his
labor.[19] Commutation, on the other hand, had two objectives: first,
the three hundred dollar fee would hopefully keep the price of substitutes down. No one in his right mind, it was reasoned, was going to
pay six hundred dollars for a substitute when he could commute for
three hundred dollars. Second, it was thought that the money raised
by the commutation fee could help pay federal bounties. The general
public, however, was unimpressed by these explanations, and a violent outcry against both substitution and commutation burst forth as
soon as the law passed.[20]

The thinking behind the Enrolment Act was that it should encourage volunteering rather than raise men directly by the draft. Under
its provisions, whenever the President issued a call for troops, all enrolled men would become liable for the draft. The call would be accompanied by quota assignments, and only if a district failed to meet
its quota in the specified time would the draft be ordered. Hence, out
of deference to the popular horror of the draft, a community was
given every opportunity to avoid it by filling its quota with volunteers.

In the history of the Enrolment Act four drafts were held, the first
in the summer of 1863. Troops were needed so badly then that orders
went out from the Provost Marshal General for the draft to begin
whenever the enrolment was completed. Districts were told to draft
20 per cent of the enrolled membership at once. In contrast to the
three later drafts, it should therefore be noted, the first draft was more
concerned with putting men right into service than with spurring enlistments. Rhode Island, on July 7, was the first state to hold the draft,
which eventually took place in eleven other states and the District
of Columbia throughout July, August, September, and October. Because a number of western states had supplied a surplus of volunteers
under earlier calls, they escaped the 1863 draft.[21]

The first draft could hardly be called a success; of the 292,441 names
drawn only 9,881 were held to service, while 26,002 furnished substitutes. The total of 35,883 men was not likely to fill the manpower gaps

created at Gettysburg and elsewhere. Even more startling was the fact that 52,288 other men who were accepted for service paid the commutation fee. Men were needed, not money, yet almost three-fifths of those accepted chose to evade service by this monetary escape route. "The large proportion of exemptions," wrote Fry, "defeated . . . the object of the law." Almost as shocking was the news that 164,395 more men were exempted for physical and other reasons.[22]

Demands for troops poured into Washington from field command- ers in such a torrent in the late summer of 1863 that on October 17 the President issued another call for 300,000 men. Districts not meeting their quotas by January 5, 1864 would "be drafted."[23] As January 5 approached, and with governors and recruiting committees beseech- ing Washington for more time, the deadline was set ahead into Feb- ruary. But before it was reached, Lincoln, under the prodding of Fry and Stanton, appealed for 200,000 more men. However, with the heavy spring campaigns of Grant and Sherman shaping up even this was found to be insufficient, and on March 14 the President called for still another 200,000, bringing the grand total for the three calls to 700,000. The quota deadline was moved up again to April 15, but no further postponements were to be granted. The second of the four drafts began, therefore, in April 1864 and was completed by early July.[24]

The second draft produced even fewer men than the 1863 draft. The names of 113,446 men were drawn in twelve states, but only 3,416 were personally held, while 8,911 furnished substitutes. Nearly three-fourths of those accepted, 32,678, paid commutation money, and 39,952 were exempted.[25] However, in this instance the draft figures did not tell the real story because of the high rate of volunteer- ing to avoid the draft. After all reductions for previous credits had been computed, the total number of troops required under the three calls was only 407,092, while 489,462 volunteers actually entered the ranks before the draft. The reason the draft was held, even though more troops were recruited than were required, was the unequal pat- tern of volunteering; a number of states were well over their quotas, yet others were still deficient, and it was in the latter states that men were drafted.[26]

Despite this fairly good showing, it was not good enough. When reports of Grant's heavy losses in Virginia got back to Washington, some influential people wanted the General's neck, but Lincoln supported him and wearily prepared for the next call. On July 18, 1864, the President appealed for 500,000 men and set the quota deadline fifty days hence, September 5.[27] But the number of volunteers who enlisted under the stimulus of this third draft was much lower than the number procured under the second. Only 188,172 men volunteered from the date of the call in mid-July until the draft commenced. Clearly the reservoir of able-bodied males was running dry.

Because of this poor showing we should not be surprised that only three states—Massachusetts, Rhode Island, and Kansas—plus those on the West Coast filled their quotas with volunteers. Of the 231,918 men drawn in September, October, and November 1864, 56,005 were accepted, of which 26,205 went into service, 28,502 furnished substitutes, and 1,298 commuted. The sharp drop in commutation resulted from the repeal of that controversial provision, except as it applied to conscientious objectors, in July 1864. In addition to these figures, 29,584 enrolled men supplied substitutes before the draft, which brought the grand total of troops raised directly by the third draft to 85,589.[28]

The third draft obtained only one-half the men—about 250,000 volunteers and draftees—called for in Lincoln's July 18 proclamation. Hence another call for troops was anticipated, and on December 19 it was issued. Even though the Confederacy was now beginning to crack, Lincoln requested 300,000 men to finish up the job, and set February 15, 1865 as the quota deadline.[29] The usual pleas for postponements were filed, and consequently the fourth draft did not begin until March, and was still in progress when the war ended. 157,058 volunteers and 12,997 substitutes furnished by enrolled men were procured before the draft commenced, while 139,024 names were drawn in the draft itself, which embraced all states except Connecticut, Massachusetts, Rhode Island, and those in the Far West. Of this number, 6,845 were held to service, 10,192 furnished substitutes, 460 commuted, and 28,631 were exempt.[30] The following table summarizes the foregoing statistics for the four drafts.[31]

TOTAL DRAFT STATISTICS (ALL STATES)

Call	Drawn	Did Not Report†	Examined†	Exempted	Held to Service	Commuted	Furnished Subs	Drafted	Troop Needs
Summer, 1863	292,441	39,415	252,566	164,395	88,171	52,288	26,002	9,881	To replace losses of Fredericksburg, Chancellorsville, and Gettysburg.
Spring, 1864	113,446	27,193	84,957	39,952	45,005	32,678	8,911	3,416	For spring offensive.
Fall, 1864	231,918	66,159	138,536	82,531	56,005	1,298	28,502	26,205	To replace losses of Wilderness, Spottsylvania, Cold Harbor.
Spring, 1865	139,024	28,477	46,128	28,631	17,497	460	10,192	6,845	To finish the job.
Totals	776,829	161,244	522,187	315,509	206,678	86,724	73,607	46,347	

Source: PMG, *Final Report*, I, pp. 175, 185, 199, 212.

† Logically, the totals in columns 2 and 3 should equal the figures in column 1. However, in each draft some people whose names were drawn and who reported, were discharged for technical reasons before being examined. In the first draft this number was 460, in the second 1,296, in the third 27,223, and in the fourth 64,419, for a total of 93,398. Fry gives no full explanation of why these men were discharged other than to write, "Discharged, quota full", or "Discharged, per order."

The Enrolment Act was amended three times, in February and July 1864, and in March 1865. In the winter of 1863-64 several attempts were made in Congress to repeal the commutation clause, and although they were unsuccessful it appeared that the clause was doomed. However, an amendatory law was approved and signed by Lincoln on February 24, 1864, which contained minor changes in the original law. Substitutes could now be secured only from exempt classes, say boys under 20 and men over 45, and the two classes of enrolled men were merged into one. While commutation was retained, those paying commutation money exempted themselves for the period of that particular draft only; if a future draft was ordered those who had commuted during the previous draft would again be eligible. This change, however, was more objectionable than the original clause, because it was felt that rich people could commute over and over again, but poor people might be able to pay the fee only once.[32]

Opposition to the commutation clause continued throughout the spring of 1864, and Fry himself, in a note to Stanton in early June, urged its repeal. Congress already had such a proposal under consideration and repeal legislation moved along with reasonable speed in June. Opponents of repeal argued that without the commutation clause substitute prices would skyrocket, but the bill went through and was signed by Lincoln on July 4. The major features of the law provided for (1) repeal of commutation except for conscientious objectors, and (2) optional enlistment of volunteers for one, two, or three years. The repeal did open the door to soaring substitute prices in the last nine months of the war, while the optional enlistment clause led to untold confusion in allotting quotas and fixing bounties.[33]

The final amendment to the act was signed by the President on March 3, 1865, but was in operation for only a brief period before the war ended. This revision dealt with a number of minor matters such as regimental organization, federal bounties, and quota computations. However, it did consider one of the major problems with which this volume is concerned—the bounty broker. By the spring of 1865 the criminal activities of brokers had become so notorious that public opinion demanded regulation. Consequently, almost one-third of the measure was devoted to putting brokers out of business.[34]

At the convenient distance of one hundred years it is easy to criticize the Enrolment Act and ridicule what appear to later generations to be undemocratic, unwise, and fraud-provoking provisions. Obviously, had all the abuses which developed been anticipated, the Enrolment Act would have been framed far differently. But experience is a master teacher. The provost marshals, AAPMG's, and the Provost Marshal General of 1863-65 all implored posterity to mobilize its armies, in time of crisis, by unrestricted conscription. The directors of the Selective Service Systems in World Wars I and II, Generals Enoch H. Crowder and Lewis B. Hershey, learned much from the misfortunes of General Fry, and never again were we to experience the problems and injustices of commutation, substitution, and bounties.[35]

· 2 ·

The Bounty System.

*F*EWER THAN 50,000 MEN were drafted into the Union Army during the Civil War, hardly an impressive figure. However, the purpose of the Enrolment Act—to stimulate voluntary enlistments—was attained. But the threat of conscription was not in itself sufficient to procure the one million and more men who volunteered in the war's last two years. The "love-of-country" boys of 1861-62 had now given way to those who had to be bribed with bounties before they would enlist. These "love-of-money" volunteers brought the Civil War bounty system to full bloom.

The bounty system was not new to the American scene, for it had first appeared in the early months of the American Revolution. Since the Continental Congress had no coercive power over the states, General Washington frequently recommended that bounties be offered to volunteers, and in every year of the war, several bounty laws were adopted. In June 1776, for example, the Continental Congress approved a ten dollar bounty for three-year volunteers, and this was doubled in September. Bounties increased as the war progressed, and grants of clothing and land were coupled with cash payments. In January 1779, the Continental Congress, in addition to earlier gifts of land and clothing, voted a two hundred dollar bounty to those who would enlist or reenlist for the duration. The figures on cash bounties are deceptive, however, because of the rapid depreciation of the Continental currency.[1]

But bounties authorized by the Continental Congress paled beside those offered by the states. In 1777 Massachusetts and New Hamp-

16

shire granted sixty-six dollars to their volunteers, while two years later New Jersey gave two hundred and fifty dollars, clothing and land, and Virginia gave seven hundred and fifty dollars, an annual suit of clothes, and one hundred acres of land. New Jersey bounties in 1780 went over one thousand dollars, in addition to all Continental Congress allowances. The high state bounties, in contrast to the modest Continental Congress bounties, created many problems, just as the high local bounties later hampered regular recruiting in the Civil War. As Upton observes,

> ... [they] put a stop to reenlistments in the old regiments, as the men naturally went home to secure the State bounty, and would not take the smaller sum offered by Congress. Further than this, the large State bounties shook the allegiance of the soldier to his colors. Desertions became ... numerous.

So even "bounty-jumping" had its roots in the Revolution and, as in the Civil War, was an outgrowth of the bounty rivalries between communities, states, and the national government.[2]

Although a small bounty was authorized in 1791 for regular enlistees, it was not until the War of 1812 that high bounties reappeared. In December 1811, before the war broke out, $16.00 bounties were offered to all five-year volunteers, who, upon their honorable discharge, were also to receive one hundred and sixty acres of land and three months' mustering-out pay. The bounty was increased several times during the war, until by the law of January 27, 1814, $124 was given to all five-year enlistees. Under this statute, $2,012,439.33 in bounty money was paid out in the first ten months of 1814. The land bounty of one hundred and sixty acres was doubled in December 1814, so that all bounty soldiers received three hundred and twenty acres upon their honorable discharge. Upton says little about state bounties in the War of 1812, but points out that the failure of recruiting in the war was ". . . due to that feature of our system which, by tolerating two kinds of troops, encourages citizens and townships to offer greater bounties to the militia than the Government is willing or able to pay to recruits for the Regular Army."[3]

Bounties also were paid to recruits in the Mexican War. Recruiting proceeded slowly in 1846, so Secretary of War William L. Marcy, in his annual report, suggested that, ". . . a small pecuniary bounty given at the time of enlistment, or land at the end of the term of service, would . . . have a most beneficial effect." Following Marcy's advice, Congress passed three bounty laws in the first three months of 1847. In January, volunteers were granted a twelve dollar bounty, six dollars of which was paid at the time of enlistment, the remainder when the man reached his regiment. The ninth section of the law of February 11 granted to all twelve-month volunteers, upon their honorable discharge, one hundred and sixty acres in land or the equivalent of one hundred dollars in Treasury scrip. Those volunteering for less than twelve months would receive forty acres or twenty-five dollars in scrip. On March 3, 1847 Congress voted a twelve dollar bounty to veterans who would reenlist. State and local bounties apparently played an insignificant role in Mexican War recruitment.[4]

When the "love-of-country" boys volunteered by the thousands at the outbreak of the Civil War, city councils, private corporations, and individuals contributed large sums of money for the families of the new recruits. While it is unlikely that many cities could match the Philadelphia council's appropriation of one million dollars in soldier family relief, liberal gifts were readily forthcoming in all parts of the North. Occasionally money was appropriated for direct bounty payments to soldiers, but more frequently the opulence of 1861 was reflected in family benefits. It was in the summer and fall of 1862, following the failure of the Peninsular Campaign and the disappearance of the "love-of-country" volunteer that the "mercenary" system, as Shannon calls it, moved out of low gear. With the Militia Draft, the bounty system proliferated, and it was not long before its many evil attributes had thoroughly corrupted the recruiting process.[5]

All three levels of government—federal, state, and local—paid bounties, and in addition to these sources, private individuals and groups also contributed to bounty funds. These bounties were by no means mutually exclusive. Conceivably, a money-minded recruit could receive all four bounties at the same time. A federal bounty was paid all volunteers—but not substitutes—throughout the entire war. Many states also paid a bounty, although this was not a universal practice.

New York, for example, provided a state bounty from 1862 on, while Ohio and Iowa, among other states, never offered any. All cities and towns, in their mad desire to fill quotas, paid local bounties, and it was here that trouble developed. Also, in many communities, private individuals contributed to war bounty funds, or while attending a quota-raising rally, offered a sum of money or gift on the spot to anyone who would enlist. At a Cleveland meeting in 1862, one man announced emotionally that he was giving his gold watch to the first volunteer.[6]

The federal bounty system was launched in May, 1861 when the War Department offered one hundred dollars to all three-year volunteers or regulars. Two years later reenlisting veterans were given three hundred dollars more, while in October 1863 this additional three hundred dollars was made available to new recruits as well. The three hundred dollar bonus was abandoned in April 1864, and until July of that year the federal bounty dropped back to one hundred dollars. Under the July 19, 1864 amendment to the Enrolment Act, the three hundred dollar federal bounty was restored, with a slight alteration. Sums of one hundred, two hundred, and three hundred dollars were allotted to recruits enlisting for one, two or three years respectively. Negro volunteers received a flat ten dollar bounty. Although national bounties never rivaled the high local bounties of 1864-65, the total federal outlay in bounties during the war was $300,223,500.[7]

The first state bounty in New York was authorized by Governor Edward Morgan on his own initiative in July, 1862, during his last year in office. Although this was a legislative matter, the assembly was not then in session, and Morgan, his comptroller, and other state officials felt that a further inducement was needed to get the men under the President's latest call. The bounty, for fifty dollars, was legitimized by the legislature February 21, 1863. Two months later, a second state bounty law was passed. Recruits who enlisted for a full three-year period were to receive seventy-five dollars, providing that half of the money went to dependents. Those who reenlisted received more: fifty dollars for a one-year reenlistment, and one hundred and fifty dollars for a two-year hitch. This law was in effect for two years, until the comprehensive New York State bounty law of February 10,

1865 replaced it. By the latter measure, state bounties under the December 19 call were fixed at two hundred and fifty, three hundred, four hundred, and six hundred dollars for draftees, one-year, two-year, and three-year volunteers respectively.[8]

The evils of the bounty system were not due to federal or state bounties where all men received fixed, uniform amounts but rather to local bounties where nothing was fixed or uniform. At first, the federal bounty was paid upon honorable discharge, and later in installments, with only a portion given to the recruit at the time of enlistment. Hence there was little incentive to desert or jump the bounty. However, the local bounties, paid in advance, were designed to promote heavy enlistments. The local districts, hastening to fill their quotas, disregarded the obvious danger in giving large amounts of money to recruits who had not yet performed a day of military service. As the provost marshal of New York's 20th District, Fred K. Emerson, wrote in his final report, "It is not the way a shrewd businessman would conduct his own business to pay a man before he does his work."[9] Consequently, while the local bounty system may have succeeded in filling quotas, it did not always procure good soldiers.

A preview of things to come was provided in the fall of 1862 during the Militia Draft. Quotas were assigned to states and districts, and as the deadline approached and quotas were unfilled, appeals went out for bounty funds to attract volunteers. Although no official statistics were kept of local bounties prior to 1863, Shannon is no doubt correct when he estimates that the Rhode Island towns, which offered volunteers three hundred and fifty dollars, led the 1862 bounty parade. Not all districts were so liberal, as for example, the Fourth Ward in Syracuse, which offered a small twenty-five dollar bounty. While that draft was in progress, prices demanded by substitutes rose swiftly. Thaddeus Stevens told of fifteen hundred dollar substitutes in sections of Pennsylvania.[10]

The bounty broker and the bounty-jumper appeared during the Militia Draft, but these practitioners were merely rehearsing for the incredibly affluent days ahead. Bounty-jumpers would shop around, frequently in groups, enlist in high bounty areas, desert at the first opportunity, and enlist somewhere else under assumed names. Despite a few concerted efforts to prevent these demoralizing practices, bounty-jumpers were highly successful in passing themselves off as bona fide soldiers-to-be to desperate, quota-conscious recruiting committees. Brokers were an even more unscrupulous lot than jumpers. Although they were entirely unnecessary in the recruiting process, they made a place for themselves, and acquired thousands of dollars in arranging for the enlistments of either innocent recruits or conniving bounty-jumpers.

In New York, the Draft Riots of July 1863 sent a wave of apprehension across the state. Demands to have the draft suspended filled the air. Little thought was given at this moment to the need for fighting troops, and consequently the possibility of offering local bounties to those who might volunteer and thus fill the quota was ignored. When the authorities refused to suspend the draft, however, the idea of paying commutation money or furnishing substitutes for every draftee in the district caught on. Fear of trouble so infected city councils and county supervisors that they cheerfully ran their locality's indebtedness into the millions just to placate rioting draftees. New York City led the way with a "draft exemption ordinance" and other cities quickly followed. After the first draft was over, the mass exemption mania died out and communities resorted to paying bounties to volunteers during the last three drafts.[11]

New York's exemption ordinance, introduced on July 15, 1863, at the height of the riots, proposed to appropriate $2,500,000 to pay the commutation fee of all draftees. A few days later the Albany Council appropriated several hundred thousand dollars to pay each draftee three hundred dollars. The Brooklyn city fathers, after first considering a proposal to pay the commutation fee for the entire quota of 4,500 men, decided also to give three hundred dollars to each draftee to use as he wished: for commutation, to furnish a substitute, to leave with his family, or to keep for himself in the event he chose to go into the service. When the Syracuse Council delayed action in providing for indigent draftees, rumors of riots were voiced in the chamber, and the aid resolution was adopted. Early in August, the town of Auburn decided to support families of draftees, and West Tarin in Lewis County voted to give each draftee three hundred dollars. The Buffalo

Council made two separate appropriations totaling $225,000 for the families of indigent draftees, although great confusion developed over just what constituted an "indigent" draftee.[12]

The practice of subsidizing draftees spread swiftly. The Jamestown (N.Y.) *Journal* in late August carried an appeal for help for indigent draftees. There may have been no connection, but in another column of the same paper it was reported that the editor had just been drafted. Some of the Supervisors of Oneida County (Utica) attempted to push through a resolution petitioning the state legislature to authorize a real estate tax with the proceeds to serve as commutation money for draftees. The resolution failed by a tie vote, but the Supervisors appropriated $25,000 for the relief of draftees. On September 6, the town council of Troy voted three hundred dollar sums for draftees, while four days later the municipal bodies of Tarrytown and Yonkers adopted similar legislation. Rensselaer County joined the parade on September 18, and on the same day Albany made a supplemental appropriation of $200,000. Early in October the "electors" of Greenbush, near Albany, voted to levy a tax for draft relief.[13]

In New York City the $2,500,000 ordinance passed on July 15 and reached Mayor George Opdyke's desk on July 27. Heavy pressure from influential citizens was brought to bear on Opdyke to approve the ordinance at once and thus placate the mob still in the streets. His Honor would not be hurried, however, and finally when order had been restored, he vetoed it in strong terms. Arguing from both the technical and practical standpoints, Opdyke said the ordinance was vague, violated the city charter, would mark a surrender to mob rule, and would defeat the purpose of the Enrolment Act.[14] The Council persisted, however, and passed another "draft evasion" ordinance on August 16, by which the city would pay three hundred dollars to each draftee to buy exemption. Opdyke vetoed this one, too, on August 25, but in his veto message announced he would support any measure that would exempt firemen, policemen, and militiamen. The Supervisors responded with a two million dollar ordinance, such as the Mayor proposed on August 29, but added a fourth exemption category of extreme indigence in draftee families. Opdyke signed the measure into law, the bonds authorized under the ordinance were readily subscribed, and a "County Substitute and Relief Committee" was set up to administer the new law.[15]

What seems most surprising about this mad resolve to buy everyone's exemption is that so few people recognized it for the absurd, cowardly policy it was, and one which gave no thought to the pressing demand for troops. This was limited patriotism with a vengeance. The Federal Government needed men badly, yet city councils in New York and other states occupied themselves solely with the need to rescue the "indigent draftee" from the unconscionable clutches of the military. In the rare instances where councils at first refused to enact exemption ordinances, so much pressure was applied that they were compelled to reverse themselves.[16] Mayor Opdyke's bold defiance of this pressure in the most "mob-oriented" city in the country was a shining exception.

The New York *Times* firmly denounced the council's "scheme for propitiating the mob," and for the most part stood behind Opdyke. Although the exemption ordinances would swell federal treasury receipts, the *Times* noted that they were in flagrant violation of sound principals of justice and patriotism. If such an ordinance was adopted, the paper bitterly observed,

> . . . it is quite certain that nobody will be sent to the army from
> New York who can give any good reason either for not serving,
> or for not purchasing his own exemption; and it is also quite
> certain that if the Common Council can get into the field
> "for the relief of the drafted," what with sham "indigents"
> and runaway substitutes, some three millions of dollars will
> pass into the pockets of the scum of the city population,
> and few or no men into the ranks of the army.

The *Times* concluded that passage of an exemption ordinance would be due to two elements which distinguished New York from all other places: first, ". . . a mob which has shown its teeth and has its partisans in high places . . ." and second, ". . . a more compact body of rich men and property-holders, to be levied on than there are elsewhere." It was a simple matter of plundering the wealthy property owners by "an unscrupulous Corporation" disguised as aid to indigents hard hit by the draft.[17]

New York's County Substitute and Relief Committee administered the limited exemption ordinance throughout September and October, when it was superseded by the County Volunteer and Substitute Committee which handled bounty payments under the last three drafts. No final figures are available for the committee's work, but through September it had disbursed $309,650 to drafted firemen, policemen, militiamen, and "indigents." Nine hundred and eighty-three furnished substitutes, forty-nine did not provide substitutes, and two, both indigents, went into service. It appears that while the ordinance did not prohibit a qualified draftee from using his exemption money to commute, the committee strongly discouraged commutation, and advertised for exemption claimants to be well fortified with substitutes when they arrived for their interviews. Practically all substitutes received three hundred dollars, although several naïve ones went for two hundred and fifty, two hundred, and even one hundred and fifty dollars. The committee predicted that it would complete its task in the remaining month, at a cost of about one million dollars, or half the anticipated amount.[18] The Conscript Relief Committee in Albany used up only $95,500 of the $200,000 appropriated by Council in furnishing substitutes and paying commutation for 339 draftees, an average of about two hundred and eighty dollars per man.[19]

When Lincoln called for troops in October 1863 the emphasis changed from buying exemptions for draftees to paying bounties for volunteers. It now became recognized that the honorable way to respond to the Enrolment Act and still avoid the draft was to encourage volunteering, and thereby fill quotas and make the draft unnecessary. County, town and even ward bounties would be raised by the political subdivision any way it could, and would be paid in addition to all state and federal bounties. Shortly after the October call, and while the draft exemption committee was still in business, the County Supervisors in New York City prepared an ordinance authorizing three hundred dollar bounties to volunteers. Brooklyn was next; on November 11 the Kings County Supervisors decided to pay three hundred dollar bounties, for which a $250,000 loan would be negotiated.[20]

Other cities fell rather quickly into step and by December 1863 practically all communities were appropriating bounty money for volunteers, just as in July and August they had adopted draft exemption legislation. In late November the Supervisors of Albany County agreed to pay three hundred dollar bounties, and during the same week the citizens of Ellicott, a little town near Jamestown, approved a one hundred dollar bounty. Up north in the 16th District, Provost Marshal George Clendon urged the citizens of all towns to demand that the authorities offer bounties and thus beat the draft. Within ten days the people of Queensbury, as one example, did initiate steps to pay a three hundred dollar bounty. Late in December at a meeting in Minerva in the same district, five hundred dollar bounties were voted which prompted eight "stalwart recruits" to come forward. In the meantime the Columbia County Supervisors, early in December, unanimously agreed on a three hundred dollar bounty, and the officials of Dutchess County copied them a few days later. A three hundred dollar bounty was voted in both Utica and Buffalo also in the first week of December.[21]

The Republican press in Syracuse advocated a bounty, but the Onondaga County Supervisors, who were uncertain about it, decided to submit the question to a popular referendum. The people had four choices: (1) a bounty ordinance; (2) a draftee exemption ordinance; (3) an appeal to the state legislature for bounty appropriation authority; and (4) no action on the matter. The county went overwhelmingly for the bounty ordinance, while the vote in Syracuse proper was 1,963 for the bounty, and 110, 6, and 11 for the other three alternatives, respectively. Conceding that it was a light vote, the *Standard* noted that the bounty ordinance was opposed only by "wealthy peace men who could not be drafted themselves." Within several days the Supervisors appropriated $360,000 for three hundred dollar bounties.[22]

Each time Lincoln called for troops there were citizens' meetings and county supervisors were petitioned to raise more bounty money. This was especially true following Lincoln's supplemental calls in February and March 1864. The Oneida Supervisors, for example, on February 2 authorized another three hundred dollar bounty, while the Onondaga Supervisors emulated them two days later. Within ten days Onondaga's $270,000 loan was fully subscribed. The Albany fathers authorized a further loan to pay bounties to the 993 men needed under the February call. In addition to bounties to new recruits, many communities, in the late winter of 1864 appropriated bounty funds for reenlisting veterans. Since the terms of the 1861 three-year men, as well as those of the nine-month militiamen, would expire shortly, it was simply good sense to keep these experienced people in service, and a bounty was the way to do it. Glens Falls paid three hundred dollars each to thirteen veterans reenlisting in the 93rd Regiment on January 18, 1864, and in New York City about a week later, the same amount was paid to seven hundred veterans who agreed to stay on. Even little Ripley voted a three hundred dollar veteran bounty.[23]

While the second draft was in progress in May and June 1864, the heavy casualty lists sent back from the Virginia battlefront made it clear that another appeal for troops would be forthcoming. Many communities, well in advance of Lincoln's July 19 call, prepared for the inevitable. Niagara County started early, appropriating $143,600 for bounty money on June 20, and New York City began raising bounty funds two days later. The counties of Saratoga, Albany and Oneida, and the town of Whitehall also authorized bounties before July 19. The Poughkeepsie Council, which was chided by the press for its inaction before the call, agreed to offer a three hundred dollar bounty on July 20, immediately after the call. Chemung County (Elmira) authorized two hundred, three hundred, and four hundred dollar bounties for one, two and three-year enlistments a week later.[24]

With the July call for troops, when commutation had been abolished, prices for substitutes commenced a steady rise. Bounty prices had to match substitute prices if a community was to fill its quota. Bounty soldiers in the last few months of the war were a poor lot who went wherever prices were highest.[25] Yet, with bounty prices rising at an uneven rate, bitter competition for even these volunteers developed.

Under popular pressure that the bounty was insufficient to "get the men," the Poughkeepsie Council, on August 15, raised its bounty to seven hundred dollars. Then like a row of agitated dominoes, other towns fell in the race for high bounties. In the next two to three weeks, as public meetings applied hot pressure on councils and supervisors, nearly every district saw their bounty figures skyrocket. A valiant effort by the Oneida Supervisors at Utica to limit bounties was quickly brushed aside, and the City Council added three hundred, four hundred, and five hundred dollar bounties (for one, two, and three-year men) on to the county figure of three hundred dollars. State and federal bounties jacked up the total for three-year volunteers to over twelve hundred dollars. Little Annsville, near Utica, late in August enlisted twenty-eight men for one thousand dollars each and cleared itself of the draft. Troy bounties were up to six hundred, seven hundred, and eight hundred dollars by late August, while Albany reached the $1,000 mark by August 29.[26]

Glens Falls offered eight hundred dollar bounties and the press hoped that amount would be sufficient to fill the quota in the one week remaining and thus make unnecessary the "heartless, grinding conscription." Bounties of six hundred and fifty, seven hundred, and eight hundred dollars were being offered in Middlefield, Maryland, Milford, Westford, and other towns in the 19th District in late August. At a town meeting in Cooperstown a $1025 bounty was suggested, but the local quota was filled before action was taken on the proposal. A money-minded Lansingburgh woman disguised her sex and tried to enlist for a nine hundred dollar bounty then being offered in Rensselaer County, ". . . but her hopes were frustrated by the searching examination of the Surgeon." Early in September, Onondaga County approved a one thousand dollar bounty for both volunteers and substitutes and the Syracuse *Journal* boasted that this was the highest amount being paid in the state.[27] Although it would be impossible to determine which community was paying the highest bounty, it is confounding to observe the boastful note used by the press of Syracuse, Albany and other cities in insisting that their bounties were highest. This spending of large sums of money on bounty soldiers—many of whom were professional bounty-jumpers—seemed not to concern anyone even though bounties were saddling monumental debts on the various communities.[28]

Town bounty rivalries soon caused trouble. In November 1863, the Syracuse *Standard* warned that there was great need to get to work and to offer high county bounties to keep local people from going to higher bounty districts to enlist. When the Albany Supervisors enacted their bounty ordinance in November, the Syracuse *Journal* complained that recruits from other places might now gravitate to the capital city. The Poughkeepsie *Daily Eagle* hoped that Dutchess County Supervisors would adopt a bounty ordinance in December 1863, but added that it would be very unhealthy if individual towns enacted bounty ordinances because this would lead to harmful rivalries. The town of Otsego offered a six hundred dollar bounty in December, causing many young men from nearby Oneonta, which had only a three hundred dollar bounty, to come over to enlist. Oneonta promptly raised its bounty to six hundred dollars and the young men returned home. It developed, however, that Oneonta could not raise the money so the men started back for Otsego. When they learned that Otsego had no money either, they abandoned the whole district and repaired to a more solvent climate. "It is a bad state of things," observed the Cooperstown *Freeman's Journal*, ". . . which the people have brought on themselves."[29]

But it was after the repeal of commutation that these rivalries assumed alarming proportions and made a farce out of legitimate recruiting procedures. At a Utica ward meeting in late July, one speaker stated that a few days before, twelve men had arrived from Syracuse ready to enlist for four hundred dollars. When they could not get it they left for Oswego. The chairman of the meeting said at that very moment Utica was filled with outside "agents" who were "picking up our floating population," and inducing it to enlist in high bounty areas. A letter to the Elmira *Advertiser* told of a recruiting agent who was about to enlist three men toward Elmira's quota when he learned that Southport's Supervisors were offering fifty dollars more per man; the agent quickly switched the men to Southport's quota and pocketed an easy one hundred and fifty dollars. Elmira must pay bigger bounties, observed the *Advertiser*, or else ". . . we will be cheated out of our just dues."[30]

Cooperstown appointed a special committee to fill its quota in August 1864, but the committee reported that the local bounty was insufficient to attract recruits. They had met hundreds of agents, representing high bounty areas, wherever they went. A man named Prosser was then sent to Buffalo to recruit 20 three-year men at nine hundred dollars each. Although the first word was that Prosser had been successful, later accounts said that just as he was to return home someone outbid him and ran off with his 20 three-year men. In Syracuse, charges of recruit-stealing between city wards prompted a proclamation by the Bounty Committee that no more bounties would be paid to volunteers unless they were accredited to the subdistricts in which they were enrolled. Meanwhile, the Saratoga *Republican* called attention to the sad fact that bounty rivalries drained off the manpower of the poorer towns, without relieving them of quota requirements.[31]

Despite widespread appeals that these rivalries be curtailed, Lincoln's final call for troops on December 19, 1864, prompted another wild wave of bounty competition. However, the state legislature was now cognizant of the evils of this competition and took steps to suppress it. In a comprehensive law of February 10, 1865, the State of New York clapped a lid on local bounties, fixing the limit at three hundred, four hundred, and six hundred dollars for one, two, or three-year enlistees respectively. Not only was a limit set on local bounties, but it was stipulated that all bounty ordinances must be approved by a popular referendum. Draftees who went into service would be paid two hundred and fifty dollars by the state, while those who furnished substitutes would be reimbursed up to six hundred dollars. If a draftee furnished a substitute for one thousand dollars, for example, he would get back only six hundred dollars. Wherever such a draftee had been reimbursed locally in whole or in part, the state would pay only enough of the difference to make up the six hundred dollars. Another provision of the bill stated that where town officers had approved a local bounty, and such ordinance had been ratified by the voters, the state would fully reimburse the town for all bounty expenditures under the ordinance.[32]

It actually had been illegal right from the beginning for any locality to increase its indebtedness for such purposes as bounties to volunteers without first obtaining authorization from the state legislature. However, many communities as early as the 1862 Militia Draft, went ahead and borrowed bounty money anyhow and later petitioned the legislature to approve such action retroactively. This procedure soon became the accepted one. On February 23, 1863, the legislature enacted a law which confirmed all bounty loans floated in the various counties in 1862.[33]

But when the mass of bounty ordinances were adopted in the fall of 1863 some doubt was still voiced as to the propriety of acting first and then asking the legislature to endorse the act later. Suppose, for example, the legislature refused to endorse the act? The Syracuse *Journal* expressed such a view in connection with the Albany bounty of November. And when the people of Erie County demanded a bounty in December the Supervisors wrote a letter to Governor Horatio Seymour asking if he would sign a law confirming local bounty ordinances. The Governor telegraphed back that he would "sign any bill the Legislature may pass with regard to bounties." In February and March 1864 the Legislature passed a whole series of laws ratifying local bounty ordinances which had been enacted in November and December 1863.[34]

Amid the trials and terrors of filling the quota, some curious things occurred. For example, in November 1864, a list containing the names of all subscribers to a bounty fund in Syracuse's Seventh Ward—with amounts contributed—mysteriously disappeared and no one knew who had pledged what. But something which must have been far more disheartening happened in the 16th District in the Lake Champlain region. By mid-September 1864 the high bounties offered had brought in enough recruits to satisfy quota needs. After a bit of unexpected quota juggling it then came out that the district was far short of the requisite number of men, and another energetic recruiting drive was launched. But suddenly it was learned that the district was not only well over its quota, but that 415 surplus men had been paid eight hundred dollar bounties! This was probably an exaggeration, but one can well imagine the general consternation when the Glens Falls *Republican* reported that over three million dollars had been spent needlessly on excess recruits.[35]

The shortcomings of the commutation provision in the Enrolment Act became so apparent in the first two drafts that it was repealed. During the exemption ordinance mania of 1863 it began to look as though no troops would be raised if every draftee were to have his commutation money paid for him. The press carried regular accounts

of how many draftees commuted and how much commutation money
was paid. Washington County conscripts, it was reported, paid $25,000
in the last week of July 1863, while $731,700 had been received by
the Internal Revenue authorities of District 28 by late September.
Six hundred and fifteen Onondaga draftees had commuted by mid-
October, while $120,500 in commutation money was paid in Columbia
County through the end of October. As an extreme illustration of how
commutation did *not* produce men, in the town of Cazenovia all but
one of eighty-seven draftees commuted![36]

COMMUTATION MONEY PAID BY STATE

State	Amount Paid	Manpower Equivalent
Maine	$ 610,200	2,034
New Hampshire	208,500	695
Vermont	593,400	1,978
Massachusetts	1,610,400	5,368
Rhode Island	141,300	471
Connecticut	457,200	1,523
New York	5,485,799	18,286
New Jersey	1,265,700	4,219
Pennsylvania	8,634,300	28,781
Delaware	416,100	1,387
Maryland	1,131,900	3,773
District of Columbia	96,900	323
Kentucky	997,530	3,325
Ohio	1,978,087	6,593
Illinois	15,900	53
Indiana	235,500	785
Michigan	614,700	2,049
Wisconsin	1,533,600	5,112
Iowa	22,500	75
Minnesota	316,800	1,056
	$26,366,316	87,887

Source: PMG, *Final Report*, I, p. 95.

Prices for substitutes rose with the end of commutation. In fact,
even before the clause was repealed, substitute prices in New York
City were quoted at six hundred dollars and were on the way up.
But after July 4, when the Enrolment Act was amended, the lid was
off and gangs of substitutes-to-be began roaming the country searching for the highest offers. Twenty-two Canadians, for example, came
to Alexandria Bay on July 18, "willing to go" for a thousand dollars

each. When no one met their price they pushed on to Oswego. The Poughkeepsie *Eagle*, a few days later, observed mournfully that the high price of substitutes elsewhere was depleting the local supply. A Columbia County man had lately been in town offering seven hundred dollars for substitutes and had carried a number of them off with him. Why not, suggested the *Eagle*, send agents South to recruit freed slaves for substitutes? And even some "love-of-country" volunteers who went off to war in 1861 without thought of compensation and had since been discharged, were ready to become "love-of-money" soldiers. An ad in the Albany *Atlas and Argus* in September 1864 announced "Two young men just returned from the war will go as substitutes."[37]

Some parents tried to help their drafted sons procure substitutes while others did not. A Lockport man, John D. Dysinger, whose son was drafted in August 1863, advertised in the newspaper that he would pay five hundred dollars to M. C. Richardson or J. W. Barker, if either would substitute for his son. "My son," wrote Dysinger, "does not believe in the policy on which the war is conducted and is opposed to conscription, which both of the former [Richardson and Barker] *profess* to endorse." Dysinger hoped to find out how deep their patriotism went. About two months later, Simon Miller, a prosperous sixty-four year old farmer from Greene County, offered himself as a substitute for his drafted son. In contrast to this spirit was that exhibited by a Negro woman of Columbia County who auctioned her son off as a substitute. The first bid was for one hundred dollars, but the mother held out and finally a local lawyer "won the boy" for one thousand dollars.[38]

Occasionally, jail or workhouse inmates would be bailed out and sent into service as substitutes. This was done in several large Ohio cities in 1864. Early in August 1864, William Morgan, imprisoned in Poughkeepsie for robbery, mysteriously escaped. It was later learned that Morgan had been released from jail and sold as a seven hundred dollar substitute. He got two hundred dollars of the money while the brokers who arranged the transaction pocketed the balance. In answer to charges of official collusion in the matter, authorities said that Morgan had received a hearing, pleaded guilty to a lesser charge than robbery, was fined and released, all in proper style. Unconvinced, the *Eagle* retorted that the case was hushed up, officials were bribed, and that the charge was improperly reduced from grand to petit larceny.[39]

In March 1865, a Cattaraugus County draftee named Bessey bailed Jacob Dailey out of the Ellicottville jail, where he was being detained on grand larceny charges. The idea was that Dailey would go as Bessey's substitute. However, when Dailey appeared at the provost marshal's office to be mustered in, the officer in charge said he knew of an unapprehended deserter named Dailey and went off to do some checking. And sure enough, Bessey's substitute and the missing deserter were one and the same. Dailey was handcuffed and packed off to Elmira, while Bessey, minus both bail money and substitute, went searching for another prospect.[40]

Where did the bounty money come from and how was it raised? It was easy enough for a board of supervisors to resolve to pay a three hundred or six hundred dollar bounty, but once that was done the real work of obtaining the money began. In many respects these fund-raising drives were similar to the United Appeal and other annual campaigns of the 20th Century, although less well-organized. And as with these modern drives, a few sacrificing civic leaders carried a great share of the responsibility, while the masses of the people did little.

Following a presidential call for troops and the fixing of quotas and quota deadlines, newspapers, provost marshals, and public-spirited citizens would urge that mass meetings be held to decide how to fill the quota and avoid the draft. In 1863 most of these meetings, instead of urging bounty ordinances, were concerned chiefly with inducing the authorities to adopt draft exemption ordinances. But for the last three draft calls, popular meetings were preoccupied with beating the draft by offering inviting bounties to volunteers. In the wake of these meetings the city councils and county supervisors would generally approve a bounty ordinance, although in some cases they either opposed the idea at first or tentatively adopted a bounty ordinance pending its approval at a public referendum. Eventually, the deed was done and attention would then be focused on raising the money needed to pay the bounties.

The problem was handled differently in different states. In Ohio, for example, bounty funds were originally raised by private voluntary contributions. But as repeated calls for troops were issued, the same people contributed to these funds over and over again, while other citizens gave nothing. In certain parts of Ohio, extreme pressure was brought to bear on chronic non-givers. Petitions began to pour into Columbus urging the state legislature to authorize local tax assessments for bounty fund purposes. Such a law was adopted in March 1864 and from that time on, bounty funds were raised by a levy on all property holders in the district.[41] Although voluntary contributions made up a much smaller percentage of bounty money in New York State than in Ohio, some funds were raised in this fashion. The largest single contribution found in a survey of New York newspapers was for one thousand dollars made by William A. Sweet, a Syracuse industrialist, at a Fifth Ward meeting in March 1865. When Skaneateles resolved to raise a six hundred dollar bounty in September 1864, it was decided to rely on voluntary donations with the hope that, when funds became available later, the money would be refunded. Private contributions were utilized in Jamestown the same month when it was necessary to double the bounty. The largest donations were fifty dollars. In March 1865, Glens Falls levied a tax to reimburse persons who had voluntarily paid $11,181 into a bounty fund the previous fall. Contributions to Elmira's bounty fund in the spring of 1865 began at ten dollars and with a top of one hundred dollars, averaged about twenty-five dollars. Even a substitute broker, Peter La France, came through with twenty-five dollars.[42]

In New York State, however, from the start the principal means of raising bounty money was a tax on real estate. All the local bounty ordinances mentioned earlier contained provisions for tax assessments. Since the tax could not be levied and collected immediately, however, the usual practice was to issue "bounty bonds" at once, and then later use the tax revenue to retire the bonds. Frequently, such bounty ordinances would be challenged on constitutional grounds, generally by copperheads or others opposed to the war and the draft, but the courts in every state upheld such legislation.[43]

Town meetings for the purpose of raising funds were lively affairs.

The Syracuse *Journal*, for example, stated that "businessmen close their stores, lawyers forsake their offices, mechanics drop their tools, and all meet in the public square at the ringing of the bell. . . ." But the enthusiasm cooled during the second draft, and on New Year's Day, 1864, the Syracuse *Standard* said that a very slim crowd had attended a recent war meeting. "The city will not escape the draft . . . unless something is done and that immediately." This was a common note. As the deadline approached and as men were needed, the appeal for large turnouts became more urgent. A town meeting in Jamestown in February 1864 was devoted to a heated debate as to the best method of raising the $10,000 needed for bounties. Some argued for an additional tax, while others proposed a twenty-five dollar compulsory contribution from each enrolled man and then a tax to make up the balance.[44]

The third draft in the summer and fall of 1864 prompted a heavy wave of ward and town meetings. At Glens Falls on July 16, labored efforts were made to impress on the citizens that with commutation terminated, volunteer and substitute prices would rise, and that more work than ever before would be required to fill the quota. Everyone was urged to attend a mass meeting in Poughkeepsie on July 18, shopkeepers being advised to close their stores. A committee was set up and council was petitioned to raise a city bounty, which council did several days later. In announcing a bounty meeting in Elmira, the *Advertiser* warned that ". . . fifty days will soon pass away, and then . . . the draft, inexorable and without commutation, follows."[45]

Meetings were held in all Utica wards in late July and August, and "ward enlistment" committees were organized to help fill quotas and "beat the draft." Although a county bounty had already been agreed upon, the money had not yet been raised; hence these ward committees kept urging the supervisors to levy a tax. Also, most of the wards assessed each enrolled man a certain sum of money to be used in securing recruits. As things got more desperate in late August, Utica ward meetings demanded a city bounty as well, which the council finally authorized. With bounty prices rising rapidly in August and September, meetings were held in a number of other cities, urging additional appropriations to meet increased bounty demands.[46]

When a bounty loan—to be repaid later by a tax assessment—was authorized, the big problem was to procure subscribers. The press carried regular accounts of the progress of subscription campaigns, and if and when the bonds were all taken up, the fund-raisers were almost as happy as if the quota had been filled. In December 1863, a $100,000 Albany County bond issue was quickly subscribed, with Erastus Corning buying $35,000 worth and four prominent banks taking the remainder. A loan floated in February 1864, following Lincoln's supplemental troop call of that month, was taken up by March 3, with Nathaniel Thayer of Boston purchasing $269,000 worth of the bonds. But the public was slow to respond to the bounty loan authorized in Albany after the July call, for by the second week of September appeals were still being made for subscribers. Men were available but bounty money was not; the *Argus* could not understand this reluctance to buy, since the interest rate was compounded 7 per cent semiannually. Again, in January 1865, Albany capitalists were slow in buying bonds even though the pending state bounty bill—later passed—would reimburse all who contributed.[47]

In New York City, banks, corporations, and private persons greatly oversubscribed the city's two million dollar bounty loan in March 1864. The New York *Times* speculated whether the subscribers would now pay up. The Military Committee of Cooperstown advertised for subscribers to the town's summer 1864 bounty loan, but no results of their appeal were published. Elmira "capitalists" were attacked for not quickly buying up Chemung County bonds in August 1864, while the Buffalo Savings Bank was praised for taking $350,000 worth of bounty bonds by October of that year. However, in March 1865, bond subscribers in Buffalo's Eleventh Ward were urged to make good on their pledges at once. And in the last week of the war, New York's Bounty Committee reported anxiously that but a fraction of the $3,500,000 in bonds lately authorized had been taken up.[48]

Onondaga supervisors advertised their bounty bonds in the Syracuse newspapers in February 1864, announcing that there was "no safer or better way to invest money." Within five days the entire $270,000 issue had been subscribed. The $400,000 loan in the summer of 1864 was also advertised in the press, a practice common to all the large cities. With the onset of the fourth draft early in 1865 the Onondaga supervisors decided that trying to borrow more money was useless, and proceeded to levy a 2 per cent personal and real property tax for bounty purposes. But months before this other communities had already resorted to tax levies, having found that they could borrow no more money. The Columbia County supervisors, for example, assessed taxpayers in June 1864 for the $75,000 to be raised under recent bounty legislation. And the Utica Council decided to finance its city bounty in August and September 1864 by real estate taxation.[49]

A clue to the increased tax rates caused by bounty appropriations was supplied by the Glens Falls *Republican* in November 1864. Comparing figures of that year with those of 1863, it found that for some property owners the rate had jumped seven times. The Commercial Bank, for example, paid only $1,715.20 in 1863, but because of the bounty ordinances paid $11,602.62 in 1864. The *Argus* published a breakdown on bounty taxes in Albany County in 1864, but made no comparison with previous years. The assessed valuation for the county was $42,457,429 while the total paid in bounty taxes was $667,197.16.[50] (See Appendix A, Table 1.)

Bounty ordinances providing for bond loans and tax assessments gave rise to a new form of litigation, for in every state there were persons who challenged the constitutionality of the laws. However, in each case the court held that county and municipal governments were fully justified, with state legislative approval, to tax property owners for such a critical purpose as raising an army in wartime. Since military bounties were directly related to raising an army, they were constitutional. Laws which permitted reimbursement of moneys to citizens who had voluntarily contributed to bounty funds were also sustained.[51]

The bounty system, which sufficed for the short wars of the past, broke down in the four long years of civil strife. The supply of patriots was limited and it became necessary to pay bounties on a large scale to obtain recruits. Unexpected abuses in the system appeared, and they proliferated as the conflict dragged on. No way out of the bounty dilemma could be found as the Government struggled to keep its armies supplied with men. Provost Marshal Isaac F. Quinby of the

28th District put the case clearly in his final report: "Human fore-sight," he wrote, "could not have anticipated the necessities of the government, and the difficulties it experienced in raising and keeping up its armies. . . . No one supposed that it would become necessary to resort to other means than volunteering. . . ."[52]

The general public and the press supported the bounty system. As Fry noted in his *Final Report*, "The anxiety of the citizens to have their respective quotas promptly filled induced submission to the evil."[53] In January 1864 the Poughkeepsie *Eagle* exulted that "The large bounties offered . . . will soon swell the ranks of the armies in the field to a greater number than was ever reached in previous wars." When the afternoon Buffalo paper complained in April 1864 that most of the men enlisted locally were credited to other districts, the *Morning Express* replied that the men were not credited to Erie County because Erie County did not pay high enough bounties. The solution was quite simple: bigger bounties.[54]

The ire of a New York *Times* reader was aroused in the spring of 1864 when the Federal Government temporarily abandoned its three hundred dollar bounty. "The Government should not be niggardly in such a matter," he wrote. The city quotas under the second draft might already have been filled had the bounty not been reduced. Furthermore, it was contended, the bounty system was the cheapest way to raise troops. With commutation abolished, the draft would fall ruthlessly on thousands who could ill afford to serve. But, the correspondent continued,

> . . . let volunteers be raised by larger bounties, their cost will
> be equally divided by taxation among all, rich and poor,
> and our armies will be *well filled,* and victory insured, and
> all this without a draft; the people will *gladly* pay any rate
> of taxation. It will be cheapest for them and they know it;
> it will allow them to remain at home if they cannot go to war,
> and relieve them from the purchase of substitutes . . .[55]

Late in December 1864 representatives of the Union League of Philadelphia petitioned Congress to make some changes in the bounty system. Among other things they proposed that local bounties be discouraged, that no one be credited to any district but the one in which he lived, that deserters should be subtracted from the quota of the district which credited them, and that bounties be paid to draftees. While hardly revolutionary, these suggestions would certainly have minimized some of the abuses of the bounty system. But in the eyes of the New York *Times*, the Philadelphia petition was a radical and unwise document. In sneering tones the *Times* pompously informed the Union Leaguers that local bounties were no concern of Congress, and that Philadelphia had no right to tell New Yorkers how they should recruit troops. Just because the City of Brotherly Love was too stingy to give bounties was no reason New York would not continue to award a "handsome bonus" to each of its volunteers.[56]

Scattered criticism of bounties (like that of the Philadelphia Union League) suggests that a few persons realized the system was morally wrong, administratively inefficient, and highly extravagant, but this feeling was well-submerged until Appomattox. With the war ended, however, there was no longer any point in continuing to laud a recruiting system which possessed such manifold evils.

"Historical Reports," written while the ashes of war were still smouldering, reveal how the district provost marshals felt about the bounty system. In these reports the provost marshals were quite generous in praising the liberality of the people in contributing so many millions of dollars to bounty funds. However, they concluded that most of it was wasted. Provost Marshal S. H. Parsons of the 14th District wrote that, "impelled by a noble patriotism," the people supported bounty payments to an unprecedented extent. "But," he added, "instead . . . of these bounties inuring to the benefit of the country . . . the money has been stolen by an organized band of thieves, and without supplying . . . any men for the service." Fred Emerson of the 20th District stated that the money went to deserters and sharpers, who robbed the soldier and the people. "The quotas have been filled on paper but the men have not gone to the field but to Canada." John T. Wright of the 27th District spoke with admiration of the "generosity" and "sublime sacrifices" represented by bounty fund donations, but concluded it was all misguided.[57]

Wright, Benjamin Snow of the 24th District, and Samuel B. Hayman, Acting Assistant Provost Marshal General of the Western Division, all condemned the bounty rivalries between towns which developed in the summer of 1864. This competition not only led to an acceleration of bounty prices, but also stimulated bounty-jumping and had disastrous effects on low income districts. Among other complaints mentioned in the final reports were the increased tax rates, administrative problems in handling bounty disbursements, and the fact that high bounties attracted low men and hampered the recruiting process.[58]

What solutions did the provost marshals propose? The recommendations bordered on unanimity: either abolish local bounties entirely, or make them uniform and carefully control their disbursement. Emerson flatly opposed all local bounties because they enhanced administrative problems, promoted brokerage and jumping, defrauded recruits, were unfair to early non-bounty soldiers, and generally degraded the profession. Snow wrote that ". . . the evil could . . . be fully remedied only by the government's prohibiting local bounties entirely, or by controlling the payment of them." Parsons recommended only small bounties at best and those to be paid on the installment plan, rather than all in advance. He argued that 98 per cent as many honest recruits could be obtained this way as when all the bounty was given out at the time of enlistment.[59]

Hayman did not expressly condemn bounties, but he did urge that they be made uniform, be deposited in the United States Treasury for later disbursement in installments, and that heavy penalties be imposed on violators. Snow observed that ". . . there were less desertions . . . when there were no local bounties offered, and as these bounties increased, desertions increased." Quinby was one of the few provost marshals who suggested that conscription should have been employed at the start of the war. Had this been done, he said, ". . . the people would readily have acquiesced in it, inconveniences and hardships inseparable from it would have been submitted to, and the general, state and municipal governments would have been saved a large portion of the heavy debts with which they are now burdened."[60] S.C.F. Thorndike of the 17th District bitterly denounced substitution as a "fraud on the government," and urged that in the future all draftees be held to personal service. William Remer of the 25th District declared that once the bounty system was entrenched nothing could be done to adequately protect the people and the government from its depredations. He did denounce the practice of substitution and urged that bounty payments be made by installments.[61]

• 3 •

The Draft.

NEW YORK, IN 1863, had thirty-one congressional districts, the first nine of which were in New York City and Brooklyn. These nine, plus the 10th District (Putnam, Rockland, and Westchester Counties) were put into the Southern Division, one of three such divisions into which the State was divided to simplify administration of the Enrolment Act. Each division, as we have already noted, was headed by an Acting Assistant Provost Marshal General (AAPMG). Districts Eleven through Twenty, embracing the east-central and northern counties, constituted the Northern Division, while Districts Twenty-one through Thirty-one, covering the central and western counties, became the Western Division. Headquarters were in New York City, Albany, and Elmira.[1] (See map, Appendix B.)

Provost Marshal General Fry warned that selection of district provost marshals and other enrolment board members was not easy because of the brief time allowed in which to check credentials, and because qualified people often would not serve. As a result, a few undesirable people who were appointed to district boards turned their offices into centers for graft and fraud. However, the boards in New York's Districts Four, Twenty, Twenty-two, Twenty-five, and Twenty-six were so well-chosen that not a single personnel change was made during the entire war. The original provost marshal, physician, and commissioner on each of those boards served the full time. But at the other end of the scale was the 27th District (Allegany, Steuben, and Chemung Counties), where four provost marshals, four physicians, and two commissioners were employed before the war

42

ended. Not far behind was the 6th District in New York City, which required three provost marshals, three physicians, and two commissioners. In all, one hundred and fifty persons were employed during the war on New York's thirty-one enrolment boards; there were fifty-seven provost marshals, forty-five commissioners, and forty-eight surgeons. (See Appendix A, Table II.)

Little information has survived to explain the fairly large turnover in provost marshals. Twenty-six of the fifty-seven received honorable discharges, seventeen resigned, two died in office, and twelve were either dismissed or had their appointments revoked. The causes of dismissal were fraudulent activity, incompetence, or political rivalry. Of the forty-five commissioners who served, three had their appointments revoked, two were dismissed, and one was simply "discharged." In some cases an official was allowed to resign under threat of dismissal.[2]

Each provost marshal was authorized to employ two clerks in his office, and two deputy provost marshals were permitted in the larger districts. Additional agents and special officers might be hired as the occasion demanded.[3] Yet the duties of the provost marshal and his board were gruelling and exacting. Enrolling all qualified men, conducting the draft, enlisting recruits, tracking down deserters, dealing with enrolment evaders and draft resisters, and contracting for supplies, sustenance, and transportation—all the while operating under heavy pressure from wealthy and politically influential people—were some of the chores which suggest the scope of the provost marshal's responsibilities. Hours were long. Thorndike reported that his board was in session daily from eight o'clock in the morning until well into the evening, oftentimes until midnight. Samuel Gordon of the 19th District complained that the pay and rank of the provost marshal was totally inadequate to compensate for the services rendered. He wrote that "an office exacting more labor, capacity, and accountability than that of a colonel in the field service, rewarded with pay (not to speak of rank) below that of clerks in the [War] Department, could not have been clearly comprehended by the law-making power."[4]

Benjamin Snow, who succeeded the discharged John A. Knapp as provost marshal of the 24th District on December 20, 1864, felt that

much of the difficulty encountered by provost marshals was due to
the novelty of the job, and the fact that no previous business experience could adequately prepare them for this kind of work. Only by
serving for a period of time could a person gain a good grasp of the
position. Snow added that trouble also resulted from the wide range
of duties provost marshals were compelled to perform, and that the
official regulations should be revised and clarified so as to spell out
their specific duties. This would also simplify their relations with the
general public, which regarded the provost marshal as a civil officer,
although he was, in fact, a military officer.[5]

Gordon liked neither the way the enrolment board was appointed
nor organized. He proposed that the provost marshal be permitted to
name his own commissioner and physician who would take their orders from and be responsible to him. Or, if the government wished to
appoint the commissioner and physician as the Enrolment Act provided, then let their duties be expressly outlined and require them to
report directly to the government. Gordon also proposed that the commissioner be replaced by a quartermaster, preferably a lieutenant
with logistical experience. The quartermaster would handle ordnance
stores, military goods, sustenance, lodging, and transportation, all routine matters which took the provost marshals away from their principal duties. As for the commissioners, Gordon stated that they "hold
sinecures without responsibility and are of little use except to help
form a quorum, or break a tie vote."[6]

❊   ❊   ❊   ❊

Most of the enrolment boards were organized by the end of April
1863. For the purposes of enrolment, each board was instructed to
organize city wards and county townships into subdistricts and appoint an Enrolling Officer for each one. Enrolment officers were to
visit every place of residence in their jurisdiction and copy down, on
specially prepared forms, the name, address, age, color, and occupation of every male between 20 and 45. When the enrolment was complete in each subdistrict, the lists of names were to be turned into
the board, which would then compile a "consolidated list" of eligible
people in the entire district. The names of drafted persons would be
drawn from the consolidated list.[7]

The process looked quite simple on paper, but in practice all kinds of problems developed. From the start it was not easy to enlist EO's, but the task became much more difficult when the news got out that some of them had been beaten up and murdered. Thorndike complained that he could not procure "persons of judgment and competency . . . who could write a legible hand and spell names correctly." So badly did they do the job that they were summoned to headquarters to decipher their scrawlings before the full Board. Also, he added, "they duplicated very many names and enrolled a large number of non-residents," which led to vexing complications during the draft.[8]

More serious were the ambiguities in the Enrolment Act itself. As Fry pointed out, certain provisions of the law called for enrolment of *all men* between 20 and 45, while other provisions required only the enrolment of *all non-exempt men* between 20 and 45. By the latter rule, only those who were not aliens, or who were not suffering from obvious physical or mental disabilities would be enrolled. Since EO's pursued both of these policies, Fry was compelled to issue Circular Number 17 on June 2, 1863, requiring the enrolment of *all* 20-45 males. The enrolment was, he asserted, "simply a census of all male citizens . . . between the ages of 20 and 45." EO's were not to exempt anyone as they made their rounds; exemptions would be made solely by the enrolment board after the draftees reported.[9]

Probably very few of the EO's anticipated the reception they would receive as they entered upon their duties. But the pages of the *Official Records*, replete with stories of violence, harassment, and murder, provide proof of the hostility and bitterness which greeted them.[10] Even if intimidation was not employed, the persons interviewed often submitted false names and addresses, which was not only exasperating in itself, but led to countless errors. This was especially so when it came to canvassing rooming houses where many people resided. An EO entering such an establishment was on his own, with few friends or sympathizers. Such an officer, at work in a Bowery barroom in late May, was badly beaten up. At about the same time, a "posse" of 24 agents from the 4th District office invaded Number 44 on the Bowery, arrested a group of men who had given fictitious names, and obtained an accurate enrolment. The New York *Times* reported in mid-June that the 4th District list was almost complete, and that the only opposition had come from "those class of men" who did not understand the laws or institutions of the country. At Kingston, most of the trouble was caused by "Irish women."[11]

After the first draft began in August and September 1863, many enrolment errors came to light. For example, on September 1 a woman was drafted in the 3rd District. The EO had copied her name by mistake off the sign over the store which she and her husband operated. About two weeks later one Katie Thomas Sackett was drafted at Geddes, near Syracuse. When the EO called, she said there was no one present qualified for military duty, but he kept pressing her and she finally gave her middle and last names, Thomas and Sackett. Enjoying her fun, she then proceeded to submit other names, all imaginary, to the unsuspecting officer. The press speculated "wittily" whether she would fight, commute, or furnish a substitute. Most incredible was the case of Edward Thompson of Troy. A 65-year old crippled alien who was sick in bed when enrolled, Thompson died a few days after he was drafted.[12]

Trouble also stemmed from a very strict interpretation of Section 25 of the Enrolment Act, which prescribed penalties for resisting the draft. Such persons were to be arrested by the provost marshal, delivered to the civil authorities for trial, and upon conviction, be subject to fine, or imprisonment, or both. The loophole in the section developed because the language did not expressly declare *enrolment resistance* a crime; only *resisting the draft* was a crime.

The case which focussed attention on this ambiguity occurred in the 3rd New York District early in June. An EO named Tompkins went to a Front Street store in Brooklyn, where he found Michael Briody. Briody insisted he did not live there, but was just "minding the store" for the boss. Tompkins returned a day or two later and again found only Briody, who was still just "minding the store." Within the next week Tompkins went to Briody's home, but the latter still refused to give any information about himself, and was promptly arrested as a draft resister. The case went before a federal commissioner, who on June 11, freed Briody because he had not resisted the draft but only the enrolment, which was not covered by Section 25.

Fry referred the case to War Department Solicitor William Whiting, who ruled that the enrolment was so closely linked to the draft that resisting the former was, in effect, resisting the latter. People like Briody, therefore, were covered by Section 25.[13]

Duplicate enrolments were a headache, particularly where a person might live in one subdistrict or district and work in another. Colonel Robert Nugent, AAPMG for the Southern Division from April until October 1863, insisted that this caused him more grief than any other phase of the enrolment. He tried first to induce double-enrollees to obtain certificates of nullification for their job-enrolment, but nobody came in for them. Next he instituted a system of exchange of lists among provost marshals to eliminate duplications. However, the July 1863 draft occurred before many of these double enrolments had been eliminated.[14]

Strong criticism developed in the 19th District over what at first looked like an attempt to avoid a duplicate enrolment. It seems that Deputy Provost Marshal Waldo did not want his son enrolled. Although the boy lived in Edmeston in Otsego County, Waldo told EO's that his son was staying in Utica. The statement was not checked out, and consequently the son was not enrolled in Edmeston. Curious townspeople, however, made some inquiries in Utica and found that the young Waldo was not enrolled there either. Irate at this deception, the public and the press demanded Waldo's dismissal.[15]

The promiscuous enrolment of people who were dead, too old, too young, in jail, already in the service, without arms or legs, blind, and lame,[16] led to a torrent of protest that the enrolment be revised. The draft officials, from Fry down to the EO's, were often the target of this abuse, but the ambiguities in the law, and the obstructions thrown up in the path of the EO's made an accurate enrolment impossible. The Allen Commission, set up in the winter of 1863-64 to investigate enrolment and quota discrepancies in New York City, gave EO's a clean bill of health. "It should be distinctly stated," the Commission reported, "that their [the EO's] fidelity or integrity is by no means impeached by any inaccuracies that may exist in the enrolment."[17]

Actually, the majority of provost marshals made every effort to prepare correct rolls. Joel B. Erhardt of the 4th District described the great pains taken—"the work of many days and nights"—to eliminate duplications in compiling the consolidated list. Every time the same name appeared, a careful check was made to insure that it was not a duplication, and where doubt remained, a deputy was dispatched to the residence of such a person to settle the matter. Provost Marshal Samuel T. Maddox of the 2nd District instructed his EO's not only to enroll all proper persons in each house or residence building, but to double-check their information by inquiring at adjoining houses. Factories, stores, and business establishments were also visited, but great care was taken not to sign up a second time a person who had already been enrolled at home.[18]

The enrolment was completed by early July 1863 in some districts, but not until August in others. Since Fry issued orders that the draft commence in a district as soon as the enrolment was finished, there was no time for revision until the draft had been concluded. The 1863 draft was over by early October, and on November 17, 1863, Fry published Circular Number 101 calling on all provost marshals to correct their lists. They were told to prepare printed lists of all enrolled persons by subdistrict, to be posted in at least five conspicuous places. Announcements were to be published in the newspapers, advising all people who were incorrectly enrolled to report to their enrolment boards and have their names expunged.[19]

However, it was not until the second draft drew near in the spring of 1864, that interest was taken in revising the enrolment. The list was corrected daily in the 24th District throughout the summer and the corrections were forwarded regularly to Washington. Provost Marshal Rogers of the 30th District ordered enrolment lists to be posted in all subdistricts in late May, and urged citizens to cooperate in correcting the rolls. "An excess of names," he properly pointed out, "increases the quota from such town and ward." Lists were distributed in the Albany area in June, and again the people were encouraged to assist in a general revision. In late July the 31st District provost marshal announced he would hold sessions in Jamestown, at which people who felt they were improperly enrolled could argue their cases. A report from Glens Falls early in August said that original quota figures were greatly reduced by the enrolment revision there.[20]

But errors persisted and Fry was compelled to order another massive enrolment revision, which he did in Circular Number 39 of November 15, 1864. It was much similar to Circular 101, although this time more stress was placed on the participation of boards of supervisors and other leading citizens in making the corrections. Enrolment boards were urged not only to remove names which did not belong on the lists, but to add others that should be. The boards were obliged to make their records available to the general public, and listen to the testimony of anyone who desired to have his name removed.[21]

A surge of interest in correcting the lists rose at the time of Lincoln's last call for troops in December and the approach of the final draft. The provost marshal's headquarters at Elmira was swamped nearly every day in January 1865 with people anxious to have their names stricken from the lists. In Albany, enrolment revision became a major civic undertaking. Governor Seymour issued a proclamation urging full citizen participation in the project, newspapers rendered strong editorial support, and the city council appointed a special committee to guarantee that every ward enrolment list would be accurate. It was estimated that two thousand names would be eliminated, which would lead to substantial quota reductions, and bounty savings of at least $200,000 to the city. Actually when the council committee made its report in late February it was learned that 3,087 names had been removed from the rolls, which constituted a saving of over $300,000.[22]

* * * *

The 1863 draft, unlike the other three, was not a result of any specific call for troops. Provost marshals were simply instructed to draft *one-fifth* of the total number of enrolled men. The enrolment was complete in most districts by early July, and Fry's Circular Number 41 of July 9 detailed the draft procedure. The names of all on the list were to be written on individual cards of uniform size. The cards of each subdistrict were then to be grouped together, placed in an envelope, sealed, and put away until the draft was held. On the draft date the board would publicly open the envelope for the first subdistrict, place all the cards in a box one foot square and one foot deep, and securely fix a lid on the top of the box, the lid containing a hole only large enough for a man's hand. After the provost marshal or some trusted person was blindfolded, he would draw a card from the box and hand it to the commissioner, who would read aloud the name on the card. The clerk recorded the name on a prepared sheet, and the other cards would be drawn until the requisite number of names had been procured.[23]

Preparing for the draft was not an easy task. At Buffalo, for example, Provost Marshal Gustavus A. Scroggs had a staff of twelve people "working day and night" for thirty days, completing the enrolment, preparing the cards, and attending to countless other duties. When things were in readiness, Scroggs announced that the draft would be held in full public view, and invited judges of the United States, Superior, and City Courts, the Mayor, City Clerk, Sheriff, Under-Sheriff, Police Jusice, Chief of Police, Aldermen, and Supervisors to attend the drawing. Provost Marshal Parsons of the 14th District at Albany also invited the Mayor, Aldermen, Supervisors, and other city and county dignitaries. This care to guarantee full publicity was perhaps a consequence of earlier criticism that both the enrolment and the 20 per cent draft notice had been handled in a "clandestine and underhanded way."[24]

Most boards proceeded with the draft in the manner outlined by Fry with a few variations. A wheel was usually substituted for the draft box because of the difficulty in mixing the cards. The 24th Board used a box in the 1863 draft, but found that the cards stuck together, and frequently the names were drawn in the exact order in which they appeared on the enrolment. For the next draft a wheel was used.[25] The draft wheel used in the 23rd District at Syracuse is now on the exhibition floor of the Onondaga Historical Association. It is a metal-enclosed cylinder, roughly eighteen inches in diameter and nine inches wide. The cylinder is rotated by a wooden-armed handle, and a small trap-door allows the removal of the draft slips. The draft slips at Syracuse and in most districts were about three inches long and one inch wide. Generally, some private citizen properly blindfolded, drew the slips, but in Utica they took no chances. The drawing there was made by a blindfolded *blind* man.[26]

The draft usually began at about ten o'clock in the morning and continued until late afternoon, with the number of districts drawn in a day varying from one board to the next. In the 19th District, for example, five subdistricts were covered each day. In some communities the subdistricts were drafted in numerical order, while in others, the subdistricts which had done the least to fulfill their quotas were drafted first. As the tickets were drawn, the commissioner or whoever was doing the drawing, would call off the names, which would be recorded on several different sheets and record books. After the day's quota was completed, the unused tickets were counted out of the wheel, and both the drawn and undrawn slips were sealed into separate packages to be reopened the next day.[27]

Although the 1863 draft encountered widespread resistance across the nation, once order had been restored it proceeded without incident and occasionally with resigned good humor. At Jamestown, the names of draftees were read aloud in the streets and amid wild cheers, the men were congratulated and paraded through the town for all to see. When word was received in Skaneateles of "the elect," the draftees "submitted with an extremely good grace to their fate, now that their first emotions of surprise have had time to cool." A rainstorm prevented a parade there.[28]

As the draft wheel turned in Rochester, a man of German origin heard his name called. He turned around, walked a few paces, and smashed his beaver hat to the ground, shouting, "Dot's my name! Dot's my name!" In a moment he retrieved the hat, brushed it off, and put it back on. But after walking a bit farther, he again slammed his hat down, repeating "Dot's my name!" Another German in Utica, taken aback at hearing his name called, ejaculated, "O mein Gott! Dot ish me!" In the Albany draft, three clerks reading the names unexpectedly called out their own. A clerk at Poughkeepsie who was drafted got a big sendoff from his colleagues.[29]

When the draft was completed for each day, notices were served personally by EO's on the draftees, or left at the draftees' last known residences. Draftees were allowed a ten-day period before reporting to the provost marshal's headquarters for examination. The records show that many draftees seized the opportunity to "skedaddle" before their time to leave.

Resistance to the 1863 draft occurred in various parts of the North, the worst trouble spot being New York City, where the anarchy of the Draft Riots held sway from July 13-16. On July 15, at the height of the New York riots AAPMG A. S. Diven reported from Elmira that the draft was "progressing quietly" in the 26th and 27th Districts, but would be delayed in the 25th, 28th, and 30th Districts because of enrolment errors. No draft had been ordered as yet in the 23rd, 24th, 29th, and 31st. In Albany, however, Major Frederick Townsend, AAPMG for the Northern Division worried about the riots that had broken out in Troy and the unreliability of the state military forces there, suspended the draft. Provost Marshal Joshua Fiero of the 13th District in Kingston removed all of his official papers to a special vault as Copperhead and anti-draft meetings were held throughout the area. Utica, according to Provost Marshal Joseph P. Richardson of the 21st District, was electric with anti-draft sentiment; he advised that no draft should be attempted there without ample military protection. Provost Marshal Moses G. Leonard reported a similar situation in the 10th District at Tarrytown. Many districts demanded military support before proceeding with the draft.[30]

Most of the violent draft resistance subsided by late July, and the draft was resumed. Ten thousand troops insured a peaceful resumption in New York City on August 19. Yet evasion of the draft was accomplished in many ways, most commonly by just running off to some other district, state, or country. Canada was the most popular refuge for draft-evaders from Michigan, Ohio, Pennsylvania, New York, and New England, and in the latter months of the war several thousand of them were congregated about Niagara Falls, Toronto, and other nearby places. A "convention" of these guilt-stricken fugitives was held in Niagara Falls in November 1864, at which a petition to Stanton, asking clemency if they would return, was drawn up. It got short shrift in Washington.[31]

Shortly after the war ended Congressman Calvin T. Hulburd of St. Lawrence County on the Canadian border wrote Stanton that many draft-evaders and bounty-jumpers were then beginning to filter back into New York, believing that no punitive action would be taken against them. Hulburd urged that a guard be posted along the boundary to apprehend these people and that they be prosecuted. Punishment of the "skedaddlers and deserters and bounty-jumpers," he noted, "would give far more satisfaction to soldiers returning and citizens generally," than any other course which might be pursued, and it would set a sound precedent.[32] Unfortunately, the government never adopted any such policy, and the skedaddlers and their fellows were allowed to carry on in peacetime as if there had never been a war.

Draft flight reached a peak just before each draft and during the ten-day waiting period following the drawing. Provost Marshal Gordon sent a frantic telegram to Townsend on the eve of the August 1864 draft, which read as follows:

> What mode or means is there of preventing persons enrolled
> and liable to draft from leaving the district or State before
> being drafted? A stampede is going on that threatens to be
> serious unless checked. I know of no remedy. Can they be
> stopped on the border of the state? Are there any means
> of checking this exodus?[33]

In the wake of the July 1863 riots, thousands of "refugees from the lottery" in Boston poured into Albany. "They do not riot against the draft," observed the *Argus*, "they simply run away from it." Prior to the last draft in the winter of 1864-65, rumors emanating from Washington spoke of a possible secret draft to prevent any more skedaddling, but this report was without foundation.[34]

But the draftees who refused to serve yet desired to stay at home, resorted to many incredible stratagems to gain exemption. The regulations required that draftees must possess a certain number of teeth. This was because of the type of cartridge used in a muzzle-loading weapon: a paper cylinder containing a lead bullet and a charge of powder. When the infantryman prepared to fire he would seize a cartridge from his belt, bite off the end, pour the powder down his gun barrel, ram the bullet home, and fix a percussion cap to explode the charge. Since teeth were necessary to bite off the tip of the paper cartridge, the Regulations stipulated that a draftee might be exempted if he had lost "a sufficient number of teeth to prevent proper mastication of food and tearing the cartridge."[35]

In view of this, tooth extraction became common in efforts to escape the draft. In August 1864 a draftee in Arcadia went to his dentist and had all the teeth removed from his upper jaw. About a month later a man in Dayton, Cattaraugus County, had sixteen teeth extracted, nearly bleeding to death as a consequence, and a dentist pulled twelve from the mouth of another man in the same town. A member of the Ohio State legislature, who thought he was drafted, had all of his teeth removed only to learn that a neighbor had played a joke on him, and that he was not drafted after all.[36] Occasionally, death was even preferable to military service. Thus August Ebner, who lived on Third Street in New York City, tried to slash his jugular vein, and though he suffered a horrible gash, he survived.[37]

Married men were not exempt, but the older ones (between 35 and 45) were put in Class Two on the enrolment list, and were not drafted until all of those in Class One had been called. Considerable misunderstanding developed over this provision of the Enrolment Act, however, and bachelors of all ages thought they could win exemption by winning a wife. An Erie Railroad official named Fisk, who lived in Buffalo, went off to Ontario County to be wed just as his name was drawn. When served his notice, he said he would be unable to go because he had already "enlisted for life." Fisk marched off to war.[38]

About a week later a young man and woman called on a judge in Troy and asked to be married. Where were their witnesses, inquired the judge? They had none because they were strangers in town. Well, replied the judge, he could not marry them without witnesses. The young man persisted, saying that he had been drafted in his native county and was told that he could exempt himself by getting married, so could not His Honor do him this little favor? Besides, he and the girl had been living together for four years, so what difference did it make? He was told to return home and enter the army.[39]

Occasionally, men who had enlisted in the army but decided they did not like it once they put on the uniform, would mutilate themselves in order to be discharged. Luke Vanderpool, a Negro, chopped off the first two fingers of his right hand four days after enlisting in February 1864. Actually, Vanderpool was not a willing enlistee. He had been arrested for beating his wife, and was given the option of going into the army or the penitentiary. A month later one McCann of Hornellsville was found with a serious self-inflicted wound in the arm. It was not thought to be serious enough, however, to warrant a discharge from the army.[40]

Aside from youth, old age, or alienage, the chief causes for exemption were physical disability, mental disability, or being the chief financial support of a family. If a draftee had a parent, or parents, or motherless children dependent upon him, he was considered to be the chief financial support of his family. Minor controversy arose over the "financial support" provision, but it paled beside the trouble which erupted over what constituted "physical disability." By far the greatest number of applicants for exemption claimed they were physically unfit to serve. It was a revelation to the older members of society to see what sad shape the younger generation thought it was in.

The regulations listed fifty-one categories of disabilities, including the major killers and cripplers, but also many other lesser ailments.[41] The regulations were sufficiently specific, but it was not always certain how serious an ailment was. Draftees were ingenious at faking illnesses, deformities, and various afflictions, and the examining physicians had to be alert. Then, too, many physicians were inexpert or were receptive to bribes.

Another problem at the outset was the appearance of a class of people known as "exemption agents." For a fee they would prepare the "proper" documents, which a draftee would present to the physician, and perhaps gain exemption. That the draftee, in such a case, might be perfectly able to serve in the army, was beside the point. He wanted to remain a civilian and the agent wanted money. Shannon reports that exemption agents

> ... thronged the county clerks' offices button-holing the conscripts as they appeared and offering "to make out and file the necessary affidavits for fifty cents." Some of them employed runners to drum up trade. They lined the corridors of the city hall in New York and had to be encountered like "a crowd of bawling hack drivers at a railway depot or steamboat landing."[42]

In early October numerous Syracuse draftees had procured exemption
through the purchase of such fraudulent papers, while the press frequently carried such advertisements as "Draft Exempts: have your
papers prepared."[43] Provost Marshal John A. Knapp of the 24th District at Auburn told draftees that these agents were imposters. He
announced

> The employment of attorneys or agents to secure the rights
> of drafted men and argue their claims for exemption, is
> entirely unnecessary, and will be discountenanced by the
> Board. Drafted men are cautioned against being imposed
> upon by parties who seek to obtain fees for pretended services
> in their behalf.[44]

The examination procedure[45] was much the same in all districts.
The draftee was usually furnished transportation to the provost marshal's headquarters, if he lived some distance away, and those who
were exempt had their expenses paid home. Upon reaching headquarters he was examined by the physician, and either "held to service" or exempted from service. Affidavits supporting exemption
claims were presented to the board, and the draftee had to testify
that they were accurate. The examination was often done in the presence of the entire board, but there were many exceptions to this.
Fraud was made easy when the medical member conducted the examination by himself. If the man was "held to service" and did not want
to serve, he was either granted a short furlough or a few hours to
procure a substitute or pay commutation. When the men were ready
to leave, they were taken under guard to the storehouse and issued
clothes. Newly enlisted draftees, awaiting transportation to the general rendezvous, were domiciled in army barracks, "Soldiers' Rests,"
armories, or any other facility that was available. When fifty or one
hundred of them had been assembled, they were then forwarded to
the draft rendezvous at Elmira or New York City.[46]

Physical examinations conducted in various districts were far from
uniform; some were rigid, while others were superficial. Judging from
the final reports of the district provost marshals, each pursued the
most rigorous policy in the state, and no draftee or volunteer examined

by his board was exempted except for good reason. Gordon, for example, said that the 19th District officials granted very few claims compared to the number who applied for exemption. On the other hand, according to a letter to Fry from Jacob Moon, who lived in Chenango County in Gordon's district, the physician there held "sham examinations," hardly looked at the men, and in many cases had made up his mind about accepting or rejecting them in advance. "Harry Duncan, Morris Brown, and H. Warner Duncan," Moon wrote, "three as able-bodied men as there are in the district, have been rejected by the surgeon. George Negus, a lame man, has been accepted. William Calvert, with a cancer, has been accepted; a man by the name of Paw, who has fits, has been accepted and Andrew Thompson, with a lame knee, also accepted."[47]

In Utica, Surgeon W. A. Babcock and Provost Marshal J. P. Richardson conducted very careful examinations. The teeth were all checked to insure the proper bite on a cartridge tip. "Every limb is examined," reported the Utica *Herald*; "if lungs are unsound, the temperament 'oplectic,' or the system wasting," the man was turned down. But in Buffalo, Surgeon John S. Trowbridge, with the approval of Provost Marshal Scroggs, accepted one Bernard H. Larey, who had already been rejected in Norwich, Syracuse, Goshen, and Utica. Larey had mutilated his left hand with an axe, could not grip anything, and was later discharged at the draft rendezvous. Yet, during his examination in Buffalo, Trowbridge called Scroggs over and said he thought he should take Larey. They both looked at the damaged hand, agreed that the injury was insignificant, and signed the man up.[48] This is not to imply fraud on the part of Scroggs and Trowbridge, but in this case they were guilty of a careless examination and poor judgment.

While many draftees submitted substantial exemption claims, many more advanced weak, far-fetched, and even ludicrous claims. The fact that some EO's signed up everyone between 20 and 45 guaranteed that there would be numerous legitimate disqualifications.[49] But those whose only problem was a fear of military service must have had a low opinion of the intelligence of enrolment boards, judging by the wild tales they told in support of their exemption applications.

For example, a husky farmer appeared before the provost marshal in Auburn in August 1863, with his husky son, who had been drafted. The father's plea was that the young man was under 20 and hence exempt. To prove his point he produced a family Bible, which purported to contain the birth dates of all children, *written in at the time they were born.* Suspicious of the story, Knapp checked the Bible's date of publication and found that it had been published ten years after the boy's supposed birth.[50] A Maine draftee feigned deafness as the surgeon was examining him. While checking the man's knee the doctor said in a whisper, "That's enough to exempt any man."

"That's what I wanted to hear," shouted the happy draftee. "What's wrong with my knee?"

"Nothing," replied the doctor, "I was talking about your ears."[51]

In the 1863 draft many confused young men sought exemption. One said that he was the only son of his widowed mother, that his father was too ill to work, and that he already had two brothers in the service. Another confidently informed the enrolment board that "I'm entirely dependent upon my mother for support." Aggrieved that the mother was so burdened, the board decided the young man should enter the army. He was still wondering what had gone wrong as he was marched off to the barracks.[52]

Hiram Snell of Easton, Washington County, was exempted in the summer of 1863 because he was the only son of aged and infirm parents. It was later learned that the elder Snell had paid taxes on sixteen thousand dollars worth of real property. Hiram was summoned to headquarters for an explanation. It came out that after the tax payment, the father had turned over all his property to Hiram, on the condition that Hiram would support his parents. Thus they were dependent on him. Along the same line, Herman Schwartz of Utica was exempted in August 1863 because he was the only financial support for his widowed mother. He was arrested the following June when it was learned that the mother was receiving a pension and owned property valued at fifteen hundred dollars. Both Hiram and Herman commuted.[53]

Among the more unusual cases was that of a Schoharie Negro, Tom Van Dyck, who was drafted three times. He was picked first in New York City in the summer of 1863, but was freed because of non-residency. His name was drawn again in Schoharie in the fall of 1863, but he was not held because he was in Class Two and Class One had not yet been exhausted. Finally, in June 1864, his name was drawn again and this time he was held. Then there was a Boston draftee who furnished a substitute who deserted. He furnished another substitute who also deserted. Weary of supplying unreliable substitutes, he decided to go himself. But, lo and behold, he was exempt for physical disability.[54]

An Orleans County lawyer established a wide reputation during the early months of conscription as a fabricator of exemption-inducing ailments. He advertised that for ten dollars he could give a draftee a set of hemorrhoids that would withstand any surgeon's scrutiny. He apparently applied mercury or some other substance to the proper area, giving a vague impression of hemorrhoids, but all such cases were quickly detected during the examination. In another instance he wrote a fifteen-page manuscript in support of some fictitious six-year old disease a draftee was supposed to have. He had another client practice pivoting on the heels of his feet for long periods of time and then claim exemption for bad legs. None of these devices worked for the draftees, but the lawyer made a good bit of money before he was exposed.[55]

An uptown New York City draftee sought to deceive the doctor by implanting a "tumor" on his side. His body was enveloped in swaths of gauze, which when removed, left a transparent patch covering the sore. The man was reluctant to remove the patch, but under the doctor's insistence did so. The surgeon examined the red swelling with great curiosity, and then told the draftee to re-swath his "tumor" and wait in the outer offiice. Soon a clerk brought out the following message:

> Mr. —— examined and found entirely healthy. Sound in
> brain, lungs, and limbs. No skin or other disease qualifying
> him for exemption. He wears, however, an ingeniously con-
> structed tumor that does not interfere with his bodily strength,
> and can at any time be removed with a little hot water and
> scrubbing brush.[56]

✻ ✻ ✻ ✻

An odd organization, devised by enrolled men to avoid military service, appeared at the time of the first draft in 1863, and reappeared with each of the other drafts. This was the "draft insurance society."(DIS)[57] Operating on the insurance principle of individual protection by group contribution, the DIS would first levy an assessment, ranging from one dollar to one hundred dollars against each enrolled member who wished to belong. If a member was later drafted, the money would be used in a number of ways to assist him. Prior to the abolition of commutation, each draftee might receive three hundred dollars with which to commute. After the commutation clause was repealed in July 1864, the money might be used to pay, at least in part, for a substitute. If the draftee did not mind serving himself, the money would help provide for his family. In the event no member of the society was drafted, or if a surplus was left over, the money was pro rated among all members. Thus, through the DIS, enrollees were protecting themselves against the draft, or providing for their families if they went into service.

The DIS should not be confused with the bounty fund drives, or the draft exemption ordinances. In the case of the bounty fund, a citizens' committee raised money to enlist volunteers and thereby fill the district's quota and avoid the draft. Exemption ordinances were local laws by which the community raised money to pay commutation or furnish substitutes for all its draftees. Both of these efforts were carried out by the citizens of the community who were personally exempt from service, and not by the enrolled men. The DIS, on the other hand, included only the enrollees themselves and was organized for their own protection.

In the larger cities the DIS often appeared at the ward level. In September 1863, a "Seventh Ward Relief Association" was established in Utica, while the enrolled men of Syracuse's 4th Ward organized one DIS in August 1864, and another in March 1865.[58] In rural areas, the DIS was formed at the village level. Thirty or forty enrollees organized one in Jamestown in July 1863. Their purpose was to "assist each other to bear the expenses of procuring substitutes, purchasing exemptions, or providing for those they leave behind in case they go. . . ." About a week later the potential draftees in Rome followed suit and in the summer of 1864, Yonkers and Schuylerville each had a DIS. One was set up in Glens Falls during the last draft.[59]

Occasionally the DIS was established along occupational lines. For example, in July 1863, the employees of Parker and Company, a carriage factory on New York City's Twenty-fifth Street, organized a company society numbering 130 members. In addition to the enrolled personnel, many employees over 45 years of age also contributed to this fund. Mr. Parker himself entered into the spirit of things with a five hundred dollar contribution. A group of Albany merchants founded a DIS in August 1864, an example Buffalo shopkeepers were urged to emulate. And while the members of a Buffalo fire brigade did not organize a DIS, they did hold a picnic to raise funds for the benefit of firemen draftees.[60]

There was one attempt on the part of an insurance company to write special policies for enrolled men in August, 1863. The North American Life Insurance Company of New York City proposed that if any enrolled man purchased a "special war permit" for one hundred dollars, from North American, and was then drafted, the company would pay him three hundred dollars.[61] There is no record that North American had any takers, but the fact that no other references can be found to formal draft insurance suggests that the insurance companies did not find this to be a lucrative field.

The amount each member of a DIS contributed varied from one community to another. In the case of the Parker Company, each member was assessed one-tenth of his weekly wage. A Yonkers group required a ten dollar down payment plus weekly contributions of one dollar until either the draft occurred or the amount paid in totalled twenty-five dollars. The enrollees in New Lotts in Brooklyn required only a weekly payment of one dollar. In Albany one hundred dollars per person was the most popular amount. Several societies organized in the summer of 1864 and in the winter of 1864-65 required that sum and restricted the membership. They ran newspaper advertisements urging men to join now, while there was still room.[62]

Somewhat similar to the DIS was another kind of organization authorized under Section 23 of the amended Enrolment Act of March 3, 1865. By this provision, enrollees in a subdistrict could recruit men in advance of a draft, and apply them as substitutes against any of their own number who might later be drafted. Fry rejected a number of petitions requesting government approval of such draft protective groups in January 1865, but following the amendment's adoption two months later, he issued a circular outlining procedures for their operations.[63] The Federal Government never took any official notice of the real DIS.

*   *   *   *

Following a presidential call for troops, little action took place until the quota deadline was practically at hand. Then, with the "dreaded draft" staring a district in the face, efforts were intensified to meet the quota and make the draft unnecessary. Frequent meetings, urgent appeals, newspaper advertisements, and fund-raising drives all became part of the pre-draft drama. The districts that had enough volunteers would breath hearty sighs of relief, while those which did not make their quotas fumed about Copperheads and traitors, and resigned themselves to the inevitable.

It was not unusual for the Provost Marshal General to postpone the draft in a given district when he was convinced that the recruiting committee there could meet the quota if given a few more days. Fry was under constant pressure from many districts in every state to delay the draft, and the frequency with which he acceded to these requests is clear proof of his determination to institute the draft only as a last resort. Only when it was clear that the quotas could not be met, the local provost marshals were ordered to proceed with the draft.

Four drafts were held during the history of the Enrolment Act, one in 1863, two in 1864, and one in 1865. All of New York's thirty-one districts saw the "wheel of fortune" turn during the first draft, but under the second draft only eighteen districts were affected, while under the third and fourth drafts the number was fourteen and twenty-four respectively. (See Appendix A, Tables III and IV.)

· 4 ·

Seymour and the 1863 Draft.

THE ENROLMENT ACT was not a popular measure, and it was not surprising that resistance developed in July 1863 when the first draft occurred. While the trouble was scattered across several states, the focus of opposition was New York City, where a predominantly Irish working-class population, encouraged by a Democratic governor, turned that metropolis into a shambles of death and destruction. Horatio Seymour, serving his second term as the state's chief executive, had been an advocate of compromise in the days before Sumter. He never adjusted to the fact that compromise had been impossible, and that war had broken out. Nevertheless, he had worked energetically to raise the required volunteer regiments, and on occasion, had been warmly applauded by the Secretary of War for his contributions. Conscription, however, was something that Seymour could not stomach. He never admitted, despite conclusive evidence, that the volunteer system had broken down, and he persisted in advocating that method down to the war's close. If the draft were abandoned, he argued, no difficulty whatever would be experienced in getting the required men. Not only was conscription unnecessary, but it was also un-American and unconstitutional. Throughout the lengthy controversy over the draft, the New York Governor continually urged that the law be suspended until the courts had passed on its validity. Understandably, Lincoln did not agree.

In addition to these objections Seymour also argued that the draft was administered in partisan fashion by a crowd of bureaucratic incompetents in Washington. Of course, the real difficulty lay in the complexities of the new law.¹ But critics of the draft, led by Seymour, could not wait for the ink to dry before attacking the Provost Marshal General, and Fry quickly became the symbol of total evil for all who felt victimized by the draft. Few of these people, least of all Governor Seymour, made any attempt to understand the size of the Provost Marshal General's problem, and criticism continued unabated.

Being a Democratic governor of the nation's largest state, disappointed at the failure of compromise and the outbreak of war, and utterly opposed to conscription, Seymour was in an uncomfortable spot. He insisted that he was loyal to the Government and would support it in all of its constitutional activities, yet he felt that some of its activities, like the draft, were unconstitutional. To oppose the war openly would be unthinkable, but he must express his disapproval in some fashion. And how to do this without being classed as a rank Copperhead? Since there was no solution to this dilemma, and since Seymour persisted in trying to find one, his behavior exposed him to charges of insincerity, duplicity, and disloyalty.

For about fifty to seventy-five years after the Civil War the standard judgment on Seymour remained a highly critical one, charging him with having done much to encourage the draft resisters and little to encourage the draft enforcers. The Governor's loyalty and good faith were not challenged, but his judgment was. Then in the 1920's, as Civil War "revisionism" began to take root, Seymour underwent a reappraisal and before long the original assessment of him was overturned. The new view was that the New York City Draft Riots should be blamed on bungling behavior in Washington rather than in Albany; that had the federal government been honest in its contacts with the Governor no trouble would have occurred. Seymour emerged in shining honor as a hard-working, dedicated public servant, and the histories were revised to accommodate this new view. Actually, the original judgment of the Governor's course was thoroughly accurate, and the revisionists, as they have often done in other matters, have distorted this unhappy page of Civil War history.²

* * * *

After the riots were put down, Seymour began a lengthy correspondence with Lincoln in which he indirectly accused Washington of fomenting the outbreak. The Governor reasoned that by (1) a fraudulent and unfair enrolment in New York City, (2) holding the draft when the city was denuded of troops, and (3) failing to advise him of the draft in advance so that he might take precautionary measures, the Administration had issued an open invitation to riot. Seymour presented his case in three letters to the President, on August 3, 7, and 8, 1863, the latter including a long report by the state's Judge Advocate General, Nelson J. Waterbury.[3]

In brief, the Governor and Waterbury contended that the enrolment, and hence the quotas, in New York City districts was disproportionately higher than it was in upstate districts. Furthermore, they alleged that those districts which voted for Lincoln in 1860 were assigned small quotas, while the metropolitan districts, all of which returned majorities for Stephen A. Douglas, had large quotas. Similarly, the districts which supported the Republican candidate, James S. Wadsworth, in the 1862 gubernatorial race, allegedly received much smaller quotas than did the districts which backed Seymour. In analyzing his figures, Waterbury commented:

> ... the discrepancies might, in charity, be ascribed to the greater incompetency, carelessness, and overzeal of some of the enrolling officers ... I regret to be compelled to say that the real truth of the case is so bad as to be inconsistent with any other conclusion than that of intentional fraud. . . .
> The enrolment is a partisan enrolment.

To which Seymour added, "There is no theory which can explain or justify the enrolment in this state."[4]

In his patient replies, Lincoln conceded the discrepancies and agreed to reduce the quotas in the most glaring cases until a reenrolment could take place. In the space of five days he ordered an almost 50 per cent reduction of the quotas in a number of districts. Furthermore, the President invited the Governor, or his agents, to witness the entire reenrolment process.[5] The charge of partisanism proved to be groundless. Fry, reported Nicolay and Hay, ". . . was a man as nearly without politics as a patriotic American can be. He came of a distinguished Democratic family, and during a life passed in the mili-

tary service his only preoccupation had been the punctual fulfillment
of every duty confided to him." Colonel Nugent, under whom the
enrolment was carried out in New York City, was an Irishman and
War Democrat. General John A. Dix, appointed Commanding General of the Department of the East on July 18, 1863, was another
leading War Democrat. The district provost marshals for the metropolitan area were all "selected with special care from those recommended by citizens of the highest character in the place." Obviously,
at the local level, it is possible that some officials might have abused
their powers and settled old scores against personal enemies by causing them to be unfairly enrolled and drafted. But for the most part,
very great efforts were made to prepare accurate enrolment lists.[6]

Bearing in mind the tremendous difficulty of the enrolling process,
and the considerable danger which enrolling officers faced in carrying
out their duties, the historian ought to be more understanding of the
errors which occurred and which Seymour advertised so widely in
August 1863. The Governor made no effort to cooperate with officials
from the Provost Marshal General's Bureau and indicated no interest
in the enrolment at all while it was taking place. Then, after the reign
of terror, he discovered great inequities in the enrolment lists and
argued that by these errors the Federal Government prompted the
riots. Fry was probably correct when he said that the argument raised
by Seymour over the enrolment was "entirely an afterthought." The
only historians to call attention to this sequence of events are James
Ford Rhodes and Sidney D. Brummer,[7] yet it would appear to be the
clue to Seymour's behavior.

*   *   *   *

Turning to the draft itself, another argument arose over Seymour's
post-riot complaint that he had not been kept properly informed of
all draft proceedings. In letters to Dix and Lincoln on August 20 and
21, he insisted that he had never been told the date of the draft in
New York City, and his friendly biographer, Howard Carroll, flatly
states that "Governor Seymour never received any official notification
that the draft was to commence, or that it had commenced."[8] The
record tells us, however, that Fry took great pains to insure close cooperation between his bureau and all governors, especially Seymour,

the most influential anti-Administration public figure save Vallandigham. For example, in selecting AAPMG's, Fry wrote that "care was taken to seek those who would be likely to secure the favor and cooperation of the authorities and the people of New York." Nugent and Diven were both War Democrats, the latter "an intimate acquaintance and personal friend of Governor Seymour."[9]

Furthermore, Fry wrote a number of messages, both to his own subordinates and to the civil officers, urging regular and cordial communication. In a letter to Seymour of April 24, 1863, the Provost Marshal General advised the Governor of the appointments of Townsend and Nugent, and hoped that they would be agreeable to him. He asked him to "communicate fully with them and secure as far as possible for all officers appointed under the Enrolment Act the cooperation of the civil officers of your State." On April 25 Fry wrote in a similar vein to Mayor George Opdyke of New York City, hoping Nugent would be acceptable to him, and requesting close and full cooperation between himself and Nugent and the local provost marshals.[10]

Letters also went out to the newly-appointed AAPMG's, instructing each one to

> ... acquaint yourself with his [Seymour's] views and wishes, and give them due weight in determining as to the best interests of the General Government, of which you are the representative. To this end you will use all proper means to gain and retain the confidence and good will of the Governor and his State officers. . . .

Fry noted that with very few exceptions this approach, which was employed toward all state governors, resulted in "harmony and cooperation between the States and the United States." Nugent and Diven reported the results of their interviews with Seymour in May, and while Nugent felt that the Governor would probably cooperate with the Federal Government, Diven, the "intimate friend," expressed serious misgivings about Seymour's attitude.[11]

In late June, when the enrolment was completed in the New York City districts, Fry ordered the draft to proceed immediately. On July 3, Seymour was advised by the Provost Marshal General that the draft

had been ordered in the 8th District, and a similar letter was sent to
the Governor on July 6, concerning the 1st, 7th, and 9th Districts.[12]
Considerable confusion subsequently developed on this point, Seymour arguing that while he might have been advised in general terms
that the draft was to begin, he was not told in precise terms what day
the draft would begin and in what district. In his August 20 letter to
Dix, he said:

> The notices sent to me by Colonel Fry advise me of the
> completion of the enrolment in several districts, the number
> to be drafted, and the fact that the draft is ordered. . . .
> They do not state when the draft will be made; and in most cases
> several weeks, and in some instances more than a month,
> elapse before the draft is made.   I therefore expected some
> interval between the notice and the draft. . . .[13]

In answering this charge Fry made three points. In the first place
it was administratively impractical to notify each governor of the precise time of each drawing in each district. So many local matters were
involved that the district provost marshal necessarily had discretionary power to proceed with the draft as soon as all was in readiness,
once he had received the green light from Washington. Secondly, had
the Governor taken the trouble to consult occasionally with the
AAPMG's, as Fry had urged all governors to do, he would have been
well posted on the exact dates of the draft. The information he desired
should have been obtained from these responsible local officials, not
from the Provost Marshal General's office in Washington. Fry, after
all, did have a few other matters to attend to besides the situation
in New York State. Seymour's attitude, wrote Fry

> . . . permitted but little, if any, intimate intercourse between
> him and the [Acting] Assistant Provost Marshals General with a
> view to enforcing the draft, and this may in some degree
> account for his lack of familiarity with operations which so
> urgently needed his aid and encouragement.[14]

And lastly, the only governor who raised these questions was
Horatio Seymour. The draft began in New England before it began in

New York, and although the governors of those states received no more information than Seymour received, none argued that he had not been informed of the draft date. All other governors accepted Fry's suggestion, and by cooperating closely with the AAPMG's, learned of all such dates first hand. They may have argued about the wisdom of the draft and the need for its suspension or postponement, but none of them contended he had not been kept properly advised of all draft orders.[15]

Turning to New York City on the eve of the riots, we find the metropolitan area without troops. Because of Lee's invasion of Pennsylvania in late June, the call had gone out to all governors to rush what help they could to the front. Seymour sent nearly 20,000 troops off to war, and was praised by Stanton for his prompt assistance. But this absence of troops gave rise to yet another controversy, once the riots had been quashed. Why, it was asked, did the government proceed with the draft in a community that was openly hostile to it [the draft], at a moment when no troops were available to preserve order? "That the provost marshals, or those behind them," wrote Howard Carroll, ". . . threw prudence, propriety, and commonsense to the winds, there can . . . be no doubt." "The day, the time, and the district were ill-chosen," concluded John B. McMaster; "a more unfavorable moment . . . could hardly have been found," allowed Stewart Mitchell; ". . . just when the city was in its most defenseless condition, the draft was ordered," complained Shannon.[16]

Although there is some merit to this charge, there is a defense against it. To begin with, it seems clear that not many people anticipated serious trouble in New York City when the draft commenced. "No apprehensions of popular tumult were entertained," noted Nicolay and Hay, while the New York *Times* predicted that "the lot in the impending draft will fall noiselessly as the snowflake." Of the first day's draft on Saturday, July 11, Rhodes reported that "the drawing took place without any disturbance whatever, good humor prevailing, even jocularity," and the doubting Shannon conceded "no trouble was encountered." If Seymour expected resistance to the draft why then did he leave New York for a long weekend in New Jersey on the day before the drawing? If he had some knowledge of possible opposition and then wilfully deserted the state, he was guilty of a high crime. It is more correct to assume that the Governor had no such knowledge, and could think of no reason for not going to New Jersey. William Hesseltine comments that Seymour had "no intimation of the morrow's trouble. . . ."[17]

Not only was there no hint of serious resistance, aside from the usual grumblings attendant on the enforcement of any unpopular law, but there were also substantial reasons for quickly proceeding with the draft. For one thing, additional troops were needed, and the draft was the only way to get them. The very invasion of Pennsylvania, which resulted in the denuding of New York City, helped convince the Government that the draft must proceed immediately. Perhaps it might have been delayed, but had this been done it would have been far more difficult to get it under way again. To surrender to the oppositionists might have been a psychological error not easily remedied. Furthermore, the draft had already been initiated in Rhode Island and Massachusetts and was proceeding without incident there. Why should New York be different?[18]

But it was different, and with a vengeance, when the Draft Riots broke out in July.[19] Seymour was at Long Branch, New Jersey, and although he tried to return to the city "as soon as possible," his actual movements remain a mystery. Carroll says he tried to get to New York on Sunday night when he "first received word that the draft was actually in progress," but was unable to secure transportation. When he received the telegram at noon Monday that rioting had broken out he left at once for the city "without having tasted food." He did not reach New York, however, until late Tuesday morning, July 14, when the rioting was well into its second day. It seems incredible that the Governor of New York, in the midst of the worst riots in the nation's history, could not get from northern New Jersey to New York City a little more rapidly than he did, but Seymour's biographer, as well as all historians of the riots, have been untroubled by that fact.[20]

While the beleaguered Metropolitan Police and the military fragments remaining in the city sought to contain the fury of the mob, Seymour, on Tuesday, issued two proclamations, urging the rioters to go home, and declaring the city in a state of insurrection. He then addressed the mob in City Hall Park, the famous "My Friends" speech,[21] and demanded the suspension of the draft. At 11:10 a.m. Tuesday Fry wired Nugent to suspend the draft, although Nugent did not officially publish the order until Wednesday, July 15.[22] Some historians believe that publishing the suspend notice broke the back of the uprising. This seems unlikely. The exhaustion of the rioters and the arrival of troops from the Pennsylvania battlefields were the two factors which terminated the riots, not the "suspension" notice. And Seymour's proclamation ordering the riots to cease could not have been less effective had it been directed at a horde of bedouins in the central Sahara.

With the riots finally suppressed, the most urgent question facing Washington was resumption of the draft at the earliest moment. From faraway places came the demand that the New York draft ought to proceed immediately. Any delay, it was held, would only embolden the opposition and make it more difficult to ever reinstitute the draft. Governor Samuel J. Kirkwood of Iowa wired that

> . . . the enforcement of the draft throughout the country
> depends upon its enforcement in New York City. If it can be
> successfully resisted there, it cannot be enforced elsewhere.
> For God's sake let there be no compromising or halfway
> measures.

A group of federal officials in Des Moines advised Lincoln that "suspension of draft in New York as suggested by Governor Seymour will result disastrously in Iowa." AAPMG Diven wrote from Elmira,

> . . . if the Government puts down the riot in New York by
> yielding to it in whole or in part by showing any disposition
> to compromise with the rioters, as Governor Seymour seems to
> propose, then I expect the resistance to be universal. . . .

The 18th District provost marshal reported from Schenectady that ". . . if the draft is enforced first in New York City and Troy . . . it would have the effect of quieting disloyalty throughout this district. . . ."[23] It is unlikely that the Administration ever considered a permanent suspension, and as soon as the air cleared a bit it moved quickly to the offensive. On July 18, General John A. Dix replaced the aging and ineffectual General John E. Wool as Commander of the Department of the East, a transfer of authority which put Dix directly in control of draft resumption.

*   *   *   *

Stewart Mitchell, who has written what James G. Randall describes as an "excellent biography" of Seymour, says that Dix's appointment was an "unfortunate" choice. In the judgment of most historians including Randall, however, Dix was an excellent choice. He was "a high-minded reliable general," "a Democrat who already had a most distinguished political career in both the state and National Governments," and "one of the best examples of a War Democrat." His good character, his non-partisanism, and his devotion to the national cause, commended him favorably to this responsible position.[24]

It should also be mentioned that certain Radical Republicans had tried to force on Lincoln the appointment of General Ben Butler for the New York command. They had little use for Dix, a Democrat and a moderate, while Butler would provide firm rule. If he caused a few hundred Copperhead corpses to clutter the streets of New York City so much the better. Had Lincoln acquiesced to this Radical pressure there is no telling what might have happened in New York. As Randall observes, "it would be an obvious understatement to say that an orderly and peaceable situation could not have been anticipated with Butler in command."[25] Thus not only was Dix's appointment a good one on its merits, but Lincoln also resisted strong Radical pressure in making it, and demonstrated again his determination to ignore party considerations in prosecuting the war.

Dix was fully resolved to enforce the federal law and resume the draft, but he was enough of a New Yorker and states rightist to hope that all of this might be accomplished simply by close cooperation with state officials. He made repeated overtures to Seymour, explaining how much he desired his help and how much he hoped resumption of the draft might be engineered without resorting to Washington. Dix's son wrote that it was a cause of "bitter regret" to his father that those hopes were not realized, and that the Governor's sullen aloofness compelled the General to request military help from Virginia.[26]

This phase of the story began when Dix arrived in New York City, on July 18, 1863. In an interview between Seymour, Dix, and General Edward R. S. Canby, Dix's second in command, Dix expressed his desire that a spirit of good will and mutual cooperation should characterize their relations. With reference to the draft resumption, he hoped that the Governor as Commander-in-Chief of the state troops "should adopt a course and take measures which would render it unnecessary to ask for assistance of the Federal authorities." In the days that followed this interview, whenever district provost marshals asked Dix for military assistance, he referred them to the Governor.[27]

It is doubtful whether Dix really expected Seymour's cooperation, but if he did, he was sharply disabused in the last part of July and early August. In an Albany speech and in his tedious correspondence with Lincoln, the Governor repeated once more that the enrolment and quotas were fraudulent, unfair, and partisan, and that the draft act was unconstitutional. He prophesied that if the draft was enforced it would bring down on this country the contempt of the civilized world. He demanded that the draft be postponed until the courts could determine the legality of the law. But Dix still tried to get the necessary assurance of help from the State's chief executive. On July 30, he wrote Seymour: "I am desirous of knowing whether the military power of the State may be relied on to enforce the execution of the law in case of forcible resistance to it. . . ." In his reply on August 3, the Governor referred to his current letters to Lincoln, and implied that the President would postpone the draft and set all their doubts at rest. Dix, growing impatient, answered in a long communication of August 8. Going over the old familiar ground, he reiterated that the draft would be enforced at all costs, that state assistance was desired, but that federal military force would be invoked if the state authorities did not cooperate.[28]

By the second week in August there was ample cause for doubt over the intentions of the state officials. Senator Henry Wilson of Massachusetts, chief architect of the Enrolment Act, had received a private letter from Saratoga Springs which said "our State militia is mainly officered by open secessionists recently appointed by the Governor. They will lead the mob in these counties. . . ." On July 31, the 20th

District provost marshal wrote AAPMG Townsend from Watertown that known "Copperhead leaders have received commissions or authority to raise companies or regiments from the Governor to fill up the National Guard, but in fact to resist the draft. . . ." And the next day Townsend informed Fry that he did not have "the slightest confidence in the State authorities in regard to the question of the draft." Seymour, he added, was a "dangerous man with a mind congenitally predisposed to lunacy." Dix was by now convinced that the "whole moral influence of the executive power of the State will be thrown against the execution of the [draft] law. . . ." It is not without reason that the General advised Fry that, in Ulster and Albany Counties, "artillery as well as infantry will be needed."[29]

Receiving no early answer to his August 8 inquiry, Dix decided to act. On August 12 he requested at least 10,000 troops to enforce the draft in New York City. General Henry W. Halleck, a War Department advisor, wired back that 5,000 soldiers would leave for Governor's Island very shortly with more to follow. The transports were slow, however, and on August 18, the day before the draft was to resume, Dix telegraphed Halleck that only two ships had cleared Fortress Monroe by 2 p.m. that day, and how could they possibly reach New York before the night of the 19th? Well, they made it somehow, because at 3 p.m. on the 19th Dix advised Halleck that "the draft is progressing quietly. The troops are arriving. . . ."[30]

On August 15, three days after Dix requested federal troops, Seymour got around to answering the General's week-old letter. In his reply the Governor made his position quite clear and it is strange that historians have paid so little attention to this document, which practically gives Seymour's case away. After lamenting Lincoln's decision to enforce the draft, the Governor got to the heart of the matter:

> . . . As you state in your letter that it is your duty to enforce the
> act of Congress, and as you apprehend its provisions may excite
> popular resistance, it is proposed you should know the position
> which will be held by the State authorities. Of course, under
> no circumstances can they perform duties expressly confided
> to others, nor can they undertake to relieve others from
> their proper responsibilities. But there can be no violations of

good order, no riotous proceedings, no disturbances of the
public peace, which are not infractions of the laws of the State,
and those laws will be enforced under all circumstances.
I shall take care that all the executive officers of this State
perform their duties vigorously and thoroughly, and if need
be the military power will be called into requisition.

As you are an officer of the General Government, and not
of the State, it does not become me to make suggestions to you
with regard to your action under a law of Congress. You
will, of course, be governed by your instructions and your
own views of duty; and it will be unbecoming in me to obtrude
my opinions upon one who is charged with high responsibilities, and who is in no degree subject to my direction, or
responsible to me for anything which he may do in accordance
with his own judgment and in pursuance of his convictions
of propriety.[31]

Not only was Seymour not going to cooperate with Dix; he was declaring war on him. For a month the General had been begging for
assistance from the Governor. Now he was cut off cold by pompous
talk.[32]

With federal troops on the way, and resumption two days off, Dix
issued a proclamation on August 17 urging compliance with the law,
and threatening punishment to anyone who might oppose it. Seymour,
having finally got it through his head that the draft would be enforced,
issued a proclamation of his own the next day, questioning again the
act's constitutionality, expressing again his opposition to the draft,
but also urging everyone to comply with it peacefully. Randall naively
hints that this belated statement by the Governor helped insure peaceful resumption, but more probably, the battle-seasoned veterans from
the Army of the Potomac then pouring into New York were the real
reason that no further trouble erupted. Seymour's habit of attaching
innumerable reservations to his official pronouncements about the
draft made them virtually worthless.[33]

Now that the draft had been resumed without incident, the Governor returned to his old complaint that he had not been informed of
the precise date of the draft resumption, and to this he added two
new complaints: (1) New York State was not receiving credit for all

volunteers enlisted prior to the draft (thus its quotas were too high),
and (2) recruiting agents were enticing young men out of the city
and enlisting them to the credit of other communities.[34] In reply to
these protests Lincoln told Seymour that in the future a running record
would be kept of every volunteer mustered into service in New York
State, so that if a draft occurred the quotas would be based on the
latest figures. Furthermore, the Governor was advised that in the future, whenever a draft date was determined in any district, he would
be personally informed of that date both by mail and by telegraph.
Neither of these services were rendered to any other governor.[35]

In addition to all of this we must also recall that on August 7 and
again on August 11 the President ordered arbitrary 50 per cent quota
reductions in a number of New York City districts, reductions justified
solely by the desire to appease Seymour. Despite these open and un-
mistakeable gestures of conciliation, the Governor still had the effron-
tery to accuse the Lincoln Administration of "a spirit of hostility to
this state. . . ." He charged that "it is governed by a spirit of malice in
all things small and great . . . I look for nothing but hostility."[36]

*   *   *   *

Having chronicled the principal events of the draft crisis of 1863,
let us compare Seymour's behavior with that of the Administration. If
we accept the judgment of many writers, the Governor's patriotism, integrity, and sincerity should not be challenged. That Seymour was an
honorable man, a courteous gentleman, and a distinguished public
servant, keeps recurring in all the literature. It is not easy to take
issue with such a body of opinion, but in fairness to Fry, Dix, and
Lincoln, issue must be taken. Admittedly, Seymour was in an awkward
spot and his entire record should not be judged by his performance in
1863. Nevertheless, his refusal to cooperate with the federal draft officers, his harangues against the draft, and his quibbling over quotas,
presents a pattern of persistent and defiant opposition to the Federal
Government.

A few writers have argued that Seymour's behavior in the draft
controversy was dictated chiefly by political considerations. The principal basis for this charge is an August 6 letter to Samuel J. Tilden.
After complaining of Washington's hostility toward him, the Governor

states that he has sent another letter off to Lincoln objecting to the draft. But, he added, "it would do no good, except making up a record." Brummer concluded that "this, then was the aim of Seymour's lengthy correspondence with Lincoln—to make a record." *Harpers Weekly* angrily accused the governor of exploiting the disturbed times to advance his own presidential prospects, while even Hesseltine concedes the Governor was "making a record."[37]

Seymour's spotty correspondence record should be admitted into evidence, to further demonstrate his bad faith toward Washington. He answered Lincoln's first letter after a three-week delay, and promised a second letter which he never wrote. Dix, after waiting nearly a month and receiving no reply to two letters, requested federal troops to insure a peaceful draft resumption in August. When the Governor did send his tardy answers he would excuse the delay by noting the great press of business. Yet Fry, Dix, and Lincoln, amid pressing duties themselves, answered Seymour's letters promptly.

Whereas Seymour's behavior in the 1863 draft crisis was characterized, for the most part, by stubborn opposition, the attitude of the Administration was marked by patience, conciliation, and moderation. Washington made repeated concessions throughout that summer in its efforts to mollify the New York Governor. With the one exception of permanent draft suspension, the Lincoln Administration softened its position on every point raised by Seymour and in many cases went beyond what he asked. The Governor's cooperation was repeatedly requested at the time of the enrolment, the draft, and the reenrolment, but these requests were ignored.

Then, after the riots, when the Governor began bombarding Washington with complaints, Lincoln typically accepted Seymour's criticism in good faith. Quotas were reduced, a reenrolment was ordered, provost marshals were instructed to advise the Governor "by mail and telegraph" the exact dates of future drafts, and enlistment figures were to be kept up to date by frequent reports from Washington. Furthermore, when Seymour sent his Judge Advocate General, Nelson Waterbury, to the capital in late July to gather material for the report which became the basis for the quota criticisms, Fry gave him complete cooperation. Waterbury wrote:

... I found that gentleman not only ready to supply the fullest
information, but also anxious to obtain a knowledge of every
wrong or injustice. The President also was decided in the
expression of his views to the same effect, and was earnest and
emphatic in the assurances he desired ... that every substantial wrong or error pointed out to him should be
corrected. ....[38]

On two occasions, in the summer and fall, Lincoln appointed special
commissions to restudy the quota system. The first of these commissions, created in response to complaints from all over the North, reported that "we have carefully examined ... the work done ... by
the Provost Marshal General, and find it has been done with fairness."
The second commission, created in early December 1863 to clarify
the New York situation, was composed of two War Democrats and a
political independent. The chairman of the commission, Judge William F. Allen, was selected personally by Seymour, as Lincoln sought
to satisfy the Governor. In its report, submitted in February 1864,
the commission stated that Fry had furnished it with all "the documents and information ... and facilitated ... all their labors." It then
expressly cleared EO's of any blame for enrolment errors, and affirmed
their fidelity and integrity. The major point of the Allen Commission's
report was that the basis of the enrolment should not be the available
able-bodied manpower of a district, but rather the total population.
Fry and Lincoln quickly disposed of this recommendation which
would make no distinction between a district populated chiefly with
old women and children and one populated with many healthy young
men, but still the President ordered a further quota reduction in certain districts.[39]

Provost Marshal General Fry is one of the most neglected figures
of the war period. No biography of him has ever appeared, and all one
can find about him are skimpy, isolated passages here and there. He
was bitterly attacked by many people as he conscientiously tried to
administer an unpopular and ambiguous law. Mitchell, having made
no effort to understand the complexities of the Provost Marshal General's job, insults Fry, disparages his character, and attributes to him
the worst possible motives for four solid pages.[40] Fry was "arrogant,"

Fry was a "desk general," Fry was "a partisan," Fry "probably secretly resented" Seymour's letters to Lincoln, the spirit of Fry's book (*New York and the Conscription of 1863*) was "none too sweet," and so on ad nauseam. If Mitchell had some basis for these remarks he might be on more solid ground, but in fact, he has no such basis. He uses the word "probably" so often that one might fairly conclude he was conjuring up some imaginary figure on whom he could vent his frustrations at Seymour's shortcomings.

Rather than being a "desk general," Fry had a fine war record prior to being summoned to Washington. Further, ample testimony to his non-partisanism can be found, and none of the responsible persons associated with him in the War Department and elsewhere ever referred to him as "arrogant." Rhodes writes that Fry "was a man of parts, of a high sense of honor and zealous for the impartial administration of the law." General Jacob D. Cox, a subordinate officer under Burnside in the Department of the Ohio in 1863, wrote that the draft law was ". . . admirably administered by Colonel Fry and his bureau. It was a delicate and difficult task, but it was carried out with . . . patience, honesty, and thoroughness. . . ." William H. H. Terrell, the Adjutant General of Indiana, commented:

> . . . The position [of Provost Marshal General] was surrounded with many difficulties. . . . The intercourse between the Governor [Oliver P. Morton] and Military Authorities of Indiana and Colonel Fry . . . was extensive and intricate, and it is but justice to say he always manifested a disposition to conscientiously and justly facilitate the efforts made by the State Authorities to raise troops in Indiana to the full extent of his power. A more faithful or capable officer could hardly have been called to the performance of this responsible trust.[41]

Nicolay and Hay note that Fry "was not only an accomplished soldier but an executive officer of extraordinary tact, ability, and industry." A representative from the Buffalo Common Council who went to Washington to obtain quota reductions, reported back that Fry was ". . . an able, industrious, and eminently just man." James G. Blaine, in the course of his notorious battle with Roscoe Conkling in

the House of Representatives in 1866 (See Appendix C), said that
Fry "is a most efficient officer, a high-toned gentleman, whose character is without spot or blemish, a gentleman who stands second to no
officer in the American army. . . ."[42] In the face of this testimony the
historian must reject Mitchell's accusations and give the Provost
Marshal General credit for doing a good job in a difficult situation.

*   *   *   *

Did Seymour provoke the Draft Riots? We know that he made
many speeches in which he strongly attacked the Administration, denounced the draft act, and suggested to his hearers that *military action
by the people* might not always be unjustified. We know also that
many anti-Seymour journals, like the New York *Tribune* and *Harpers
Weekly* openly accused the Governor of instigating the trouble by
these inflammatory speeches. No evidence exists confirming a direct
connection between the speeches and the riots,[43] but many students
of history conclude that Seymour helped create such an explosive atmosphere by his speeches that when other combustible elements were
introduced the riots resulted. A public officer who excites a mob to a
white fury and then tells it not to be violent, must bear a good bit of
the blame if violence results. For these various reasons we consider
the original, not the revisionist interpretation of Seymour's role in the
1863 draft crisis to be the correct one.

· 5 ·

The Jumpers.

THE TERM "BOUNTY-JUMPER," gained wide currency in the last two years of the Civil War. It was applied to persons who would enlist for no other purpose than to pocket one or more large bounties. Drawn principally from the dregs of society, the bounty-jumper, totally immune to patriotic impulse, was dedicated to the acquisition of as much money with as little effort as possible. He differed from the typical deserter only in his monetary motivation, and by his repeated reenlistments in new localities under new names for new bounties. Once enlisted, he would stop at nothing to gain his freedom, occasionally losing his life in the attempt. The most successful jumpers accumulated thousands of dollars in a short space of time. Of course, the hard-working communities, which raised bounty funds, and the United States Army, which needed troops, were both badly cheated by this form of rascality. But efforts to check bounty-jumping were either inadequate or belated, so that the practice flourished right down to the end of the war.[1]

The Poughkeepsie *Daily Eagle*, it is true, did insist that bounty soldiers were good material for the army. "Once in the ranks," it argued, "and with three months drilling and discipline they will make obedient soldiers." For proof it cited "Billy Wilson's Zouaves," originally a collection of thieves, pickpockets, emigrant-runners and prize-fighters, which quickly adjusted to the army way and became a well-disciplined, hard-fighting outfit.[2] But since such testimony is contrary to everything else ever said or written about bounty soldiers, it cannot be taken seriously. That same paper listed some twenty-two separate

81

items on bounty-jumping crimes from July 1863 to April 1865, and
New York's most notorious jumper of all, William Provost, came from
Hudson, only forty miles from Poughkeepsie.

Several hundred New York bounty-jumpers who had been sent to
the front in irons in 1864, were captured by the Confederates before
they had an opportunity to desert, and were shipped to Andersonville
prison in southwestern Georgia. Things were bad enough anyhow in
that concentration camp, but with the arrival of these "N'Yaarkers"
the situation worsened appreciably. A clue to the bounty-jumper type
is provided by John McElroy's account of these criminals at Andersonville. "The lice," wrote McElroy, "worried us by day and tormented
us by night; the maggot-flies fouled our food and laid in sores and
wounds larvae that speedily became masses of wriggling worms. The
N'Yaarkers were human vermin that preyed upon and harried us un-
ceasingly."

The N'Yaarkers banded together in raiding parties, each com-
manded by a "bold, unscrupulous, energetic scoundrel." At first the
Raiders would cross over the polluted creek which cut through the
middle of the camp and seize money and other valuables from the
new arrivals. Originally carried out at night, these expeditions gradually came to be executed in broad daylight in full view of the entire
camp. So dispirited, physically weakened, or unfamiliar with what
was going on were the mass of men in the enclosure that little was
done to stop the raids. The Confederate authorities provided no internal supervision of the camp. McElroy reports that the Raiders'
methods ranged from sneak thievery to highway robbery:

> All the arts learned in the prisons and purlieus of New York
> were put into exercise. Decoys . . . would be on the lookout for
> promising subjects as each crowd of fresh prisoners entered
> the gate, and by kindly offers to find them a sleeping place, lure
> them to where they could be easily despoiled during the
> night. If the victim resisted there was always sufficient force
> at hand to conquer him. . . . I have known as many as three of
> these to be killed in a night.[3]

Or listen to the story of Frank Wilkeson, a lad of 16 who ran away from his Hudson River farm in the winter of 1863-64 and enlisted in the 11th New York Artillery at Albany. The month he spent in the Troy Road Barracks awaiting shipment south was an experience he never forgot, and was exceeded in horror only by the actual trip from New York City to Alexandria, Virginia, and service at the front. But even the latter circumstance, with shells bursting over him and comrades dropping at each side of him, may have been anti-climactic when compared to the nightmarish happenings on the way to the front.[4]

As he entered the Barracks in Albany he was swallowed up by about 1,000 of the most repulsive characters he had ever seen. A gang of them quickly clustered around Wilkeson demanding to know what bounty he had received and how many bounties he had jumped. Naively, the young boy shot back that he had received no bounty, had never jumped one, and had entered the army to fight Confederates.[5] For this remark, he was assailed with sarcasm, insults, and foul names; the thugs told him that he was worse than an idiot. Within a day or two Wilkeson was robbed of all of his belongings, and soon thereafter was savagely beaten up. Had not the guards rushed to his rescue, he might have been killed.[6]

The jumpers dominated life in Troy Barracks; they were the social elite. The more bounties a man had jumped the more highly was he regarded by his fellows. Non-jumpers, who had somehow gotten in there, were complete outcasts. As Wilkeson reports it,

> ... the social standing of a hard-faced, crafty pickpocket who had jumped the bounty in say half a dozen cities, was assured. He shamelessly boasted of his rascally agility. Less active bounty-jumpers looked up to him as to a leader. He commanded their profound respect. When he talked, men gathered around him in crowds and listened attentively to words of wisdom concerning bounty-jumping. . . . His right to occupy the most desirable bunk, or to stand at the head of the column when we prepared to march to the kitchen for our rations, was undisputed. If there was a man in all that shameless crew who had enlisted from patriotic motives, I did not see him. . . .[7]

❂ ❂ ❂ ❂

On the boat trip to New York City, two men jumped overboard, one being killed, while in the march through the city to the dock at the Battery, four more who tried to flee were shot dead. The boat which took the men to Alexandria was, in Wilkeson's words, a "floating hell." Whiskey flowed freely and the drunken brawling which followed left hardly a man unscarred. By some miracle no one was killed, although broken heads and empty pockets were commonplace. Then the gambling commenced, the losers began to assault the winners, and soon anyone with a wad of bills was fair game. Wilkeson believed that professional gamblers, "in league with high officials," were planted on the boat for the purpose of swindling the men of their bounty money. He estimated that $170,000 was taken by the gamblers between New York City and Alexandria. Summing it all up, Wilkeson observed that "False history . . . say[s] they were brave Northern youth going to the defence of their country. I, who know, say they were as arrant a gang of cowards, thieves, murderers, and blacklegs as were ever gathered inside the walls of Newgate or Sing Sing."[8]

In other words, most bounty-jumpers were common criminals who were taking advantage of the war crisis to improve their own financial situation. They were associated with almost every kind of law-breaking deed. For example, a man named "Brick" Boyd, who was arrested in Albany in January 1864 for bounty-jumping, was wanted in a western city on a counterfeit charge. Rodney McGee, arrested for assault and battery in November 1864, proved to be a bounty-jumper and horse thief as well. Had one McCloskey, who was found guilty of attempted murder in Buffalo, been acquitted, he would have been seized by the military for "having extensively practiced bounty-jumping."[9]

Ira Fryer, a many-time, Albany delinquent, was finally thrown into jail in December 1864 for assault and battery, attempted murder, entering a house of ill-fame, and bounty-jumping.[10] The 192nd Regiment garrisoned in Albany, consisted chiefly of jumpers, and in the latter months of the war, the press carried stories of its escapades almost every day. The *Argus* doubted that "there ever was a regiment that suffered more from this class of villains known as bounty-jumpers than the 192nd, and we suggest that it would be safer for the public to have all of them on their march down Broadway, handcuffed."[11]

Although it thought bounty volunteers could make good soldiers, the Poughkeepsie *Daily Eagle* complained constantly about the activities of hoodlums and bounty-jumpers. It was charged that Albany "roughs" regularly came to the town to assist the escape of new recruits. In February 1864, the *Eagle* reported that "some of the thieves, robbers, bounty-jumpers, pickpockets, scoundrels, and roughs," who had been hanging around for a few days left their hotel without paying their bill, "completely outwitting the landlord." The following month, the "recent thieves" were alleged to have transferred operations to Kingston and Rhinebeck, where they robbed recruits without interference from anyone. Shortly after this Poughkeepsie was again invaded by a number of people with "villainous-looking countenances, short thick necks, and bullet-shaped heads." The newspaper presumed that these people were bounty-jumpers and advised the local police to look sharp.[12]

Captain James Forsyth, provost marshal of the 15th District, wrote Townsend from Troy in December 1864, that "bands of bounty-jumpers, deserters and stragglers infest this district, but when arrested nothing can be proved to identify them, as they enlist in other states under assumed names, and desert with pockets full of money and then congregate in cities and towns with perfect impunity." Fort Erie, Ontario, just across the border from Buffalo, was a favorite haven for bounty-jumpers, who wanted to allow the "heat" to subside prior to returning for another jump. One late visitor to that town counted twenty-four of "those sneaking thieves . . . hanging around the various taverns." He noted that they were impudent, yet cowardly, and held in as much contempt on the Canadian side as on the American.[13]

This is not to say that everyone who received a bounty did so intending to desert at once. Of course, many—there are no statistics—needed the money, but also recognized that an obligation to serve in the army went with the money, and they accepted this obligation. For example, a Negro who had just enlisted at the Poughkeepsie office in January 1864 was observed carefully counting out the money to his wife with detailed instructions to use the cash to pay off the family debts. That very same week one Henry Van Arnum enlisted at Troy and bought a home for his father with his bounty money. And perhaps some bounty recruits may have been just "wholesome American boys" who wanted to live it up a bit before entering the military. One was a 6th District recruit who deserted with two hundred dollars in substitute money in September 1863. Two weeks later, broke but happy following a "jolly good spree," he reported back to the provost marshal, announced that his private affairs were in good shape and said he was ready to go.[14] But the fact remains that a great many bounty soldiers were unscrupulous rogues, concerned only with acquiring more cash, and giving no thought to serving their country.

In effecting their escape, bounty-jumpers employed boat-jumps, dig-outs, mass breaks, and tricking gullible guards. However, since most troops were transported by train, train-jumping quickly became the most popular method of desertion. A number of recruits, on a train heading for Elmira in August 1863, put the lights out in several of the cars and attempted a general break. Five were either killed by bullets from the guards, or by the fall from the moving train. One guard also jumped and caught a substitute, who tried to bribe the guard with half of his bounty. Instead, the guard marched the jumper twelve miles at bayonet point to the next station and had him jailed. About a month later, a body in an advanced state of decomposition was found in the woods near Corning. Riddled with bullets, the dead man was presumed to be one of those who had jumped from the Elmira train.[15]

Water closets, on occasion, were favorite points from which to jump, since they were concealed from public view. John McKelver, on a train to Riker's Island in October 1863, changed to citizen's clothes in the water closet and leaped to freedom near Hyde Park. He left his wife and child on the train without a cent. Two months later, while a squad of conscripts was passing through Chatham in Columbia County, a recruit forced the door to the platform open, and tried to stab the guard. The latter saw the thrust coming, made a wild swipe with his gun, and knocked the draftee clear off the car. The train was stopped, but not in sufficient time to apprehend the knife-wielding jumper.[16]

Twenty-eight substitutes were being brought down to Albany from Malone in August 1864, when a malfunction in the brakes caused the train to stop. When it was ready to proceed, however, only twenty-four substitutes were found on board. A guard of three men was detailed to recapture the four escapees, while the train moved on to Albany. The next morning the guard reported that the fog and darkness had prevented the recapture of the fugitives, although they did find the cap of one, which they brought back "as a trophy."[17]

Two chained-together deserters were being shipped to Washington in January 1865, when one slipped his wrist from the ring and jumped from the platform. He was found groggy on the track with a broken back and was barely dragged off in time to avoid being crushed by another train. Train-jumping was even popular well after the war was over. In July 1865 a handcuffed deserter being returned to Syracuse leaped from a train proceeding at a thirty-five mile per hour clip. He was found a day later with head wounds and in a delirious condition. But the most gruesome such episode occurred near Schenectady in January 1864, when an Albany recruit jumped into the path of an express train moving the opposite way, and was sliced in two.[18]

One of the best places to attempt a break was in the depot itself, where recruits were transferred to other trains or taken to restaurants for meals. With many people milling around, it was easy to hide or to run for the exits. The fact that the guards might hit innocent bystanders if they fired worked to the jumpers' advantage, although this did not always deter the trigger-happy guards. Two hundred substitutes arrived in Albany from Boston in late June 1864, and despite a heavy guard posted in the station, six got away. Then as soon as the train left the city a dozen more successfully leaped out of the car windows. In March 1865, when a squad of men from the infamous 192nd was moving through the East Albany depot, five escaped, the guards shooting indiscriminately at soldier and civilian alike. As the train carrying these 192nd recruits stopped in the Ossining station, two more fled, and while the unit was marching through New York City, sixty-two others vanished.[19]

Recruits brought from Boston destined for New York City, Elmira, or points west, came through Albany, and frequent breaks occurred at that point. Escape was facilitated by the fact that the railroad had no bridge over the Hudson River, so all passengers were unloaded at

East Albany, put on a ferryboat, floated across to Albany, and transported or marched to the Albany depot. One such train carrying 150
recruits, many of them admitted bounty-jumpers, left Boston early in
June 1864. Although the men were heavily guarded—one guard for
every five men—a group of them in one of the cars sealed the doors,
cut a hole in the floor, and tried to lock the brakes. Apparently the
train was partially stopped in this fashion, for ten did escape through
the hole. Several others were not so lucky, however, for on the following day four dead soldiers with torn and mangled bodies were found
along the tracks near Schodack and Kinderhook.[20]

When the train arrived in East Albany the depot was thronged
with a hostile mob, which appeared bent on freeing all the Boston
recruits. The jumpy guards took every precaution to avoid an escape
or a rescue. When two young men named Cleary and Murray, who
had been on the train but were not connected with the jumpers, refused to return to a car when ordered, a guard struck Murray with his
rifle butt and repeated his orders. The two started to run and had
gone some fifteen feet when the guard fired twice, the first shot missing both men, but the second killing Murray instantly. Although a
coroner's jury ruled the slaying unjustifiable and ordered the arrest
of the guard who fired the shot, one cannot help but feel sympathy
for the guard. Considering the difficulty of watching bounty-jumpers,
it was understandable that guards should shoot first and ask questions
later.[21]

When the ferryboat transporting what remained of the Boston recruits arrived on the Albany side a mob of cutthroats, similar to that
in East Albany, was waiting to try another rescue. However, all efforts
to distract the guards failed, and the recruits, kept in a compact body,
were marched to the depot without further loss.[22]

Late in the war the city of Utica negotiated a contract for the filling
of its quota under the December 1864 call for troops with a broker,
Aaron Richardson. Richardson rounded up his men in several cities,
drawing a large number, most of whom were master bounty-jumpers,
from New York City and Albany. As these new recruits were being
forwarded from Utica to New York they began to disappear. When
one train containing sixteen of them reached West Albany, three used

the water closet routine. Two were successful, but the third struck his head on a stone as he dropped, and died a few hours later. When the train reached the depot the agent in charge of the thirteen remaining men, for some unaccountable reason, took them to a hospital, where nine escaped. The remaining four were delivered to the barracks.[23]

Another shipment of Utica recruits, also signed up by Richardson, was sent to Albany a day or two later, but thirty-two quickly escaped en masse from the barracks. The following night nine more reached the Albany depot from Utica, accompanied by a four-man guard. Suddenly a "captain" appeared, who relieved the surprised guards and marched the men off to a secluded spot, where men and "captain" together, all became civilians.[24] The whole business was naturally looked upon as an outrage in Utica, and the new provost marshal, Peter Crandall, came under heavy fire. Crandall, in turn, denounced Richardson the broker, and demanded either more men or his money back. The matter exploded into the famous Haddock court-martial, a subject to be examined in detail later in this volume.[25]

Occasionally recruits, desperate for freedom, jumped from boats. A group of five "noted vagabonds" from Mercer Street in New York City went to Connecticut to enlist in August 1864. After being mustered in for three hundred dollar bounties, they were placed aboard transports headed for camp at New Haven, but all jumped overboard before the ship was fairly underway. As they swam for the shore, three drowned and two were shot dead. Their bodies were washed up on the beach in a day or so, and early passers-by rifled the dead mens' pockets of all bounty money.[26]

At about the same time, a boat with two hundred conscripts from New Haven was pulling into New York's East River when two substitutes leaped overboard. One was shot in the arm, and the other in the back by a guard. Meanwhile boats were dispatched from the shore by friends of the jumpers to rescue them, and boats were sent from the transport to recapture them. In an exciting melee in midstream, the man shot in the arm was hustled away to freedom, while the man shot in the back was recaptured. About a year later, a bounty-jumper leaped from the Albany ferry as the boat neared the western bank. A volley of shots rang out, and "he sank to rise no more."[27]

For those recruits who were confined in cells and hence unable to jump from trains or boats, there was little else to do but dig out. A group of men from New York City, who proposed to capitalize on higher substitute prices in New England, went to Worcester, Massachusetts, to enlist in July 1863. After being sworn in they were placed in a dungeon, and promptly commenced to dig under the wall to freedom. They were shortly found out, however, and put under close guard. Five recruits dug out of the Poughkeepsie Armory in April 1864, and headed toward Albany. When the escape was discovered, orders were sent to stop the northbound express at nearby Hyde Park. This was done at one-thirty in the morning to allow the deserters, presuming they were still in the neighborhood, to get on board. They fell full into the trap and were seized as soon as they took their seats. In the last month of the war, several bounty-jumpers being detained in a room at the Albany provost marshal's headquarters tried to cut a hole in the floor with a jackknife. After going through one layer of flooring, they found it was a double floor. Undaunted, they started in on the second layer and were practically through it when caught.[28]

Fewer bounty-jumpers would have escaped had their guards been either more intelligent or less gullible. Frequently the jumper would ask for a small favor or privilege, which seemed innocent, but generally resulted in his escape. In Syracuse in September 1863, a substitute induced his guard to take him to the theatre, where he fled during the intermission. A few days later, in Dunkirk, a substitute talked his guard into accompanying him to the express office to send money home. When they reached the doorway the guard was slugged by a confederate of the substitute, who was waiting in ambush, and the two ran off down the nearby railroad track. In August 1864, near Buffalo, an officer tried to apprehend four bounty-jumpers, and after a shooting and wrestling match, finally overpowered one of the men. On the way to the station house, however, the bounty-jumper asked for a drink of water, gained a momentary advantage over the officer, and escaped.[29]

A miscellaneous listing of a few other escapes would read something like this: four substitutes in Troy "skedaddled" from the provost marshal's guard (September 1863); five bounty-jumpers fled from the barracks in Dunkirk (February 1864); eleven recruits escaped from the Soldiers' Rest at Poughkeepsie (February 1864); eleven men crawled out of a window of the provost marshal's office in Syracuse while the guard was asleep, taking some $5,200 in bounty money with them (March 1864); eight substitutes exited from the Albany Barracks (April 1864); four men were shot while trying to flee from a train travelling west from Albany (June 1864); four Boston substitutes, each with $1,000 in bounty money, jumped a train near Troy and vanished (August 1864); forty-three stampeded from Barracks Number One at Elmira (September 1864); on a train from Buffalo bringing twenty-five men to Albany, five jumped successfully, while two more were shot while trying to leave the depot (October 1864); several dozen escaped from the Albany Barracks in two breaks in one week by simply battering the guards with clubs and disappearing in the darkness (February 1865); and several bounty-jumpers fled while being marched to the Albany dock (March 1865).[30]

Three bounty-jumpers escaped from Albany Barracks in March 1865 by sawing through iron bars, lowering themselves to the next roof by a blanket rope, creeping along this roof to a neighboring shed, and then dropping down to the street. An impatient substitute named Lamotte got out of his cell in the Troy provost marshal's office by sliding down the gutter to the street from the fourth story. A suspected bounty-jumper, trapped in Elmira's Hoffman Hotel in September 1864, jumped wildly from the roof, only to be captured after he hit the ground.[31]

One bounty-jumper with a glass eye took clever advantage of the rules regarding sight. The Regulations published by the Provost Marshal General stated these disqualifying conditions: "Total loss of sight; loss of sight of right eye; cataract; loss of crystalline lens of right eye." The requirement was based on the need of the right eye to sight down the gun barrel. Apparently, after this young man was inducted, he would extract what the examining surgeon had thought to be a good right eye, and demand to be discharged. He jumped twelve bounties before he was caught and sentenced to be shot. An industrious two-time jumper named Coates fled from the Albany Barracks in March 1865 although handcuffed and with a ball and chain attached to his leg. A nonchalant jumper from the 192nd was caught earlier the same month and lodged in the provost marshal's headquarters in Albany. Weary of confinement, he arose, walked out of his room and down the stairs and out the front door, without a hand being laid upon him. So casual was his manner that none of the many guards lining the corridor had the slightest notion that he was a deserter.[32]

A sensational "escape" was engineered at Norfolk, Virginia, by a man named Freeborn, and his common-law wife, one Mary Louisa Linder. Freeborn had already quit the Army of the Potomac which then, in the winter of 1864-65, held Petersburg in an iron grip. He did not feel safe in Norfolk, however, and wanted to go north. He proposed that his wife ship him in a trunk to Baltimore, and then on to Chicago, where he would enlist for $1,000, and jump with her to Canada. Although the wife did not like the idea, they secured a trunk, cut a small hole and inserted a pipe through which Freeborn could breath while in transit. After Freeborn got into the trunk, his wife sealed the lid and sent it off. Everything went well until Mary Louisa opened the trunk in her Baltimore hotel room. To her surprise, Freeborn was dead! Later, she was found guilty of aiding a soldier to desert, fined five hundred dollars, and sentenced to two years of hard labor.[33]

The two military forts that were deserter favorites were the Troy Road Barracks at Albany and Fort Porter at Buffalo. Although we have few details of the numerous stampedes from the former, some accounts have survived of the Fort Porter escapes. For example, in August 1863, a substitute for a prominent citizen got away despite earlier remarks by the officer in charge that no one ever escaped from Porter. On the night of May 5, 1864, fifteen recruits made a break for the door where a sentry stood guard. One tried to throw snuff into the sentry's eyes, but missed, striking his chest. It knocked him off balance, long enough, however, to allow the men to get out into the yard. When the guard recovered, he fired several shots, hitting one man in the thigh, and causing other guards to rush to the scene. But it was too late, and even though a dozen more shots were fired, the remaining jumpers escaped in the dark.[34]

In late December 1864 some twenty-seven prisoners were incarcerated in a "modern building" at Fort Porter, in a room twenty-five feet wide, forty feet long, and with one door. Some ten or twelve feet outside the door a sentinel was posted, sole guard of the twenty-seven men. At one o'clock in the morning of December 26, the officer of the day, accompanied by the corporal of the guard, visited the prisoners and sentry, and found everything in order. Upon leaving, the officer told the corporal to take the lamp, the only light in the hall, and escort him from the building. When the corporal checked the prisoners again, he found twelve of them missing. It seems that earlier in the evening, these recruits had huddled at the far end of the room, where they could barely be seen in the dim light. Pulling blankets over themselves to deaden the noise, they began to cut a hole in the wall with a set of mysteriously acquired sharp knives. In several hours they had an opening, about twelve to seventeen inches across, through to the outside. After the officer of the day had left, the sentry apparently went to sleep and the men wormed their way through the hole and escaped.

The incident caused a stir, but a special investigation board absolved all military personnel at Fort Porter of any blame for the escape, stating that the real cause was "the utter worthlessness of the building, as a place of safekeeping, in which the men were confined, and to the insufficient number of men placed as a guard over the recruits. . . ."[35] The next instance of "jumping" from Porter was even more ironic, for this time the sentry on guard also joined in the escape.[36]

The reckless shooting by guards attempting to halt escapees in public places was another serious problem. Often, when a break occurred, they would panic and fire crazily into crowds of bystanders, even when the men had already escaped. Many times guards would fire at men who were merely suspected of being bounty-jumpers. Late in January 1864, at the Buffalo railroad depot, a bootblack was mistaken by a guard for a substitute about to desert. The boy was ordered to halt, and when he gave an impudent reply, was shot dead. The anti-Administration *Argus*, which had never liked the draft, and blamed bounty-jumper crimes more on the draft than on the bounty-jumpers,

denounced the killing of a jumper in February 1865. Arguing that the
man had already been wounded in the leg and hence could not have
escaped, the *Argus* insisted that this was but another example of the
inhumanity and irresponsibility of the government and its draft system.[37]

When five members of the 192nd made a break at the East Albany
depot in March 1865, the guards shot promiscuously into the crowd,
missing the fugitives, but wounding two small boys. As a sequel to
this, the *Argus* observed about a week later that when several bounty-
jumpers escaped while being marched to the dock, the guards fired
and missed again, but luckily this time they hit no civilians either.[38]

Many bounty-jumpers received aid and comfort from their families,
either during their escape, or after the escape when a hideout was
needed. A deputy provost marshal at Watertown arrested Wesley Ar-
nold in April 1864, for harboring his brother, who had deserted at
Albany a short time before. A seventeen-year old boy, Asa Waldorf,
from Otsego County, was arrested in June 1864 as a deserter from
the 152nd. Waldorf, who was said to be simple-minded, blamed it
all on his mother, who, he charged, had induced him to desert and
took him to Canada. "He must be simple-minded," commented the
Argus, "thus to attempt to implicate his mother." A woman named
Catherine Whittington was arrested at Buffalo in April 1864 for aiding
her son to escape across the Suspension Bridge. As she was being
taken to jail, an unsuccessful attempt was made by her husband and
friends to rescue her.[39]

Another mother anxious to assist her wayward son, was a Mrs.
Muckle, who visited him in an Albany jail where he was classified as
a "bounty-jumper-desperado." She tried to pass a letter to him, was
detected, and threw the missive out the window. When it was recovered, the note was found to contain plans for a jail delivery of Muckle
at five o'clock when the guard was being changed. The jumper was
to run the guard at that time, and his friends were to wait for him in
a hack outside and hustle him to freedom. The mother was promptly
put in jail herself. A girl friend visiting her bounty-jumping boy friend
in a Boston jail facilitated his escape by transferring a key to his mouth
while bestowing a farewell kiss. The key permitted the inmate to

loosen the irons holding him and flee. In Fort Erie, Ontario, a police constable named John Magwood assisted his son, William, in enlisting and deserting seven times, in each case splitting the bounty with him.[40]

* * * *

Not every escape try succeeded. Sometimes it was luck and sometimes it was cleverness which permitted custodial officers to foil "jump" attempts. A man from Troy named Duffy went as a substitute in Poughkeepsie in September 1863, and unsuccessfully tried to bribe his way out by offering the sentry first seventy dollars, and then two hundred dollars, asserting he had enough money to buy up a whole regiment. When four or five roughs arrived, demanding to see Duffy, the suspicious guard summoned help from the provost marshal's office. The leader of the gang, one "Troy Bill," was alleged to be a "leader of substitute dodgers," and was promptly jailed along with Duffy. Duffy was found to have eight hundred dollars in counterfeit greenbacks on his person, but the Poughkeepsie *Daily Eagle* didn't venture a guess as to where it came from.[41]

While a squad of naval enlistees was being escorted to the Buffalo depot in March 1864, two made a sudden break, running "from their colors faster than they ever will towards the enemy." They were retaken, however, after a short but spirited chase. Two recruits from the 11th Regulars who fled from the Albany depot several weeks later were caught behind a nearby freight station, where one was in the process of pulling off his uniform, worn over a civilian suit. At about the same time, a squad of seven deserters was shipped from Albany to Washington, all carefully manacled. Prior to their departure they had tried to cut their way out of their rooms, and had already removed one iron bar when discovered. The ringleader, a veteran bounty-jumper named Dwyer, made the trip in irons as well as handcuffs. Rumors of a mass rescue effort of 120 recruits coming into Albany from Boston in August 1864 brought forth special security precautions at the depot. If any such rescue had been planned, it was abandoned.[42]

In recapturing deserters, force was usually necessary. Many bounty-jumpers on the brink of capture would shout defiantly, "I will never be taken alive," and would have to be shot into submission. One Luther Greenfield, claimed by at least three regiments, was traveling to Syracuse in September 1863 under the care of a special agent named Adams. At one of the stops Adams decided to step off the train momentarily, and turned Greenfield over to a gentleman passenger. Greenfield quickly slipped his cuffs, leaped from the car, and lit out across an open field. Agent Adams was alerted and was soon on the prisoner's trail, shouting, "Halt or I'll shoot!"

"Shoot and be damned!" replied Luther, "I'll never be taken alive." Well, Adams shot, and in spite of his boast, Greenfield *was* taken alive.[43]

A middle-aged man named Sullivan, who enlisted at Oswego for a $1,300 bounty in August 1864, deserted while home on a short furlough. The local provost marshal dispatched a Sergeant Whalen to apprehend Sullivan, which he did on the train at Minetto, just south of Oswego. But as the train stopped at Baldwinsville on the way to Syracuse, Sullivan broke free and ran from the station with Whalen, armed only with a dirk, in hot pursuit. The younger sergeant soon caught up to the older bounty-jumper and ordered him to stop, but Sullivan slugged Whalen, yelling he would never be taken alive. The persistent Whalen went after him again, and this time plunged his knife up to the hilt in Sullivan's chest. The latter staggered on for a short distance, but soon collapsed. He was right; he was not taken alive.[44]

David Morgan, multiple bounty-jumper, most recently from the 124th, was found working the coal fields of Orange County in the late summer of 1864. A deputy provost marshal was sent after him, and seeing him in the pits, ordered him out. Informed that he was under arrest, Morgan scrambled out the far side, shouting the usual, "You'll never take me alive." Like Sullivan, Morgan spoke the truth, for the deputy's aim was true to the mark. A switch on the "I'll never be taken alive" theme occurred at Elmira. A recruit ran the guard at Barracks Number Three and plunged into the nearby Chemung River. Several guards began shooting, slightly wounding the swimming bounty-jumper. The man did reach the opposite shore, but as soon as he emerged from the water, he screamed back to his tormentors, "For God's sake, don't shoot! I'll give up." He was allowed to swim back and was promptly placed in irons. So at least one deserter *wanted* to be taken alive.[45]

Another Elmira bounty-jumper also tried swimming to freedom. James Kelly enlisted in July 1864, but deserted before his group left town, and was accidentally found in a barbershop getting a haircut. With his locks partly trimmed and with shaving soap all over the back of his neck, Kelly was marched to the provost marshal's office. Just at the door he raced off along the Chemung Canal towpath, finally jumping into the canal itself. He reached the opposite shore without difficulty, but when he got there he was greeted by Provost Marshal Samuel M. Harmon in person. Harmon and an aide had run down the other side of the canal unbeknownst to Kelly, who thought he had shaken his pursuers.[46]

Sometimes the difficult phase of apprehending deserters was not the actual capture, but the removal of the man to jail. Messrs. William Kingsley and George Wright, army detectives looking for a three-time jumper named George Coffin, finally located him on South Street in lower Manhattan. While the three walked to the provost marshal's office, Coffin made a break and led the detectives a merry chase for several blocks, but was recaptured on Beekman Street. As they proceeded along Beekman, Coffin again dashed away ignoring all shouts to halt. Kingsley thereupon fired three shots, which dropped Coffin to the ground, and he was seized for the third time in about twenty minutes. Without further ado he was jailed.[47]

Physical endurance naturally was responsible for the success of many bounty jumps. In an age that knew nothing of the automobile, telephone, or two-way radio, a strong-winded bounty-jumper could escape by simply outdistancing his pursuers. By the same token many of the failures were owing to the superior fitness of the guards. Two bounty-jumpers at the Soldiers' Rest in Poughkeepsie fled in early February 1864, but were chased up hill and down dale for a mile or so by several guards and finally recaptured. Later the same month John Duly, a two hundred dollar bounty soldier, escaped at Dunkirk, but the guard remained close behind for over four miles. Full of buckshot, breathless, and leg-weary, Duly finally surrendered to the persistent soldier.[48]

Occasionally the capture of deserters occurred under unusual circumstances. Two Syracuse bounty-jumpers who had fled from the 185th Regiment in September 1864 were captured in Madison County by authorities who trailed two prostitutes to their hideaway. The deserters were sent to the front. A New York City police sergeant, who returned a deserter to the Soldiers' Rest at Poughkeepsie in February 1864, recognized among the new recruits three notorious metropolitan thieves, who were no doubt about to make a jump. A deserter was arrested in downtown Elmira in February 1865, when recognized by his former commanding officer on the main street.[49]

Perhaps the size of the problem would have been substantially reduced if more convicted bounty-jumpers had been promptly executed. A potentially effective example took place at the headquarters of the Army of the Potomac in August 1863. Before an assembled crowd of 25,000, five deserters "of recent immigrant stock," the newspapers dutifully reported, were executed as an object lesson to other troops. A soldier of the 146th, who witnessed the event, was properly impressed, writing home that "the sight was the most solemn one I ever saw."[50] But many of the captured bounty-jumpers were merely sent off to the front after forfeiting their bounty.

Charles McCarty and John Riley, veteran bounty-jumpers from Cohoes, north of Albany, went off to Vermont in April 1864 to practice their art. They enlisted at Brattleboro for five hundred dollars, and without waiting for further formalities, made an immediate break. Captured quickly, McCarty and Riley were transported to Fort Warren in Boston Harbor, tried by a military court, convicted, and sentenced to be shot. The sentence was carried out before a sizeable throng on April 22. The families of the two men requested that the bodies be returned to Cohoes. Two days later, the funeral and burial took place there, one of those present being the intended bride of McCarty.[51]

Everett Babbitt was another one-eyed multiple enlistee, but one whose missing eye—apparently the left—had nothing to do with his bounty-jumping operations. At the age of seventeen, he readily confessed to having jumped twenty sizeable bounties. He was sentenced to be shot, but friends intervened in his behalf with Lincoln. The

President commuted the death sentence to three years at hard labor in a military prison camp at Dry Tortugas in the Florida Keys. Not so lucky was William "Polly" Lynch, a noted and shrewed bounty-jumper from Albany, who was sentenced to death in September 1864. Although the actual execution was delayed for over a month, Lynch was finally shot at Washington.[52]

A perusal of several dozen New York regimental histories reveals only one execution of a bounty-jumper. This occurred in December 1863 in the 76th Regiment, then camped along the Rapidan River. Winslow N. Allen had enlisted in that organization in the spring of 1862, but deserted soon afterwards while his outfit was stationed near Washington. Allen went to Jefferson County, New York, took the name of William Newton, married and settled down. By the fall of 1863, however, the lure of the bounty proved too great to resist, so he enlisted as a substitute for three hundred dollars. Then, as fate would have it, he was not only assigned to his old regiment, the 76th, but even to his old unit, Company H. On the night of September 27, 1863, he came marching down the Company street with seven other new men, and was at once recognized by his old comrades. He was arrested, confined, tried, convicted and sentenced to be shot. On December 18,

> . . . the condemned man was placed upon the foot of his coffin; the bandage placed over his eyes; his hands pinioned. The charges, specifications, findings and order for his execution had been read. The Captain bent over him, and his heart almost too full for utterance, whispered: "Winslow, I can go no further with you; the rest of your dark journey is alone. . . ." The Captain stepped back a few feet; the officer gave the signal to his executioners; the report as of a single gun rang out, and Winslow N. Allen fell lifeless upon his coffin.[53]

The most celebrated execution of a bounty-jumper took place at Governor's Island in New York harbor on February 3, 1865. James Devlin, about thirty, "of compact, well-built form, and five feet nine inches high," had deserted from the 1st Connecticut Cavalry and the 43rd New York. Several years before the war he married a woman ten years his senior by whom he had three children. In June 1864 he deserted his wife and family and moved in with a girl friend on Mott Street. His wife, bent on revenge, finally went to General Dix's office and told all she knew about her bounty-jumping spouse. Devlin, who had enlisted again, was consequently arrested on January 20, 1865, while aboard the recruiting ship *North Carolina*, anchored in New York harbor. He was tried by court-martial, convicted, and sentenced to be shot between twelve noon and two o'clock in the afternoon of February 3. Dix reviewed the sentence and confirmed it with a ringing denunciation of bounty-jumpers in general.

In the meantime, however, Mrs. Devlin was overcome with remorse for having tattled on her husband and went rushing to Governor's Island to plead for his release. Several tearful, agonizing sessions followed, one in the presence of Devlin himself, who seemed totally unperturbed by the wailings of his distraught wife. At about one o'clock on the fateful day, Devlin was brought out from his cell onto the parade ground, and accompanied by a priest, was marched to the execution site. Numerous delays interrupted proceedings and it was not until nearly two o'clock that the prisoner, surrounded by some four hundred soldiers, was ordered to kneel in front of his coffin down near the beach. Mrs. Devlin's screeches and moans were heard all over the island, moving everyone except the impervious husband. The court-martial sentence was read, the prisoner was blindfolded, and the preliminaries were over. At precisely two o'clock, the captain in command shouted, "Ready," "Aim," and then flourished his sword. Ten shots exploded. Devlin's body shivered momentarily and then fell heavily forward, as Mrs. Devlin continued to sob.[54]

*   *   *   *

The story of William Jackson, who passed himself off as an Englishman, is unusual. Jackson enlisted in the Confederate Army under the name of Hyatt, and was captured early in 1864. He appealed to Lord Lyons, the British Ambassador in Washington, and through the latter's intercession, Jackson was released from detention. He then enlisted in the Union Army in April, deserted, was caught, escaped, was caught again, escaped again, and was caught for the third and last time in August.

A captured Confederate soldier, "Bad John" Wright, escaped from an Ohio prison and made a fortune by multiple bounty-jumping. Then with his pockets full of greenbacks he went south and rejoined his old unit.

A bounty-jumper named Day got a room in a Utica boarding house run by Miss Phillips in December 1864. In a short time Day induced his landlady to marry him, and took her to New York for a honeymoon, where he deserted her after appropriating all her money and gold watch.[55]

Bounty-jumper Michael Waters became the center of a violent controversy between civil and military authorities in the spring of 1864. While being marched through New York City to the depot in April, Waters tried to desert, but was shot in the head by the guard and died instantly. The New York police, unaware of the circumstances, seized the guard who killed Waters and put him in jail. When General Dix learned what had happened, he ordered the release of the guard and the arrest of the policemen for interfering with military officers in the discharge of their duties.[56]

A celebrated bounty-jumper named Chauncey Cosselman from the Syracuse suburb of De Witt proved a king-sized headache until he was put safely away. Cosselman was drafted in the fall of 1863, but did not like army life, so he discharged himself and went home. When deputy provost marshals learned of his presence in De Witt in November, they went to apprehend him but ran into armed resistance from Cosselman, his mother, sisters, brothers, and brothers-in-law. The defiant family had turned their house into a fortress in their resolve not to surrender their beloved Chauncey. After one deputy was seriously wounded, the siege was temporarily lifted. Later another assault was launched on "Fort Cosselman" and this time Chauncey was shot and captured, while the relatives were kept silent at bayonet point. Cosselman was shipped to Washington, but in mid-December deserted, and returned to the comfortable environs of De Witt. The weary deputies trudged again to the Cosselman home, flushed Chauncey out of an upstairs window, shot him three times, and took him into custody. Several of the relatives were also jailed for aiding a deserter.[57]

But New York's most famous bounty-jumper was the incredible William Provost of Hudson in Columbia County. A rugged individualist and neighborhood roughneck, Provost enlisted in the 134th Regiment in the fall of 1863 for three hundred and twenty-five dollars. He deserted before his outfit ever left Poughkeepsie and returned to Hudson where he appeared to be a law unto himself. In February 1864 his whereabouts were discovered, and after a police posse apprehended him, he was sent to Governor's Island in irons. A few days after his arrival on the Island, Provost managed to slip his irons, run the guard, dive into the Bay, and swim to the Brooklyn shore about a half mile away. From there he worked his way back to Hudson. A federal marshal named Seymour, advised that the bounty-jumper might be in Hudson, went to that village, arrested Provost, and took him back to Poughkeepsie. On the way Provost wagered Seymour that he would be back in Hudson in a week, and just for fun, unlocked his handcuffs with a pin.

From Poughkeepsie he was forwarded to a stragglers' camp at Alexandria, Virginia, fitted with a ball and chain, and sent on to his regiment in Kentucky. As might be expected, he escaped en route and was back in Hudson within the week's time he set for himself. How he disposed of his ball and chain, unfortunately is not disclosed. When news of his escape reached Poughkeepsie, Marshal Seymour again went to Hudson where he arrested Provost on April 14, handcuffed him and clapped him into the local jail. While in jail Provost amused himself by beating and mutilating a fellow prisoner with his handcuffs, for which he was put in solitary confinement. But within a day or so he was transferred to the Soldiers' Rest and chained to a post to await shipment to Washington. Disgusted at the prospect that Provost would go again to the front, the Poughkeepsie *Daily Eagle* demanded that he "be hung immediately."[58]

On the evening of April 29, 1864 while the guard was being changed, Provost escaped by crawling through a hole he had dug under the back fence. But Marshal Seymour was soon on the train to Hudson, and on May 1 he caught Provost in a house of ill-fame. When Provost saw Seymour enter the front door he went out the back door. Seymour fired two shots and set out in pursuit, gradually closing in on his quarry along a narrow lane. Provost now halted, drew a knife, and began to advance menacingly toward Seymour. Seymour fired and Provost, slightly wounded, fell to the ground and surrendered. He was returned to Poughkeepsie and jailed. Three weeks later, recovered from his wounds, he was placed in irons and again sent to Governor's Island.[59]

Provost's activities for the next few months went unreported in the press and it was not unreasonable to assume that he had been either forwarded to the front or detained in some military prison. But in late July, the *Argus* reported that three or four rowdies in Hudson, the chief of whom was Bill Provost, were making nuisances of themselves by roaming about the community and "exercising their muscle" upon whom they pleased. So fearsome a gang was it that the police were afraid to arrest any of its members.[60] Nothing was said about Provost's escape from the Island, or that he was a bounty-jumper. It just seemed natural that he should be making trouble in Hudson.

But Provost's downfall came about when he roused the anger of a woman. The young lady turned the matter over to a friend, a big and rugged Dutchman named Hank Van Buskirk. Hank found Provost on a main street in Hudson, and after giving him a savage beating, dumped him on the doorstep of the provost marshal's office. For the last time Seymour took Provost back to Poughkeepsie, put him in irons, and shipped him off to Governor's Island.[61]

A number of "outstanding" bounty-jumpers came from Canada, even though enlisting in a foreign army was illegal under British law.[62] A number of young men came across from Fort Erie, Ontario, to enlist for bounties in Buffalo and go back home again. One man, Thomas Denby, arrived in Buffalo to enlist with three other Canadians in March 1864, only to be arrested for a previous jump. Mistakenly he thought no one would remember him. Three Canadians who enlisted at Elmira were found three weeks later, back in Elmira among a batch of captured Rebel prisoners. It seems that they had deserted near Washington, passed themselves off as Confederates escaping to Union lines and sought sanctuary there. Taken at their word, they were locked up with bona fide Rebel prisoners, and shipped to the Confederate prison at Elmira, where they were recognized.[63]

What methods were used to punish captured bounty-jumpers? Major Van Rensselaer, in command of the Barracks at Albany in March 1864, compelled deserters to wear the barrel shirt and march alongside the guard at the rate of twelve inches each step. Others were stationed on wooden horses in front of the barracks with placards on their backs bearing some appropriate inscription such as, "I am a thief," "I am a coward," or "I am a bounty-jumper." However, little evidence of physical chastisement in other places has survived. Late in the war seven captured bounty-jumpers at Albany confessed their crimes after being thumb-tied.[64]

One method of keeping bounty-jumpers under control was to assign more guards to their care. An increasing number of escape attempts at Elmira's Number One Barracks in September 1864 caused additional sentries to be placed there. In the West, toward the end of the war, so many men who were headed for Tennessee deserted at Toledo that one armed guard was assigned to each man for the remainder of the trip.[65]

Public humiliation was used occasionally, although not in New York. In May 1864 a bounty-jumper named Phillis was publicly shamed in Zanesville, Ohio. With head shaven and an insulting placard on his back, he was marched down the town's main street to the "Rogues' March" and the jeers of the crowd. Over one hundred jumpers were put on "dress parade" in Indianapolis in December 1864. The imaginative commandant had the men lashed together in pairs by a long rope. They were marched through the downtown section, led by a "herculean African" ringing a bell. Each bounty-jumper carried a placard advertising his achievement, two lines of bayonets restrained the curious mob, and "the soul-stirring notes of the 'Rogues' March' kept tune to their tramping feet."[66]

A new method to prevent bounty jumping was devised in the fall of 1864. Physicians would mark an "I" in nitrate of silver on the backs of rejected substitutes and volunteers, at first without the knowledge of the men involved. For a short time all accepted recruits were marked as well, although a subsequent order from Fry put a stop to it. The purpose was two-fold: to let other surgeons know a man had already been rejected, and to allow easy detection of bounty-jumpers.

It is not clear how the practice started, whether by voluntary agreement among physicians or by orders from Washington. Provost Marshal General Fry's chief medical officer, J. H. Baxter, did send a communication to an enrolment board surgeon in Illinois approving
"branding," as its critics labelled the custom, but this was a private
note. At any rate, by September 1864 reports of branding were published in New York, New Jersey, Illinois, Wisconsin, and other places.

Two letters from recruits at Hart's Island tell something about the
process. "After an examination of knapsacks," wrote one, "we were
marched out in front and formed in two ranks and went to the Doctor's to be marked. . . . One of our boys . . . fainted on being marked."
The other wrote that they were ordered to line up in front of the
hospital to be "vaccinated." "Of course," he added, "we had to submit,
but I made up my mind that we were only being branded like
horses." The Democratic press shared this hostility toward branding,
and the *Argus* in particular devoted columns to the subject. Denouncing it as an insult to free and honorable men, the *Argus* claimed that
branding also was physically harmful to the body and left a mark
for life. Branding of slaves with hot irons was trivial alongside this.

The furor subsided by October and no further reference to the
practice can be found. However, despite the wailings of the *Argus*,
this seems to have been an excellent way to handle bounty-jumpers.
As for the charge that nitrate of silver might leave a permenent mark
and damage the skin, reputable physicians issued a flat denial.[67]

The conviction gradually grew, however, that the only effective way
to put an end to bounty-jumping was to put an end to the bounty-
jumper. Following a wild wave of bounty-jumping at Elmira in the
summer of 1864, the *Advertiser* despairingly cried out that "they had
better be shot and done with." On the arrest of five bounty-jumpers at
Buffalo in March 1865, the *Morning Express* demanded that if the
men were found guilty they should be shot. "More healthy shooting,"
it observed, "will not prove disadvantageous to either the service or
the pockets of those so heavily taxed to pay bounties."[68]

But it was the Devlin execution at Governor's Island on February 3,
1865 which crystallized "executionist" sentiment, and had the war
lasted any longer, it appears certain that bounty-jumpers would have

been given short shrift. In endorsing the court's sentence Dix expressed a view which won wide approval. The General wrote that Devlin's case

> ... is one of those in which bad men, tempted by enormous bounties, enlist into the service for the sake of making money, with the deliberate purpose of deserting, and in which the profit is proportioned to the number of successful repetitions of the crime. By common consent these infamous men are designated by the expressive appellation of "bounty-jumpers." They might more properly be termed traitors and public plunderers; and the Major-General Commanding, in approving the sentence of death pronounced by the court, deems it his duty to the army and the country to announce that, *in all cases, he will cause the punishment awarded to a crime subversive of every principle of moral and political obligation to be executed with the utmost inflexibility and promptness.*[69]

To which the Elmira *Advertiser* appended a warm "Amen!" Denouncing the "mistaken clemency" which had saved bounty-jumpers from their rightful fate, it insisted that if the war were conducted with "terrible exaction alike against the enemy in the field and deserters from our own ranks . . . its duration will be shortened."[70] This was the only realistic approach, and it was most unfortunate that Washington did not set forth a policy statement in keeping with Dix's views when the bounty system first appeared.

• 6 •

The Brokers.

ALTHOUGH MOST ASPECTS of the Civil War bounty system seem unwise and unfair, that which merits the greatest criticism is the brokerage function.[1] Bounty-jumpers were bad, certainly, but much of their wrongdoing was directly stimulated by the brokers. By enticing young men to desert, reenlist, and desert ad infinitum, brokers made jumping a profitable practice. But far worse than aiding and abetting jumpers were the brokers' ruthless practices of kidnapping, immigrant-running, grand larceny, assault, and murder.

It is true that the army paid a small cash bonus to anyone who was instrumental in inducing a man to enlist. Recruiting regulations provided for a premium of two dollars to be paid to any citizen, noncommissioned officer, or soldier for each *accepted* recruit brought in. If the recruit presented himself, he received the bonus. Thus, while the recruiting machinery did allow for a middleman, the premium—"hand money," as it was called—was scarcely sufficient to explain the rise of the Civil War broker. But the hand money did open the door for the broker, and once he gained entrance he was able to convert the whole process to his own advantage.

Brokers, then, though not necessary to recruiting procedures, were permitted, and soon thronged so thickly about recruiting and provost marshal offices that it was, in fact, virtually impossible for a volunteer to enlist without broker assistance. So gullible and misinformed were the young men of the day that they actually believed brokers were required to process their enlistments and were entitled to a good portion of the bounties. Yet it is easy to understand why the young

107

men had faith in brokers, when they observed the trust placed in them by recruiting committees in their communities. Although the belief that brokers performed a valuable service prevailed during most of the war, Provost Marshal General Fry and the district provost marshals strongly condemned the brokers in their final reports, urging that they never again be allowed to control wartime recruitment.[2]

Brokers appeared with the blossoming of the bounty system in the fall of 1862 and became ever more important as the war progressed. They advertised in the newspapers, opened offices in or near recruiting and provost marshal headquarters, and posted convincing signs. They were on intimate terms with provost marshals, recruiting officers, and district committeemen, and often employed "runners" to explore the countryside for prospects. They overlooked nothing in their efforts to convince the public and the government that they alone could supply the needed troops.

*   *   *   *

To begin with, broker advertisements couched in the most appealing terms appeared daily in the metropolitan press. Jacob Chapman, for example, advised his fellow Syracusans that he could pay substitutes more than any firm in the state. Peter La France of Elmira asserted, "We are prepared to take contracts to fill the quotas of towns, which we guarantee to do . . . at very low figures," and Tompkins and Company of New York City advised, "We are daily furnishing large numbers of substitutes . . . to individuals . . . in Pennsylvania, New England, and New York." Thomson, Wilcox, and Thomson of Utica promised to find substitutes before the draft at much more reasonable terms than other brokers. Lewis Clapp of Buffalo and the firm of Garner and St. Ange in Syracuse pledged to supply alien substitutes on the shortest notice and for the lowest rates. O'Dea and Warren of Buffalo not only guaranteed the "highest prices for aliens willing to take the places of conscripts," but also offered to furnish room and board prior to enlistment for all non-residents rendering their services.[3] Newspapers frequently endorsed particular brokers, as when the Elmira *Daily Advertiser* announced that brokers La France and Kirby were "enterprising men . . . [who] will honorably fulfill all contracts." The Buffalo *Morning Express* apparently had more than an incidental interest in substitute brokerage, for in August 1863 it advertised that those interested in being substitutes should apply at the "counting room of this paper."[4]

Town, city, and county recruiting committees, whose job it was to fill quotas, often worked with the brokers, believing that this was the most reliable way to get men. The Onondaga County Supervisors Military Bounty Committee, for example, advertised that recruits should apply at the office of brokers Maynard and Griswold.[5] But the most open and frank dependence on brokers was exhibited by the County Volunteer and Substitute Committee of New York City. In the summer of 1863, the New York County Board of Supervisors authorized a bounty of three hundred dollars for each volunteer, and created the committee, with Orison J. Blunt as chairman, to disburse the money. After studying the problem, the Committee concluded that the most efficient way to hand out the bounty money was through the bounty brokers. When a recruit was mustered in, either at a provost marshal's office or at a regular recruiting center, the broker who brought him in would pay him the amount previously agreed upon between broker and recruit, and the recruit would assign the full bounty of three hundred dollars to the broker. The broker would then take the assignment to Blunt's office and be reimbursed to the amount of three hundred dollars.[6] Blunt's system quickly came under heavy fire and General Dix forced him to modify it.

It was not uncommon, toward the close of the war, for recruiting committees to abandon all efforts to meet their quotas and contract with brokers to do the job for them. Provost Marshal Parsons of the 14th District at Albany reported that several towns in Schoharie County "generally filled their quotas by making contracts" with brokers. The town authorities of Waterford in Saratoga County arranged with a New York City broker for the filling of its entire quota in August 1864.[7] The most celebrated broker contract was one referred to in the preceding chapter, in which the Supervisors of Oneida County agreed to pay Aaron Richardson $750,000 to fill their entire quota.

Brokers in different localities corresponded with one another whenever the need for substitutes or volunteers became urgent. For example, in December 1864 broker E. W. Mosher of Middleville in Herki-

mer County wrote to broker Richard Dalton at the Brooklyn Navy
Yard, requesting a set of substitute papers. Mosher would sell the
papers to a draftee, who could apparently file them with the district
provost marshal and be exempt from the draft. While the details of
this transaction are not spelled out in the correspondence, all Mosher
needed was a set of substitute papers. Dalton was advised to

> ... be sure and have an alien for this substitute. You must
> make the price a little less than $550, as that is all I get for him.
> I guess you can let me have him for an even $500. I will send
> you a draft for the amount on receipt of the papers. ... I
> would like the papers as soon as you can send them, as I have
> promised to deliver them in Utica next week. ...[8]

*   *   *   *

Among the many kinds of fraud committed by brokers, the forging
of enlistment papers was perhaps the most ingenious. No doubt the
papers Dalton sent Mosher were forged since those brokers who
worked the Brooklyn Navy Yard were the principal authors of such
false papers. Another popular practice employed by brokers, when
recruits happened to be in short supply was the kidnapping of young
boys or the seizing of unwary immigrants. The victims were either
threatened with violence, or enlisted while befuddled by drug or
drink. For example, eighteen-year old Michael Kelly was met by two
men in Chambers Street in New York City on the afternoon of January
9, 1865, and was invited into a saloon for a glass of ale. When Kelly
awoke on the morning of January 10, he was in the barracks at Governor's Island and a member of the 19th United States Regulars.[9]

Two Troy brokers went across the Vermont border in August 1864,
and seized a fifteen-year old boy, Edward Wheeler, got him drunk
and brought him to Poughkeepsie. When the boy refused to testify
that he was eighteen years old, he was kept shut up in a house for
two days. What happened there we are not told, but young Wheeler
was enlisted as a substitute and sent to Hart's Island before his parents
were able to locate him. Albany brokers were accused of going to
Scoharie, getting ignorant Negroes drunk and taking them off. The
victims would be "tumbled into a sled and hurried off to the railroad

station, where they are packed into a small room partitioned off at one end of the car and there locked in until they arrive at Albany."[10]

Stephen Green was drunk in Dunkirk one afternoon in September 1863 when he was accosted by Eli Standish, Buffalo saloonkeeper and sometime broker. Standish induced Green to enlist as a substitute in Buffalo and then helped him desert. Green, who received two hundred dollars of his three hundred and fifty dollar bounty, was later captured near his native Troy and sent to the front. A veteran combat soldier on leave in Elmira in January 1865 was persuaded by some brokers at the railroad depot to join them in a drink. Soon he was quite drunk, whereupon the brokers took him to Syracuse and sold him as a substitute. When he regained his senses, the soldier resolved to rejoin his old outfit, which meant he was forced to desert the organization in which he had just enlisted. In trying to desert, he was shot, arrested, and brought up for court-martial. Even officers were not spared. On recruiting duty in February 1865, one of them was drugged by a broker while on the train to Syracuse and was enlisted at Auburn as a private in the notorious 192nd Regiment.[11]

Generally, however, the drink and drug device took too long, and most brokers relied on simple force or outright falsehood to gain their quarry. In March 1865, a broker conveniently named Smith, was alleged to have abducted two sixteen-year old boys in Brooklyn and sent them off to Boston in a closed car. A friend of the boys, who informed General Lafayette C. Baker of the matter, closed his letter by urging Baker to "ferret out and arrest these body-snatchers." Late in December 1863 a Negro named John Alexander was passing near Lafayette Hall, a large recruiting station on lower Broadway in New York City. Suddenly, he saw another Negro grabbed by the collar at the front door of the building and dragged inside. Alexander went over to investigate and was himself thrown into a "pen." The guard was told that if Alexander tried to escape he should be "run . . . through with a bayonet."[12]

Many abductions reported in the press carry no suggestion of force, but it is doubtful that the victims went willingly. Thus, two sons of a Greenbush farmer named De Freest were taken off by brokers and enlisted in Boston in November 1864. And perhaps it was so with

Orlando Golder who went with Harlan Van Wagner from his Rhinebeck home to enlist in Syracuse in February 1865. And it must have
been so with a Canadian boy kidnapped by two men in September
1864 and brought over to Dunkirk in a small boat for enlistment.[13]

The hardships and indignities inflicted on some of the bounty brokers' hapless victims is well illustrated by the story of Lonson Putnam
of Syracuse. Putnam was a moron, barely able to handle his own
affairs. On the night of December 4, 1864, two men posing as policemen came to his home, routed him out of bed and forcibly abducted
him. He was taken by train to some city in the western part of the
state (Putnam did not know what one) and brought before a provost
marshal. When checked by the physician, he was found unfit for service and rejected. The exasperated brokers thereupon turned Putnam
loose, without funds or friends. Somehow in a week or so, he managed
to make his way back to Syracuse, where in a wretched state, he was
finally located by relatives. In similar fashion, earlier in 1864, two
young men, Thomas Harwood and Robert Allen, were brought from
New York by "flesh brokers," but when they failed to pass they were
turned adrift with no means to return home.[14]

Without question, however, many boys and men went willingly
with a broker, intrigued by the fascinating stories of wealth and fame
awaiting them in the service. A broker dressed in a military uniform
stopped by the farm of William Henry, near Albany, in July 1864.
The visitor asked for food and was obliged. Later he was seen near
the road, flashing large sums of money and talking to the hired hand
and Henry's two teen-age sons. When last seen, all four were marching
down the road to Albany.[15] An ungrammatical letter from Smith's
Mills, dated June 27, 1864, tells a similar tale:

> I write to you for to know whether there is a boy by the name
> of Gildray Gould I supposed him probly to be there at almira
> or somewhere else in the army he run away from home on the
> 11 of June and if he is there please let me now yours respectfully
> James Gould smiths mills co NY. . . . he is only 17 years old and
> was coxed up to run away I followed him to buffalo and there I
> understood that some fellow got holt of him and sold him
> for $50. . . .[16]

Transporting people, either by force or peaceful persuasion, to high bounty communities, was called "running," a vicious practice which was generally condemned by government, press, and public. Legislation was finally adopted to prohibit it. What would seem more objectionable, however, was the abduction of ignorant immigrants fresh from the boat, and either enlisting them in New York or carrying them to distant places for enlistment. Brokers were actually permitted aboard immigrant boats while they rode at anchor, and once aboard, they would coax and flatter Germans and Irishmen with promises of quick wealth. If this did not work, the broker would resort to intimidation, and many frightened foreigners were actually bound to the broker before they ever set foot on American soil. One man down from Rochester, in August 1863, raided an immigrant vessel and carried off a batch of "raw Irishmen," whom he later sold for over three hundred dollars per head.[17]

An example of immigrant-running which came to the attention of the United States Secretary of State was that of Ebenezer East. A native of Buckinghamshire, England, East travelled to the United States in September 1863 for his health and to visit friends in Utica. When he arrived at the Emigrant Depot at Castle Garden in New York harbor, he headed for the Albany boat station to begin his trip to Utica. There he learned that no more sailings were scheduled for that day. Looking around for aid, East asked a man standing nearby where he might find a night's lodging, and the two men walked a short distance to a public house. After East rented a room, his new companion offered to buy him a drink before he retired. Before long, the Britisher passed out and remembered no more until he awoke in military garb on Riker's Island.

East said later that he never suspected a conspiracy since he would have surely been rejected from army service because of a lung ailment. After being robbed of all his money, East was shipped south as a private in Company A of the 47th Regiment. On November 1, 1863, "nearly dead with the disease," he wrote to the British consul in New York, E. M. Archbold, asking for help. Archbold sent the note to Lord Lyons, the British Ambassador in Washington, who transmitted it to Seward, who referred it to Stanton. The file ends at that point so we do not know what disposition was made of the case. In view of Lyons' insistence on an investigation, however, it is safe to conclude that East was freed and allowed to go on to Utica.[18]

Complaints of kidnapping immigrants were made by the French, Belgian, Italian, Danish, Swedish, German and British governments. A Prussian chargé d'affaires, von Grabow, visited an island in Boston Harbor in September 1864, when he learned that a number of newly-arrived Germans were being diverted into the army. After his investigation, he wrote Seward a strong note warning of serious consequences if these people were put into the army against their wishes or by means of fraud. A few months before this incident a boatload of Germans landed in Boston, each of them under contract for specified non-military employment. When they were all enlisted in the army, Boston's German population advertised a protest against immigrant labor contracts.[19] British immigrants—often Canadians—were victimized to a far greater degree than those from any other country. Seward was advised by Lord Lyons as early as February 1863 that British subjects were being kidnapped and forced into the army with great regularity. The final national figures of reported cases by country were Britain—235, France—50, Italy—22, Scandinavia—11, and Prussia—undetermined. The kidnapping of immigrants, in the opinion of the foremost student of Civil War immigration, was "the worst scandal of the war period, and indeed, it remains one of the darkest blots on the history of the United States."[20]

Occasionally, nationals of a European state would contract to come to the United States for military service, but would be swindled after enlistment. Two teen-age boys arrived in New York in December 1864 and went as substitutes for five hundred dollars. A broker retained the money for "safekeeping," so safely in fact that the boys never saw it again. A young man named Edward Bourke, six months in the country, enlisted in the 12th Regulars on April 5, 1865, and planned to use his bounty money to bring his parents to the United States. He received only one hundred dollars, however, and wrote Baker a letter demanding that something be done about it.[21]

A knotty problem was raised by the immigrant-labor contracts. On July 4, 1864, Congress passed "An Act to Encourage Immigration,"[22] which authorized private persons or companies to make contracts with foreign nationals to come to the United States and work under stipulated conditions. By such a contract the immigrant, in a fashion reminiscent of the indentured servant, would pledge his wages for twelve months to the company to pay for the cost of his transportation. Shortly after the law was passed the American Emigrant Company was organized to negotiate labor contracts in Europe, bring the immigrants to American shores and turn them over to employers in need of labor. But many of the contracts, while not specifying military employment, actually meant just that.

The big question is whether these immigrants understood that they were going into the army. Four hundred Prussians who arrived at Deer Island in Boston Harbor in August 1864, apparently knew they would be soldiers, for their contracts stated that they would (1) be paid thirteen dollars per month and (2) turn all bounties over to their employer. During the trip over, it was clearly explained to them that they were headed for the army, and the tenor of their casual conversation was military. On the other hand, many immigrants were blithely unaware of their true destination. When they wound up in the army they felt that their contracts had been brazenly violated. Although Mayor Godfrey Gunther of New York City bitterly denounced such fraudulent practices, the New York *Times* and the Springfield *Republican* defended them, arguing that no one really was hurt, and insisting that the ignorant Germans never made so much money as they were making in the army.[23]

A Canadian newspaper frankly accused the American government of collusion in the kidnapping of Swedish immigrants for military service while pretending to employ them under labor contracts. The Quebec *Chronicle* said that about two hundred and twenty people who arrived in Quebec in August 1864 had signed agreements with United States Consul Teft in Stockholm before they left. The Swedes were given a free passage and promised employment in their particular trades upon reaching their destination at Portland, Maine. They were bound, however, to pay for transportation costs and incidental expenses from the one hundred and twenty-five dollars' annual wage each was supposed to earn. But to the *Chronicle* this veneer of legality was too transparent to be taken seriously. What Teft's contracts authorized was "a traffic in human flesh . . . which resembles but surpasses in atrocity the worst phases of the 'coolie' trade." The object of the scheme, continued the *Chronicle,*

> is to crowd the Atlantic ports with thousands of destitute foreigners, whose wretched condition must at once force them into the ranks of the army. . . . The agency of the United States Consul establishes the official nature of the speculation. A rush of starving immigrants might afford sufficient war material to render another conscription unnecessary, and thus 'stave off' the disturbance another draft is sure to create.[24]

Many brokers travelled north of the border and found their prey on Canadian soil, while a few Canadian brokers ran their fellow citizens over to New York for enlistment. This was called "crimping" in the Canadian press and the brokers were called "crimps." Advertisements were placed in the newspapers of Ontario and Quebec offering fanciful inducements to the enlistee, and when these were banned by the British government, brokers posted placards and distributed handbills throughout the border towns. Principal targets of these efforts were British soldiers stationed in Canada. Pay in the British Army was low and the prospects of great financial dividends in the Union ranks were hard to resist. As one military dispatch put it, "The inducements to desert are too much for the 'virtue' of any British soldier." In addition to this, brokers played effectively on the Anglophobia of the troops, many of whom were young Irish boys from Belfast. A sergeant at Toronto said that "every Irishman would desert from the 16th when there was an opportunity to do so."[25]

Of course, where the British soldier or Canadian civilian was unwilling to go voluntarily across the border, the usual "drink-or-drug" strategem was employed and the victim was carried off unconscious. Nine merchant seamen wrote to the British consul at Boston in September 1864, saying that they had been made drunk in a Quebec boarding house and then run off to Lebanon, New Hampshire, where they were enlisted. They were paid two hundred dollars, but their captors received one thousand dollars for each man. Numerous complaints were also made to the authorities of drugging and kidnapping of teen-age boys. The consul at Buffalo wrote Lord Lyons:

> ... the question arises, are British youth of less than 16 years of age ... to be enticed away from their homes, and enlisted into the military service of the United States, by United States officers who are well aware of what they are doing, and who would not have these youths brought to them by the crimps if the latter thought there would be any difficulty thrown in their way.[26]

The most famous of the Canadian crimps was one F. B. Bonter, who owned a fleet of small boats at Kingston in which he shipped his cargoes over to Watertown. "I have got a good many men out of Canada," he once reflected. In the wintertime Bonter and others employed sleighs on frozen Lake Ontario. In Hamilton, women were known to use drugged tea to befog soldiers of the 47th and cause them to desert. Hutton's and Egeners Taverns were favorite haunts, while McCarthy's and Rob Roy's were "veritable nests for crimps." In Kingston it was Cockran's; in Sandwich it was Mears Tavern. Tavern-keepers often operated in collusion with crimps; for a cut of the proceeds they would put drugs in the drinks of promising victims. These brokers, much like deserters from the Union Army, were a plague on Canadian society. One official reported that it was unsafe for peaceful citizens to go abroad at night, while others protested that they would be awakened at night by the screams of people being kidnapped.[27]

Brokers scoured low bounty districts for prospective recruits who would jump at the chance of enlisting in some other city or state for a high bounty. Many brokers had runners in western states to round up prospects for shipment east. Such a swindler was jailed in Cleveland in November 1863.[28] In mid-August 1863 a New York broker, Charles Miller, took a flock of deserters to Providence to serve as substitutes for draftees, but their guilt was detected just prior to muster. Miller, as well as his men, wound up behind bars. In the wake of New York's Draft Riots, a "Jew broker" took a dozen men, still bearing riot scars, to Philadelphia. Although half of them were disfigured about the face and hands, one even having the "end of his nose taken off," they all duly enlisted and later, just as duly deserted.[29]

On April 14, 1864, a broker named Sam Gordon[30] arrived in Utica with a gang of jumpers and went straight to the provost marshal's headquarters. They signed enlistment papers, but when they learned that they would not receive their bounties until they got to the rendezvous in Auburn they lost interest. That night Gordon and his men slipped out of their hotel and caught a train to Syracuse where they enlisted in the 149th Regiment the next morning. An agent from the Utica headquarters went after them, found them in the provost marshal's office, and shipped the whole lot back to Utica under heavy guard. At a hearing, it was ruled that the men were not deserters, since, although they had signed enlistment papers in Utica, they had not been mustered into service. Hence, the men were legally members of the 149th and were sent on to the Auburn rendezvous. Gordon was freed, much to the disgust of the local press.[31]

At Little Falls, a small town east of Herkimer, three brokers and thirteen jumpers held a meeting in late August 1864. The brokers, Albert Fralich, Levi Fralich, and John Korberth, told the men that if they went to Buffalo and enlisted at a certain recruiting office, not only would they be paid one hundred dollars, but when they left the office they would be free to return at once to Little Falls. It was a "soft thing," the men were told, since the brokers had already paid off the recruiting officers. The plan seemed a good one, so on September 1 the men went to Buffalo where everything proceeded without incident. They liked the idea so much that on September 15 they travelled again to Buffalo, received two hundred dollars each, and again returned to Little Falls. Five of the men, led by a farmer named Countryman, could not shake the habit and late in September they went to Sacketts Harbor where they picked up still another two hundred dollar bounty before returning to Little Falls.[32]

Reports of frauds in the 13th District, composed of Greene and Ulster counties, reached Albany and Washington in the winter of 1863-64, and Captain W. W. Teall of the Provost Marshal General's Bureau was ordered to Kingston to investigate. Teall reported that eleven men had been victimized by several brokers, chief of whom were George S. France, who doubled as a deputy provost marshal, and Daniel D. Bell, who held a captain's commission from Governor Seymour. Nine of the eleven were Negroes and completely ignorant of the workings of the bounty system. The brokers generally threatened their prey with jail sentences for some fictitious crime, then permitted them to escape punishment by enlisting in the army. And because the brokers were such good fellows they would give the men twenty-five or maybe fifty dollars. Teall closed his report by demanding France's removal as deputy provost marshal, and denouncing this exploitation of ignorant people.[33]

In December 1863, John J. Robinson of Albany presented himself for enlistment in the cavalry through broker James Cook in New York City. The uniformed Cook, formerly an officer in the 6th N.Y. Cavalry, pretended he was still on active duty, recruiting for his old outfit. Provost Marshal Theodore B. Bronson of the 6th District refused the eighteen-year-old Robinson because he lacked the written consent of parent or guardian. Thereupon, Cook had himself made Robinson's guardian at a nearby surrogate's office. Bronson, now accepting the young man for service, asked if he had received his bounty, and Cook said it had been taken care of. Actually, Cook had given Robinson fifty dollars out of three hundred. Cook was prosecuted for obtaining money under false pretenses in March, 1864.[34]

Two other devices sometimes employed by brokers should be mentioned: the "fictitious mother," and "doping." A broker would sometimes find an unscrupulous woman to cooperate with him in the kidnapping and enlistment of a young boy by posing as the boy's mother. The woman would testify before the provost marshal that she was perfectly willing to have her "son" enter the army. "Doping" was the process of "prettying up" a human derelict to make him acceptable to recruiting officers. He would be taken to a nice hotel, given a good meal, treated to a haircut and shave, then have his hair dyed and his cheeks rouged. Finally, resplendent in a new suit, he would be marched to the provost marshal's office or run off to some other town and enlisted.[35]

A St. Louis broker, in August 1864, found an old man who agreed to be "doped" and enlisted as a substitute:

[The broker] first administered to his patient a liberal dose
of the essence of rye; then took him to a barber's shop, had his
neck and face washed and powdered his hair and whiskers
neatly and the wrinkles in his cheeks smoothed over. . . .
Another snifter of rye was poured down the patient's throat
to straighten his spine, clear the rheum from his eyes, and
make his breast swell out in martial style. . . . A pair of substantial brogans was purchased, and a nice yellow linen duster
added, and the old man presented the appearance of a biped
of not more than thirty. . . .

Trouble developed on the way to the recruiting office, however, when
the broker, pleased at the prospect of easy wealth, decided to stop at
a saloon and treat his man to a drink. After three shots of rye, the
latter, feeling as "independent as a newly-appointed corporal," underwent a change of heart and decided against a military career. In spite
of pleas, threats, and a flying beer mug, the doped one went home,
and the broker was out nineteen dollars and thirty-five cents.[36]

Violence was a way of life for brokers, just as it was for jumpers.
If the victim did not submit to persuasion, he would be threatened,
beaten, and even murdered. William Coyne went to Rochester from
Syracuse to volunteer in September 1864. He was badly beaten by two
brokers who wanted him to go as a substitute.[37]

Brokers fought violently among themselves. A general melee
erupted in the provost marshal's office in Albany in June 1864, when
several brokers disputed "ownership" of a substitute prospect. Then
again, Frank Cotten and Aaron Richardson got into a struggle over
Negro recruits in the Utica provost marshal's office in September 1864.
Cotten, who received a blow on the head and a bite on the nose,
swore out a warrant against Richardson who was held in two hundred
dollars bail for violating a city ordinance.[38]

*   *   *   *

Although many brokers made fortunes from their illicit practices,[39]
a number of them were caught and either thrown into jail or compelled to disgorge their money. Robert Barrett persuaded a soldier
to abandon the 15th Cavalry and to go as a substitute at Auburn in
August 1863. Found guilty in the federal district court in Buffalo,

Barrett was sentenced to two years' imprisonment and fined five hundred dollars.[40] Most of the brokers brought to justice by General Baker were prosecuted—not for swindling recruits—but for either enticing soldiers to desert, or forging and selling false enlistment papers.[41]

A broker named Malloy swindled a New York City resident out of two hundred and seventy dollars bounty money in December 1863. The victim's angry wife went to Supervisor Blunt, who told Malloy that he must pay the wife the balance or lose the right to do business with Blunt's committee. Rather than forego such a "privilege," Malloy paid up. In the case of Orlando Golder, mentioned earlier in this chapter, his broker, Harlan Van Wagner of Rhinebeck, was compelled to return five hundred and fifty dollars to his victim. A broker named Brady, who persuaded two boys to enlist in Albany in the fall of 1863, was forced to pay the full bounties to the parents of both, since the boys were away with the Army of the Potomac.[42]

General Dix disliked brokers intensely and constantly crusaded against them. Whenever a broker accused of fraud was brought before him he would demand that the money be refunded. A young man named John Richler thought two New York brokers were helping him secure transportation to Iowa. When he wound up on Riker's Island, he notified General Dix, the case was investigated, and the brokers were forced to return one hundred and fifty dollars to Richler. The following month Dix launched a campaign against swindling city brokers, and for a short time was forcing them to return $1,000 a day. "He is determined, if possible," wrote the New York *Times*, "to break up this swindling business, and the brokers finding they cannot keep the money are getting tired of it."[43] Naturally, when Dix relaxed his energies the brokers returned with their old fervor. There was no unofficial way to dispose of them. Only city, state, or federal law could do the job, and there were no such laws until the last weeks of the war.

Those unwilling or unable to give up the bounty money went to jail. James Weaver, apprehended in New York City in February 1864 for enlisting a boy and appropriating two hundred and fifty-five dollars of his three hundred dollar bounty, was ordered by Dix to refund the money. He refused and was confined at Fort Lafayette. A belligerent broker named John Connell defied Dix, shouting that he would rot in jail rather than return a penny of the four hundred and fifty dollars he had stolen from three recruits. After a few days, however, he cooled off, paid the money and was released. Broker John Crocker told Dix he would return the money he had taken if he could go home and procure it. Accompanied by officers, he went home, but alas, no money. He then took the officers on a tour of several places in which he was well known, but still no money. Weary and impatient, the officers returned Crocker to Dix, who confined him at Fort Lafayette. In Dix's crackdown in March of 1864, other brokers unable to raise the money were jailed. And poor old "Bowery Sam" Garman was also sent to jail because he was unable to return the two hundred and seventy dollars he had swindled from William Coeler; it had been spent for "refreshments."[44]

On several occasions, brokers who had induced young boys to leave home and go to other cities to enlist were apprehended before they carried out their plan. One of them took two brothers, aged twelve and fourteen, from Syracuse to Buffalo in August 1864, but the father arrived just in time to thwart the kidnappers. Early in January 1865 Buffalo police freed four teen-age boys who had come from Rochester without their parents' knowledge. The broker had promised them five hundred dollars each and a furlough if they would enlist. In both of these cases it is obvious that had the boys been enlisted the brokers would have appropriated most, if not all of the bounty money.[45]

Although ignorant Negroes were regularly exploited by brokers, once in a while the deception was uncovered. In February 1864 a Buffalo broker brought a Negro to Albany and enlisted him, demanding two hundred of the man's three hundred dollar bounty. The officers gave him twenty-five dollars. Another time, two Columbia County brokers persuaded a Negro to let them enlist him for one hundred and fifty dollars. They took him to Massachusetts where, before the brokers could stop him, he blurted out that he did not live in Massachusetts. Rejected there, he was taken to Poughkeepsie and enlisted. The brokers demanded one hundred and seventy-five dollars for their costs. The provost marshal ignored them, awarded the full three hundred and twenty-five dollar bounty to the recruit, and sent him to the Soldiers' Rest under guard so the brokers could not rob him en route. In January 1865 a broker told the Poughkeepsie provost that the Negro he had brought in was from Canada and thus eligible to go as a substitute. When the man was questioned, it was obvious he knew nothing about Canada. He finally admitted that he had been liberated by Sherman's army and shipped north by boat. Here he fell in with the broker, who promised him a hundred dollars if he would sign up. The provost marshal told him that he could not go as a substitute since he was not an alien, but that he might volunteer and receive a three hundred dollar bounty. This he did as the angry broker stomped out.[46]

Brokers were sharp and shrewd but once in a great while one of them was really "taken" by his intended victim. In the summer of 1864, a Poughkeepsie broker spied a promising Irishman on a street corner, got him drunk, and took him to the provost marshal's office. The broker's cleverness earned him nothing, however, because it turned out that the man had an incurable leg ailment. If the Irishman realized what the broker had in mind, he must have been chuckling over his free drinks. Some months later another Poughkeepsie broker checked into Rutzers Hotel with a recruit whom he planned to enlist the following day. That night, while the young man was writing a letter, the broker fell asleep. When he awakened next morning he found a brief note on the table: "Dear Sir—You consider yourself pretty smart. You thought you had me all right. You also had $200 in greenbacks. I love greenbacks so I'll just take them with me. Good-bye."[47]

Another sleepy broker riding on a train from Dunkirk to Buffalo in September 1863 awakened only to find he was minus eight hundred dollars. "As far as heard from," observed the unsympathetic *Morning Express*, "the light-fingered gentleman has not offered himself as a substitute." Some time later, a New York City broker who had just swindled a group of recruits in Goshen, tried to escape with his loot by boarding a moving train. He misjudged the distance and lost his leg under the wheels of the train. On one occasion a broker's wife suffered for the misdeeds of her spouse. A woman wearing a veil over her face appeared at the door of a Cohoes home in February 1865 and inquired for the broker. The man's wife, who answered the knock, said that her husband was out of town and was brutally assaulted.[48]

By far the most delightful tale of a taken broker appeared in the pages of *Harpers Weekly*, entitled "John Waggoner's Recruit." John Waggoner, it seems, had a high tolerance for liquor and a low opinion of brokers. He decided to teach broker C. E. Miggs a lesson, so he answered Miggs' advertisement in the newspaper, met him in a downtown street, and invited him into a saloon for refreshments. Playing the hale fellow, Waggoner kept joshing Miggs, refilled his glass several times, and began to feign intoxication. "Miggs—hic! old boy, I b'lieve I can lick Deff Javis or any other man. I b'lieve you an' I could, anyhow."

"Of course you could," replied Miggs. "I tell you what, Waggoner," continued the broker, feeling pretty good by now, "I've half a notion to enlist myself."

"Bully f'you," rejoined Waggoner. "Come up and drink," and Miggs' glass was again full. After about two more refills, Waggoner marched, or dragged, the broker across the street to a recruiting office, and enlisted him in the army. "There is one mighty mean man wearing the army blue," concluded Waggoner, "and that man is John Waggoner's recruit."[49]

The above story cannot be verified, but at least one broker was actually victimized in this fashion. A Poughkeepsie operator saw a country greenhorn in town one day in August 1864, and invited him into the inevitable saloon. But it was the broker who got drunk, and the farm boy who enlisted the broker and pocketed the full bounty. The broker had a chance to sober up on Hart's Island along with several of his own victims.[50]

Although brokers were usually considered necessary evils, the press continually reminded recruits that they need not enlist through brokers. Young men wishing to enter the service, it was noted, might go directly to the provost marshal's office and not only receive the full bounty but also the "hand money," which was the legal bonus due anyone who enlisted a man. During the summer draft of 1864 the Elmira *Advertiser* published such a notice: "The recruit himself," it pointed out, "by volunteering in his own person, will be entitled to the agent fee [hand money] and the entire bounty." In February 1865 a Syracuse paper reminded recruits that they would receive more money by going straight to the provost marshal.[51] However, alongside such announcements the papers continued to publish conspicuous broker advertisements, which probably destroyed the effect of the anti-broker warnings. But even the *Argus*, which led the "necessary evil" school of thought, boasted in January 1864, that the county had filled its quota "without the aid of bounty brokers."[52]

Orison Blunt, chairman of the New York County Volunteer and Substitute Committee, exasperated the public and the press, first because he tried to work with the brokers, and then because he refused to work with them. The trouble began over Blunt's plan to pay the county bounty to any broker who appeared at his office bearing the recruit's bounty assignment. Blunt felt the best way to disburse the bounty was through the brokers, and as long as they possessed the assignment they should receive the bounty. When told that recruits were being defrauded, Blunt said he did not care and that the Committee had resolved to execute all bargains made between recruits and brokers.[53]

Reports of fraud began to pour into General Dix's office and on December 3, 1863, he instructed General William Hays, AAPMG for the Southern Division, to take steps to protect all recruits. A week or so later Hays ordered that every recruit mustered into service in New York City must receive the full three hundred dollar bounty, and it should be paid directly to the recruit either by the committee or an agent of the committee. Somewhat pleased, the *Argus* predicted that this ought "to put an end to the bounty swindles on volunteers.[54] The New York *Times*, however, was greatly disturbed by Hays' order. Though prompted by the best of motives, it had led to a 50 per cent decline in recruits the first few days it was in force. It would be nice, the *Times* conceded, if the men enlisting could receive the full bounties, but unfortunately the only people who could obtain the men were brokers, and rightfully they expected expense money for their services.[55]

At the height of this controversy Hays stated that brokers were deliberately withholding men, even paying them not to enlist, just to embarrass him and force him to rescind the order. He added that he would rescind it if the supervisors' committee would publish a signed statement, endorsing the broker system and assuming full responsibility for settling all complaints of swindled recruits. He was particularly irked that the public should blame him and the Federal Government for a series of frauds which he felt were the logical results of Blunt's mistaken methods.[56]

Since the committee was unwilling to do this, Hays offered a substitute proposal by which a recruiting officer would be established in Blunt's headquarters with a provost marshal in constant attendance. Then, whenever a recruit was mustered in by the provost marshal, Blunt could hand the three hundred dollars directly to him. This plan was put into operation, but did not work too well. Because the recruit had already made his arrangement with the broker he merely passed the agreed amount on to the broker as soon as he received his money from Blunt. However, Major Charles G. Halpine, a member of Dix's staff, wrote a few weeks later that although recruiting did fall off under the new system at first, it picked up again, and before long the results were better than before.[57]

Blunt was in the middle again late in the war, by which time he had changed his strategy and was no longer cooperating with the brokers. In January 1865 the supervisor was accused of treating them "as if they were dogs," insulting them in front of their recruits, and giving the hand money to the recruits instead of the brokers. If the broker argued with the supervisor, it was reported, he would be evicted. Was it any wonder that Blunt was unable to procure any men? The upstate districts, the *Times* noted, were having no problem filling their quotas and many of the men were coming from New York City. It was hoped that Blunt would change his ways, so that the brokers would keep their men in the city and fill local quotas.[58]

The broker question came into sharp focus in Albany in mid-summer 1864 as the outgrowth of an incident which occurred in the headquarters of the 14th District. A runner named Holley, who had brought two men down from Canada to serve as substitutes, called on an Oswego broker, A.B. Pratt, to ask if Pratt could find principals for his substitutes. The broker eventually located two draftees in Scho-harie County who needed substitutes. A bargain was struck whereby the principals agreed to pay the substitutes one hundred and fifty dollars each for entering the service in their places. When they reached Provost Marshal Parsons' office one of the men was rejected, while the other, Joshua Long, was accepted as a substitute for draftee James Spore. Parsons then asked Long how much he was getting and when he said one hundred and fifty dollars, he was told that he could get three hundred dollars. When Pratt then tried to speak with Long, Eliakim Chase, a clerk in the office, seized him and flung him to the door where a guard shoved him down the stairs. It is not quite clear why Chase attacked Pratt, and Parsons testified later that he had not ordered the broker's eviction, but Chase was arrested for assault and battery. In late July 1864 the court ruled for Pratt.[59]

The *Argus* capitalized upon this episode to reiterate its "necessary evil" position. Hounding the brokers simply caused them to take their recruits elsewhere. The *Argus* denied "the right to interfere where a fair bargain has been made between two men of common sense, [simply] because the man agreed to go for a less sum than some third person thinks he ought to."[60] The *Argus* missed the point when it spoke of a "fair bargain" between men of "common sense." Broker bargains were inherently unfair, and the officers who interfered with them were trying to protect naive young men who had been badly tricked into making unfair bargains. If the bargains had been fair there would have been no problem.

As the war progressed and as broker swindles spread, it was gener-ally conceded that many brokers were brazen thieves, but that many others did not defraud recruits. Enlistees were strongly urged to seek out the latter and shun the former. The brokerage business itself, ob-served a Rochester newspaper, was not dishonorable. The broker must "make no false representations, he must split the money liberally with the recruit." By so doing he made three people happy—the principal, the substitute, and the broker. However, since the commutation clause had been repealed, the prices for substitutes had shot up and many unscrupulous people were entering the field. These must be guarded against.[61]

The Elmira *Advertiser* commended honest brokers for their important services but warned against "interlopers," who had invaded a legitimate business and "deserve all the scorn and punishment which has been heaped upon them." Even the New York *Times*, which had agreed with the *Argus*, lost patience with the brokers. Condemning "the extravagant and often dishonest system of bounty brokerage," in August 1864 it urged draftees or prospective volunteers to "club together" and find agents of their own who would arrange for their enlistment without exacting the usurious tribute common to brokers. "Clubbing" would also result in a better class of substitutes than brokers normally supplied. Thousands of young men, the *Times* concluded, "are repelled from the service solely by the rascally agencies which meet them at the very threshold of military life."[62] However, the *Times* receded from this commendable position in January and February 1865, when Blunt was talking brokers out of their hand money. As for "clubbing," it apparently never caught on because no future reference to it can be found in the *Times*.

Actually, strong condemnation of the brokers had appeared in other states by late 1863, not too long after passage of the Enrolment Act. "Cannot something be done to stop this nefarious practice?" beseeched the angry Cleveland *Herald* in December of that year.[63] However, New York State seemed undisturbed by the crimes of the broker system for many months after the first reports of large-scale swindles.

When anger against brokers started to mount, the Saratoga *Republican*, after describing the many ways by which brokers defrauded recruits, suggested that "if all the frauds and rascalities . . . could be truthfully and fairly written it would form a good appendix to Greeley's *History of the Great Rebellion*." But more significant was the *Argus* itself, which by early 1865 had abandoned its position that the broker system was a necessary evil. When brokers were accused of running recruits to more affluent communities, it complained that they had an obligation to their home districts and had betrayed this trust. Then, in a final fit of despair, the *Argus* cried out that "three or four policemen . . . would be able to effectually check the operations of these brokers. . . ."[64]

*   *   *   *

The first steps to regulate brokers were merely efforts to prohibit "running" or to guarantee the recruit his full bounty, but as the frauds continued unabated, absolute prohibition of broker activity became mandatory. By the time such regulation had been enacted, however, the war was all but over and the laws served little purpose. Had strict anti-broker legislation been adopted in 1863, it might have saved the taxpayers of New York State a large portion of the $86,000,000 paid in bounties and provided real troops instead of a collection of criminals or nonexistent "paper" credits.

John T. Sprague, Adjutant General of the state, in his annual report for 1863, strongly urged the legislature to curtail the activities of out-of-state recruiters. He reported that at one time seventeen such agents were active in New York City, while others were operating in Utica, Rochester, Lockport, and Buffalo. Their interference was adversely affecting and discouraging the various county, town, and city committees. Taking their cue from Sprague, the legislature, on January 29, 1864, passed a law prohibiting running recruits to other states.[65] The only significant running activities after this were intra-state, rather than inter-state.

What was more important was the effort to undercut broker strength by paying the full bounty directly into the hands of the recruit in the presence of the provost marshal. Something like this had been tried in the Hays-Blunt affair with mixed results. But in the spring of 1864 the indomitable Dix, continuing his war on the brokers, revived the idea. In March he learned that Richmond County and certain towns within his command had authorized a three hundred dollar bounty, with the unusual stipulation that "at least $100" of the bounty must go to the recruit. This wording would help brokers convince recruits that the remaining two hundred dollars rightfully belonged to the broker. This, said Dix, must cease.

In General Orders Number 23 of March 25, 1864, the Commander of the Department of the East instructed all provost marshals under his authority to refuse to muster any recruit from a county or town which had a bounty ordinance similar to that of Richmond County, unless they were positive that each recruit received the full three hundred dollars. Dix would not tolerate a situation where money was specifically appropriated for bounties yet only a portion of it was required to go to the recruit. Still, the order was difficult to enforce and was probably ineffective. In December 1864, for example, Major Haddock, AAPMG of the Western Division, was compelled to re-issue it.[66]

Several ineffectual attempts at broker regulation were made prior to the statutory prohibitions. In Rochester, in August 1864, each broker was required to pay a license fee of seven dollars and fifty cents if he wished to continue in business. It was also suggested by the Poughkeepsie *Daily Eagle* that United States Assessors and Collectors check up on the brokers and scrutinize their income tax statements.[67] In the last two weeks of the war, an Albany recruiting committee opened its own office in Parsons' headquarters to assist recruits to enlist without brokers. At the committee's request signs were posted near the various broker offices to discourage recruits from going there.[68] Voluntary circumvention of the brokers had been tried in Cleveland and Cincinnati in 1864, but with poor results.[69] No major city in New York State, except Albany, attempted it, and the office there was not in business long enough to judge its effectiveness.

New York City did not pass an ordinance strictly regulating broker activity, such as was adopted in Ohio in January 1865. The only regulatory legislation enacted in New York was the state law of February 10, 1865, when the war was all but over. Section Five provided that all bounties must be paid directly to the recruit and that any agreement between a broker and a substitute or a volunteer, by which the bounty money would be divided, was void. Furthermore, any money paid to a broker in the future might be recovered by the substitute or volunteer, his heirs, or legal representatives, with full interest from the date of the first payment. The Congress also amended the Enrolment Act in March 1865 so that a broker who defrauded a recruit of "any portion of the State, local, or United States bounty," would be jailed for from three months to two years and be fined from two hundred dollars to $1,000.[70]

After the war, when the provost marshals had put their notes together and submitted their final reports, it became clear they did not think that brokers had been necessary. Parsons reiterated that under the system the taxpayers were robbed. John T. Wright of the 27th District affirmed that the only way to stop the outrageous swindles was "by prohibiting entirely and radically the operations of so-called substitute brokers." S. B. Haynam, who succeeded Haddock as AAPMG for the Western Division, urged an absolute ban on brokers, and recommended that all such recruiting activities be carried out by authorized ward and town committees. Lastly, Fry in his *Final Report*, endorsed all these recommendations and urged that, in future wars, we employ some other system to raise troops.[71]

· 7 ·

Baker and the Brokers.

COLONEL LAFAYETTE C. BAKER, mentioned previously, was a special detective for the War Department. Baker's investigations into broker frauds in New York City in January, February, and March 1865 illustrated the growing concern over broker depredations and the new resolve to stop them. On January 16 he received the following order from Provost Marshal General Fry:

> ... you are hereby directed to make an examination ... with
> a view of detecting and bringing to punishment men who
> are violating the laws as bounty and substitute brokers and
> bounty-jumpers, and also any officer or employee of this bureau
> who may be taking part in or conniving at frauds or imposi-
> tions in connection with the raising of troops ....[1]

The detective caught the first train for New York City, the acknowledged center of the frauds, got a room at the Astor, and began his investigation of broker operations in the nation's largest city.[2]

Baker was just the man to undertake the difficult job of flushing out the unscrupulous brokers who had defrauded individual soldiers and countless communities of thousands of dollars. In 1852, at the age of twenty-seven, he had left a new bride in Philadelphia and had gone to California where he became a vigilante. He developed a capacity for ruthless, relentless pursuit of lawbreakers and an indifference to human suffering. He mastered the techniques of disguise and deception by studying the life of the celebrated French detective Vidocq. Back in Washington early in the Civil War, he was soon attached to

Secretary of War Stanton's office with instructions to build up his own detective force and track down every spy, deserter, and subversive he could find. Baker promised the Secretary that "the air of the Old Capitol Prison will be foul with the odor of the traitors I throw into its cells."[3]

He employed the midnight raid, the arbitrary arrest, and the third degree. He held his victims incommunicado—many dying unnoticed in Old Capitol—and ignored their civil rights. He tangled with generals, cabinet officers, and congressmen. He went on missions behind the Confederate lines, exposed frauds in the Treasury Department, broke up the Johnson's Island conspiracy, and later organized the capture of John Wilkes Booth. Cold-blooded and dedicated, Baker drove ahead, unmoved by criticism, loyal alone to Stanton.[4]

Yet, in spite of his broad experience in dealing with lawbreakers, Baker was appalled by the massive fraud operations he found in New York City. He wrote:

> ... A large number of persons, of the most desperate and
> disreputable character, were engaged at the different rendez-
> vous in filling the quotas. The great and urgent demands of
> the Government to fill up the ranks of our depleted army, were
> seized upon by these individuals, known as bounty brokers
> or receiving agents, as a fit time to perpetrate those forgeries
> and frauds upon the Government and soldiers, the extent
> and enormity of which, I believe, are unparalleled in the history
> of the world . . . .[5]

He returned to Washington and told Fry to find somebody else to round up this vast array of thieves. It took Fry's best powers of persuasion to get Baker to go ahead with the job.

After some thought Baker hit upon a plan which he hoped would smash the most fraudulent practice he had found—the forging and selling of false enlistment papers. The plan was to pose as a supervisor or a committeeman from upstate New York, who was in the city to fill his district's quota under the December 1864 call for troops. Baker knew that some officials had bought hundreds of forged enlistment papers from brokers who were in collusion with corrupt recruiting officials. If the word got around that he was looking for recruits, he reasoned, the brokers would soon find their way to his Astor House rooms. He was right.

On January 28, 1865, two notorious brokers, James Devlin and James Cabron, visited Baker and offered him sixteen sets of enlistment papers. The detective purchased them at once for two hundred and twenty-five dollars a set. He told them to bring him some more and to tell other brokers that he was in business. Baker continued to purchase forged documents for several days. On February 2 he arrested Devlin and Cabron, and another Devlin named John, a Brooklyn notary public. From them he learned how the forgers operated, as well as the names of other culprits. Baker continued to gather information until he had enough evidence to move against the principal brokers. Then he invited nine of them to prepare a lot of phony papers and come to his rooms. Several of his aides were in an adjoining room with instructions to enter at the signal.

Everything proceeded smoothly. The brokers arrived, their hands filled with papers, and lined up for the payoff. After they had all made their marks[6] on the receipts, the signal was given, and the other detectives came quickly in. Baker announced, "Gentlemen, this joke has gone far enough; you are my prisoners. I am General Baker,[7] the Chief of the Detective Bureau." Dumbfounded at this unexpected turn of events, the brokers either dropped speechless into chairs, broke into tears, or began to laugh awkwardly. A defiant one dared Baker to arrest him, but when the detective flashed his revolver, the defiance vanished. They were all shortly packed off to the Old Capitol to await trial.[8]

The methods of preparing the papers, explained to Baker by Devlin and Cabron, was ingenius. The Naval Rendezvous on York Street in Brooklyn, although not under the authority of the Provost Marshal Bureau, had been the center of the illicit activity. Two clerks in charge of the books at the rendezvous copied down the names of all recruits who had been legitimately enlisted each day. The list had been sent to Devlin and Cabron, who put the names on enlistment blanks with which they had already been amply supplied. These forms were then taken to the Brooklyn notary public, John Devlin, who

MULLIGAN'S BRIGADE!

LAST CHANCE TO AVOID THE DRAFT!

$402 BOUNTY!

TO VETERANS!

$302 to all other VOLUNTEERS!

All Able-bodied Men, between the ages of 18 and 45 Years, who have heretofore served not less than nine months, who shall re-enlist for Regiments in the field, will be deemed Veterans, and will receive one month's pay in advance, and a bounty and premium of $402. To all other recruits, one month's pay in advance, and a bounty and premium of $302 will be paid.

All who wish to join Mulligan's Irish Brigade, now in the field, and to receive the munificent bounties offered by the Government, can have the opportunity by calling at the headquarters of

CAPT. J. J. FITZGERALD

Of the Irish Brigade. 23d Regiment Illinois Volunteers. Recruiting Officer. Chicago. Illinois

Each Recruit, Veteran or otherwise, will receive

Seventy-five Dollars Before Leaving General Rendezvous,

and the remainder of the bounty in regular instalments till all is paid. The pay, bounty and premium for three years will average $24 per month, for Veterans; and $21.30 per month for all others.

If the Government shall not require these troops for the full period of Three Years, and they shall be mustered honor out of the service before the expiration of their term of enlistment, they shall receive, UPON BEING MUSTERED O the whole amount of BOUNTY remaining unpaid, the same as if the full term been served.

J. J. FITZGERALD.

Chicago, December, 1863.

Recruiting Officer, cor. of North Clark & Kenzie Stre

An early poster. In later months of the war no one would enlist for this paltry sum.—from The Granger Collection, New York City.

Satire on spurious, but successful,
draft exemption pleas.
—from *Harper's Weekly* (August 23, 1862).

AN EXEMPT.

OFFICER. "You're a Foreigner, you say?"
APPLICANT. "Born in Tipperary, yer honor."
OFFICER. "Did you never get Naturalized?"
APPLICANT. "Ne'er a time."
OFFICER. "Did you never Vote?"
APPLICANT. "Oh! for the matter of votin', yer honor,
allus Votes. Many's the Vote I've guv FERNANDY WOOD
an' av' he were Mayor now———(*is marched off.*)

The easy way out, all other means
of evading the draft having failed.
—from *Harper's Weekly* (November 8, 1862).

ABUNDANT DISQUALIFICATION.

"Ugh! How d'you make out that *you* are exempt, eh?"

"I'm over age, I am a Negro, a Minister, a Cripple, a
British Subject, and an Habitual Drunkard."

"Doping".
—from *Harper's Weekly* (January 23, 1864).

THE RECRUITING BUSINESS.

VOLUNTEER-BROKER (*to Barber*) "Look a-here—I want you to trim up this old chap with a flaxen wig and a light mustache, so as to make him look like twenty; and as I shall probably clear three hundred dollars on him, I sha'n't mind giving you fifty for the job."

Brokers were ". . . enterprising men . . . [who] will honorably fulfill all contracts." Elmira Daily Advertiser.—from Collection of Astor, Lenox and Tilden Foundations, The New York Public Library.

THE CONSCRIPT BILL!

HOW TO AVOID IT!!

U. S. NAVY.

1,000 MEN WANTED, FOR 12 MONTHS!

Seamen's Pay, - - - - - - $18.00 per month.
Ordinary Seamen's Pay, ...   14.00 " "
Landsmen's Pay, ...   12.00 " "
$1.50 extra per month to all, Grog Money.

$50,000,000 PRIZES!

Already captured, a large share of which is awarded to Ships Crews. The laws for the distributing of Prize money carefully protects the rights of all the captors.

PETTY OFFICERS,—PROMOTION.—Seamen have a chance for promotion to the offices of Master at Arms, Boatswain's Mates, Quarter Gunners, Captain of Tops, Forecastle, Holds, After-Guard, &c.
Landsmen may be advanced to Armorers, Armorers' Mates, Carpenter's Mates, Sailmakers' Mates, Painters, Coopers, &c.
PAY OF PETTY OFFICERS,—From $20.00 to $45.00 per month.
CHANCES FOR WARRANTS, BOUNTIES AND MEDALS OF HONOR.—All those who distinguish themselves in battle or by extraordinary heroism, may be promoted to forward Warrant Officers or Acting Masters' Mates,—and upon their promotion receive a guaranty of $100, with a medal of honor from their country.
All who wish may leave HALF PAY with their families, to commence from date of enlistment.
Minors must have a written consent, sworn to before a Justice of the Peace.

For further information apply to U. S. NAVAL RENDEZVOUS,

E. Y. BUTLER, U. S. N. Recruiting Officer,

No. 14 FRONT STREET, SALEM, MASS.

FROM WRIGHT & POTTER'S BOSTON PRINTING ESTABLISHMENT, No. 4 SPRING LANE, CORNER OF DEVONSHIRE STREET.

A Join-the-Navy-and-avoid-the-draft poster.
—from National Selective Service Headquarters, Washington.

Recruiting in City Hall Park, New York City, 1864.
—from Paul F. Mottelay and T. Campbell-Copeland, *The Soldier in Our Civil War* (Stanley Bradley, Publishers, New York, 1890).

Major General John Adams Dix.
—from *Harper's Weekly*
(August 2, 1862).

Resumption of the draft at the Sixth District Provost Marshall's Office,
New York City, August 19, 1863.—from The Granger Collection, New York City.

Ruins of the Ninth District Provost Marshall's Office, Third Avenue and 46th
Street, New York City, July 13, 1863.—from The Granger Collection, New York City.

DESTRUCTION OF PROVOST MARSHAL'S OFFICE 3ᵈ AV

Police dispersing draft rioters at *New York Tribune* office.
—from *Harper's Weekly* (New York, August 1, 1863).

Sacking Brooks Brothers Clothing Store, New York Draft Riots.
—from The Granger Collection, New York City.

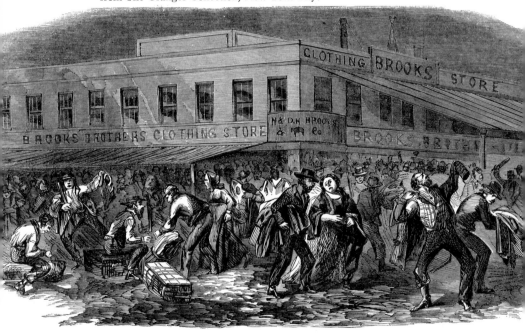

Horatio Seymour.
—from *Harper's Weekly* (November 22, 1862).

Brigadier General LaFayette Curry Baker, "Special Detective, War Department".
—from L. C. Baker, *History of the Secret Service* (L. C. Baker, Philadelphia, 1867).

OPPOSITE:
Classified advertisements for substitutes, both wanted and furnished.
—from Cincinnati Daily Gazette, 1864.

Highest bounties? Some, reputedly, went as high as $1,500.
—from Poster Collection of Norm Flayderman, New Milford, Connecticut.

The "alien" was often drafted.
—from *Harper's Weekly* (November 29, 1862).

JOHN CHINAMAN. "Me no 'Merikan Man — you no Draftee me — you Draftee me, me *appeal to my Government*. My Government be *Much Mad!*"

Baker springs his trap at Hoboken.
—from L. C. Baker, *History of the Secret Service* (L. C. Baker, Philadelphia, 1867).

Execution of bounty jumpers, Fifth Corps, Army of the Potomac.
—from *Harper's Weekly* (September 26, 1863).

SCENE, FIFTH AVENUE.

HE. "Ah! Dearest ADDIE! I've succeeded. I've got a Substitute!"
SHE. "Have you? What a curious coincidence! And *I* have found one FOR YOU!"

Contrary to
the implication,
those who furnished
substitutes were not
objects of contempt.
—from *Harper's Weekly*
(August 30, 1862).

The "Rogues"
march at
Indianapolis,
December, 1864.
—from
Fletcher Pratt,
*Civil War
in Pictures*
(Henry Holt
and Company,
New York, 1955).

certified that the recruits whose names were on the forms had appeared before him and had been properly sworn in. He then affixed his seal and signature.[9]

Seemingly authentic, these papers were now hawked by the brokers in the streets, saloons, and hotels of downtown New York. Unsuspecting agents from upstate districts, hard-pressed to fill their quotas, bought all the recruits they needed. If the agent wanted to see the names of his recruits properly recorded before he paid his money, the broker would take him back to the Naval Rendezvous where, of course, the names had already been enrolled. The recruits, unknown to the upstate agents, were already legally credited to other districts. To circumvent this difficulty a simple subterfuge was employed. When the broker and agent appeared, the clerks produced the enlistment books in which fly-sheets identical to the original pages had been loosely inserted. These fly-sheets were properly lined and marked, and when the agent saw the names of his recruits written on them and credited to his district, he paid over his money and went away happy. Naturally, as soon as he left, the fly-sheet was removed and destroyed. Baker reported that "in the town of Delhi, St. Lawrence County, a quota of two hundred and twenty-three men was filled by these forged papers, and not a single man was enlisted."[10]

The detective learned that numerous officers and clerks at the Brooklyn Navy Yard had received large sums of money from brokers for supplying them with forged enlistment papers, lists of fictitious names, and hundreds of forged shipping receipts. Only a select band of brokers was allowed into the York Street station or on board the receiving ships at the Navy Yard. The gatekeeper at the Yard was also on the crooks' payroll, permitting just the favored few into the compound. The commander of the rendezvous agreed to aid the brokers for one-fourth of the profits. Bank checks drawn in favor of naval officers by the brokers were produced which mounted into the thousands of dollars.[11]

When Baker had commenced his investigations, the commander of one of the other naval rendezvous offices was an aged cripple named Captain Young. Because of his disability, Young relied on a broker firm, Fay and Dalton, to take him to and from his office and to assist him in his work. Little by little, John Fay took over the Captain's duties, and before long was running the office. Fay was soon forging enlistment papers under Young's very eyes and was always armed with a hundred or more sets of papers whenever recruiting agents arrived. He proved such an expert forger and seller of these papers that "from a penniless hackman of three years ago, he has come to be the real estate holder in Brooklyn to the amount of more than $200,000."[12]

If the brokers, reviewing their circumstances from the dungeons of Old Capitol, were unhappy over the Baker disclosures, the defrauded supervisors and agents were in a purple rage. From the day the newspapers picked up the story, these victims thronged Baker's parlors in the Astor, demanding credit or refunds for their forged enlistments. Dozens of agents had filled their quotas entirely with these phony papers from the York Street rendezvous and they wanted satisfaction. All Baker could do was show them the enlistment records and check to see whether they happened to be the lucky ones whose recruits were actually listed on the books. In answer to a recurrent question, he had to tell the recruiters that Fry would view "as so much wastepaper" all false papers.

Crowded in the hotel corridors, these agents jostled against the same mustachioed, bejeweled crooks who had swindled them. Surprisingly, the encounters did not erupt in mayhem. One elderly supervisor from Lewis County was unperturbed by the uproar. "The old lady cautioned me," he remarked confidently, "to beware of sharpers, and before I paid over my money I saw the names that are written on these certificates recorded on the great book at the office of the Naval Rendezvous." When he got in to see Baker, the detective brought the enlistment volume over and asked the unworried supervisor to find the names of his recruits. When he was unable to find them, the clerk of the rendezvous showed him how the facsimile flysheet was inserted in the book for the recording of false enlistments. The supervisor's "old lady" no doubt had something to say to him when he returned to Lewis County.[13]

In many cases the forged papers were easy to detect, so conspicuous were certain errors made by the forgers. For example, one "recruit" signed the first paper in a fine "Roman hand," while on a second document he could only affix his mark, an "X". Numerous sets of papers had widely contrasting signatures, while some had no signatures at all.[14]

Another kind of error brought about the downfall of Captain James Mooney, a recruiting officer for the 19th United States Infantry, with offices at Number 4 Chambers Street in Manhattan. Mooney first sold a set of forged papers to agents from Delaware County in the 19th District, and later peddled additional papers to agents from Columbia County in the 12th District. Through some mixup, he gave the same sets of papers to both sets of agents. After the New York *Times* published the story of Mooney's arrest, the Captain wrote an irate letter to the editor, denying all allegations and protesting that he had actually been one of the first to report the frauds to the police. The *Times* responded by publishing a deposition from one John Oliver, who testified he had purchased two sets of papers from Mooney for the 12th District only to be informed by the AAPMG at Albany that the same men had already been credited by Mooney to the 19th District. In the National Archives today may be found three sets of duplicate enlistment papers, all signed "James Mooney, Capt., 19th U.S. Infantry."[15]

Baker also put a stop to the fraudulent practice of "putting through" new recruits at the rendezvous stations on Governor's and Hart's Islands. At the stations, the guards had been bribed to allow the new men to go ashore, where they would promptly enlist under a new name and be put through again.

Arthur Carron, a broker who was himself a deserter, had an agreement with Sergeants Mulhern, Brown, and Keegan for putting recruits through Governor's Island. Carron would enlist a man for a large bounty, and then offer to get him off the Island for two hundred or two hundred and fifty dollars. If the recruit accepted the offer, Carron would accompany him to the rendezvous, pay one of the sergeants fifty to seventy-five dollars and the man was free to leave. Mulhern later admitted that he accumulated $14,000 in this fashion, with which he bought a large farm in New Jersey.[16]

Carron also had arrangements with officers on the Island to purchase passes for the new recruits which would allow them to leave the rendezvous. To test Carron's connections, Baker detectives, on April 8, paid over five hundred dollars to the broker to secure the release of a number of recruits enlisted the day before. Accompanied by the detectives, Carron went to Governor's Island, put the five hundred dollars in a Bible on the desk of one of the officers, secured the passes, and brought the men back to New York. They were reenlisted that same day, taken to the Island, returned to the city the following day, and enlisted again. In his confession, Carron stated, "I think I have brought off, in all, about four hundred men, about two-thirds of whom I re-enlisted." One Thomas Patterson confessed that Carron had put him through seven times.[17]

One of Baker's detectives cultivated the friendship of a "Captain" Richard McGuire, a broker in Nassau Street. The detective got the "Captain" drunk. The latter then revealed his method of operation and invited Baker's aide to be put through. The detective enlisted, received his bounty, was "put through", and upon his return from the Island, inquired of the possibilities of bounty-jumping in New Jersey. McGuire enjoined caution because "Colonel Baker's detectives are in town and they may nab you." McGuire was himself "nabbed" within minutes.[18]

Baker compiled impressive statistics to show that many recruits enlisted at the various stations never reached the rendezvous. For example, of the 1,284 men signed up at the Cedar Street station between May and October 1864, only eight hundred and thirteen reached Hart's or Governor's Islands. James Lee, a broker located in Tammany Hall, guaranteed his recruits that they would either be freed on the way to the rendezvous, or at the rendezvous itself. Sergeant McCue, attached to the same Cedar Street office, was reported to have made $20,000 through recruiting fraud operations.[19]

For the honest, law-abiding recruit, who fully intended to serve in the army at the front, the stay at the rendezvous was less than pleasant. In response to numerous complaints, Baker ordered one of his men to enlist and go to Hart's Island for a first-hand investigation. He found that bounty-jumpers had turned the place into a black hole of crime and violence. The detective assumed the guise of a thief and was soon admitted into the rogues' inner councils. The practice was to rob the recruits of their funds while they were asleep during the first night on the Island. If the thieves were caught in the act, they would immediately commence a "fight" among themselves, and the rookie's pockets would be picked while he was watching the put-up fight. On Governor's Island, the scoundrels took no chances; they chloroformed their victims first.[20]

A lover of disguises and something of a ham actor as well, Baker enjoyed impersonating the type of person he was investigating. Early in February he dressed himself up like an experienced jumper, and walked to a recruiting office near the Astor House. He was at once accosted by a broker who enlisted him, gave him one hundred dollars, and asked, "Have you ever been on the Island?" Baker said he had, whereupon the broker told him to come to Tammany Hall as soon as he got off the Island and he would be put through again.

But now his adventure began. As he stepped outside, Baker was invited to a nearby saloon and treated to a drink. Certain that it was drugged, the detective appeared to swallow the drink, but actually poured it inside his shirt at the neck. After a few minutes he feigned drowsiness, and was taken along with a number of really drugged men to the Cedar Street recruiting station. His hat was jammed down over his face as a recruiting officer asked him if he wished to enlist. One of the brokers, standing behind him muttered "yes," and Baker was in the army again.

The detective was now dumped into a room with a crowd of befuddled rookies, but quickly escaped by dropping out the back window. Returning uptown, Baker entered another recruiting office and told an inquiring broker that he wanted to enlist as a clerk for six hundred dollars. The broker obliged, and the detective entered the army for the third time in one night. Again he was invited to a saloon, this time meeting the brokers who had arranged his earlier enlistments. They were not at all surprised to see him, and, in fact, welcomed him into the club as a "perfect trump."[21] It was an eventful day for Baker, followed by the triumphant arrest of countless brokers, jumpers, and recruiters.

Another ruse paid off successfully when Baker had two of his aides enlist with a State Street broker who was reportedly an expert at putting men through Governor's Island. After they had been sent to the rendezvous, another of Baker's men applied to the broker for the release of the first two. For two hundred dollars this was agreed to. Even better, the broker let the third detective go with him to the Island to see for himself how cleverly the matter was handled.

Upon reaching the Island the detective could easily see that the broker was on intimate terms with the officers and enlisted men. A sergeant at the gate was paid fifty dollars for which he issued the two men a pass signed in the name of the provost marshal of the Island. Another sergeant at the end of the dock, after receiving his cut, examined the passes, reminded the men with a wink that they were due back for evening roll-call, and permitted them to leave.

Baker arrested the broker when he returned to New York, but kept the arrest secret for several days. This alarmed the two Island sergeants who, fearing their friend had been murdered, came to the city and sought the help of the city police. The latter directed them to Baker. They told their story excitedly to the chief detective, noting that when last seen the broker had a lot of money on his person and was in the company of a suspicious-looking stranger. They offered five hundred dollars for help in locating the missing man. Baker informed them he would find their friend without charge and instructed an assistant to bring the broker in from an adjacent room.

> The scene was a rich and rare one [wrote Baker]. The glad
> surprise of the sergeants was soon toned down by the myster-
> ious gravity of their friend, and also my own. I then took out
> a pair of handcuffs, and said to the young men, "I am very glad
> you have saved me the trouble of sending for you, as I in-
> tended to do tomorrow."[22]

It was not uncommon for a gang of jumpers to organize under a broker and travel in a body from town to town, enlisting and deserting at every stop. Baker assigned one of his detectives to accompany one such band of thirty-six. They left New York City about midnight, March 17, 1865. The next day at Poughkeepsie, eleven enlisted, four escaping in the afternoon, two at night, and the rest in the early morning. The next day the whole crew enlisted at Albany, many having already signed up at nearby Troy. Most of them escaped in the evening, when they pushed on to Utica for a rendezvous. In the five days at Utica, twenty-one enlisted, four of them twice, one, three times. They travelled on to Buffalo, Cleveland, Chicago, and Detroit and back home by way of Rochester and Elmira. Not all of the crowd made it back to New York, but those who did were gone thirty-two days, and accumulated profits totaling $32,000.[23]

Besides brokers, there was another element to cope with. Baker estimated that there were about 10,000 bounty-jumpers and deserters in New York City. They were described by the New York *Times* as "the outscourings of the city slums, old prison birds, graduates from the city institutions . . . and Tombs repeaters." To snare such a motley crew, careful planning was required. It was decided at length to open a phony recruiting office in Hoboken, New Jersey, where bounty-jumpers would be enlisted and allowed to escape for several days until the news spread that it was a real "walkaway." Then, suddenly, the trap would be sprung on the unsuspecting victims, and they would be hustled off to the Old Capitol.[24]

To staff the Hoboken office Baker was assigned Colonel Guido Ilges, of the 14th United States Infantry, as mustering officer, and Lieutenant J. B. Rife, of the 6th United States Infantry, as commander of the guard. These two were not at all happy with the scheme, but accepted the assignment. The recruiting office was opened in the basement of the Odd Fellows Hall in Washington Street, Hoboken. The recruiting room was in front, then came the surgeon's office, next the mustering room, and finally the escape hatch in the rear. From the mustering room a spiral stairway led to a large hall above. When the trap was to be snapped shut, the victims would be directed up the stairway to the great hall, rather than allowed to escape out the back door.[25]

The news was spread that a "perfect gift"—a recruiting office where bounties were high and guards corrupt—was open. To advertise the "gift" Baker had enlisted the services of Theodore Allen, the most notorious bounty broker in New York City. It was Allen's job to mobilize his gang of brokers and have them direct all the jumpers they could locate to the Odd Fellows Hall.[26]

It is not quite clear whether Baker was aware that Allen had a lengthy criminal record, or if he chose to disregard it. Or perhaps he simply felt it fitted his purpose; Baker had often demonstrated that he would use any means to obtain a goal. And Allen seemed to be eminently suited to help Baker at this time.

In 1864, Allen had formed the brokerage firm of Allen, Reilly, and Hughes with offices at 25 Chambers Street, which quickly became the "leading establishment in the city." It had reportedly amassed $100,000 and had agents in Philadelphia, Harrisburg, and Washington, as well as in New York. Long Island was supposedly overrun with his people. Allen and his associates often made $5,000 in profits in a day and in one stretch of twelve consecutive days they took in over $60,000. Allen was credited with being a man of great tact, executive ability, and persuasiveness.[27]

Allen obviously did not care which side he was on, as he had helped Baker in exposing the bogus enlistment paper frauds. Because of this, Baker felt he could trust Allen at Hoboken. At Baker's suggestion the broker went to Washington on February 28, 1865, and discussed the entrapment scheme with Fry, who gave it his full support. It is astounding to realize that the government, in its effort to destroy the broker fraternity in New York City, placed full reliance on the most infamous broker of all. But A. G. Riddle, Fry's counsel during the Fry-Conkling investigation of 1866, effectively defended the strategy.

> Enormous frauds [he said] were in full tide when Baker, at
> the instance of General Fry, was launched against them. The
> campaign was brief but decisive, and resulted in the utter
> extermination of the whole obscene brood; and when I hear a
> man condemn the means used, I am inclined to suspect that
> he dislikes the results.

In other words, it was a calculated risk to use Allen, but the enormity of the frauds being committed in New York demanded extreme measures.[28]

The recruiting office in Odd Fellows Hall opened on March 1, 1865, and in the first nine days of operation fifty-four men were mustered, three of whom were legitimate recruits. They were forwarded to their regiments. The remaining fifty-one, acknowledged bounty-jumpers, were allowed to escape through the back door so that they might return to New York and spread the word about Allen's "walkaway." As news circulated to "the dens in Houston Street, in the 4th and 6th Wards, and in Mackerelville" that men were receiving sizeable bounties in Hoboken and allowed to escape, the traffic picked up at Odd Fellows Hall. The New York *Times* reported, with some exaggeration, that the ferryboats to Jersey were crowded each morning with jumpers who returned in the evening with their pockets stuffed with greenbacks.[29]

By March 9 Baker thought the trap had been open long enough, so he ordered it closed the next day. In other words, from now on the "recruits" would be led up the spiral staircase instead of out the back door. Lieutenant Rife arrived with a company of guards late on the 9th, and he and his men spent the night in the upstairs ballroom. The jumpers began arriving in droves on the morning of the 10th. Allen greeted them at the door and sent them on to the surgeon, who passed them to the mustering room in the rear where clerks made out their enlistment papers. As they prepared to leave through the rear door, however, a guard unexpectedly directed them up the stairs where they found themselves under arrest. Since the men outside had no way of knowing what was going on, the jumpers kept entering the building throughout the morning and early afternoon.

At about half past one, however, a guard in the ballroom inadvertently shoved aside the curtains covering the windows looking out on Washington Street, allowing the men outside to see Rife's troops uniformed and armed. Then several of the jumpers raced around to the rear of Odd Fellows Hall and, finding no fresh footprints leading from the door, gave the alarm that it was a trap. A mad rush now ensued for the Hoboken ferry, with brokers and jumpers jostling one another in their haste to reach New York City before being caught. Some twenty-seven brokers, who had been furnishing men at Odd Fellows Hall and had been marked with chalk on the shoulder by Baker agents, were apprehended at the ferry. But the jumpers, who had not yet been enlisted, had to be allowed to board the boats.[30]

Baker was disappointed that his plan broke down when it did, since he only captured one hundred and eighty-three jumpers out of a hoped-for thousand or more. Despite his lack of complete success, he still derived some satisfaction from the discomfiture of those he did catch. His own account reflects this attitude:

> It would be difficult to imagine the scene in the Odd Fellows
> Hall of Hoboken, on the afternoon of that day of arrest.
> Formed in a ring were many hundred soldiers, armed for any
> emergency; within it, seated on benches, were nearly two
> hundred prisoners. With the dawning of the truth upon the
> minds of the wondering crowd of arrested men, a sudden and
> amusing change went over the faces of all. They had been
> especially careful to avoid me, and now, awakened from a
> dream of security to find themselves in my toils! Some looked
> blank with amazement and despair; others had an expression of
> demoniac hate; while a portion of the arrested seemed
> strongly inclined to treat their imprisonment jocosely, and re-
> gard it as a trivial affair. They were caught in the net set by
> hands most dreaded and carefully avoided.

That they had not all lost their sense of humor was evident when one chap inquired, "When will they let us have our bounty?" He practically broke up the assemblage.[31]

The New York *Times* reporter observed that no one could look at this collection of humanity without glimpsing the features of the thief. Fifty of the victims were understood to be "dissipated sons of re-spectable and wealthy people in this city," and practically all of them were readily recognized as multiple bounty-jumpers, if any doubt still remained on that point. One of them had a record of twenty-five jumps. Among the twenty-seven brokers ensnared was one Dennis Sullivan, indicted but acquitted for murder some years before, and a man named McAnnally, a recent escapee from Sing Sing Prison. The captives included "nearly one-half of an uptown fire company." The valuables seized from the jumpers would have equipped a regiment of footpads: dirks, jimmies, skeleton keys, revolvers, and poinards. They also were carrying gold and silver watches, rings, breastpins, assorted jewelry, obscene pictures, $2,000 in greenbacks, and several empty pocketbooks.[32] The one hundred and eighty-three jumpers were imprisoned at Fort Lafayette for three weeks and then allowed to go free. Allen stated that some of them later "waylaid me and fired upon me in my house."[33]

Whatever might be said of the success or failure of the Hoboken entrapment, the events which followed were most unsatisfactory to everyone, except perhaps Allen, Reilly and Hughes. The trouble stemmed from a monumental misunderstanding as to the crediting of the one hundred and eighty-three men enlisted and caught on March 10. Obviously neither Fry nor Baker intended that these jumpers should be credited. The whole scheme was designed to catch these men, and by allowing credits for the recruits mustered prior to March 10 the authorities were simply baiting the trap.[34]

However, Mayor Cleveland of Jersey City, who had bought the enlistments from Allen, also had the impression from Baker that even the men of March 10 were to be credited, and both he and Allen kept pressing the mustering officer, Ilges, to allow the credits. For several days Ilges was torn with indecision, but at length—probably on March 14—he agreed to issue certificates of enlistment for the one hundred and eighty-three jumpers. These certificates would be given to Allen, Reilly, and Hughes, who would then sell them to Cleveland to apply to the Jersey City quota. Ilges acted without express instructions, although he later said that Fry's telegram of March 5 contained the proper authorization for his decision. It is true that neither Fry nor Baker gave any orders *not* to credit the men of March 10, but as Riddle observed during his defense of Fry, common sense should have told Ilges not to credit them.[35]

On March 14 Mayor Cleveland, Ilges, and Peter Reilly, who acted as Allen's treasurer, gathered in the Mayor's office to settle accounts on the one hundred and eighty-three men. Certificates of enlistment for the bounty-jumpers had been given Allen & Company by Ilges, and Reilly was now to sell them to Cleveland at the going bounty prices. Since bounties then being paid ranged from six hundred and seventy-five to seven hundred dollars per man, Cleveland had over $125,000 with him. Before things had proceeded very far, however, Ilges pointed out that he had orders to retain three hundred dollars of each man's bounty until he reached his regiment. Consequently when Cleveland gave the $125,000 to Reilly, the latter passed $54,900 of it on to Ilges. When Allen learned of this, he went to Washington on March 18 to urge Fry to order Ilges to release the money to him. It was at this interview in Fry's office in the War Department that, according to Allen, the Provost Marshal General promised to have the $54,900 returned to the broker if Allen would travel to Utica and gather incriminating evidence against Roscoe Conkling and Peter Crandall, provost marshal of the 21st District.[36]

On the following day, Fry wired Ilges that the credits were disallowed and that he should return the money "to the parties who advanced it." Since Jersey City could no longer claim the one hundred and eighty-three men, the entire $125,000 which Cleveland paid for those men should rightfully have been returned to him. Obviously, however, Allen would not return the more than $70,000 he had received. Still, the Mayor could expect Ilges to return the $54,900 in his possession. But Ilges was reluctant to part with the money, and it required another telegram from Fry on March 23 and a telegram from Fry to Baker on March 24 to make him do it. At last on the 25th Ilges was prepared to dispose of the $54,900. But here he blundered again. Fry, in his telegram, had said to return the money "to the parties who advanced it." The obvious meaning of the message was to return the money to Mayor Cleveland. Since, however, the money had technically passed through the hands of Reilly, Ilges gave it all back to Reilly and Allen.[37]

The unhappy Cleveland went to see Baker and reminded him that he had promised that all the men enlisted at Hoboken would be credited to Jersey City and that now the credits had been disallowed. Baker, while sympathizing with the Mayor, denied he ever made such a promise and in fact recalled that he had advised Cleveland to pay over no money to the brokers until the validity of the credits was fully settled. When Fry learned of what happened, he wrote Baker instructing him to tell Allen to give all the money back to Cleveland. By now Allen and his partners were getting worried, and on April 4 Hughes fled to Canada. Fry ordered the arrest of Allen and Reilly on April 6, but it was too late; Allen had also left for Canada and Reilly was in Europe. The case dragged on throughout the summer of 1865 with Jersey City trying to locate and arrest Allen, Hughes and Reilly, and also convince the government that the credits should be allowed. Early in September the credits were finally allowed and thus Jersey City no longer had any legitimate claim to the $54,900 or the $125,000.[38]

It is incredible, from our point of view, that in all this wrangling about credits and bounties, the fact that the supposed purpose of both was to provide fighting men for the war effort was completely disregarded.

The Hoboken entrapment brought a shower of criticism down on Baker's head. His critics were relatively unconcerned over bounty frauds, but violently concerned over Baker's use and misuse of arbitrary power, and insisted that he had gone too far. In the months ahead, Baker would be sued unsuccessfully forty times for false arrest, while his victims spread the story that the entrapment scheme was designed solely to enrich the detective by shaking down captured jumpers and brokers.[39]

Another story that brought discredit to Baker involved a testimonial fund that was started in April 1865 to honor him for his prosecution of the bounty swindlers. The treasurer of the fund was astounded to receive contributions of over $5,000 from only three persons. Baker quickly investigated and learned that the money had been donated by—guess who? Allen, Hughes, and Reilly! It was alleged that there had been an "understanding" that Baker was to receive a cut of the proceeds. The detective indignantly ordered that the money be returned and stated flatly, "I have never received, directly or indirectly, from any person or persons, the value of one farthing from my connection with any investigation, either at New York, Hoboken, Jersey City, or elsewhere."[40]

Baker's agents were also accused of fraudulent and abusive behavior on occasion. A man named Fred Wall, who was searching for a substitute for his drafted brother in March 1865, was arrested and locked up by two men named Lewis and Kearns, who said they represented Baker. Wall was charged with running recruits out of the state. John Williams testified the following month that a Baker detective falsely arrested him in Buffalo and robbed him of his money, clothing, and valuables. Baker's people also allegedly seized the property and money of Charles W. Cheshire, commissioner for the 2nd District, in May 1865 and in July Cheshire's attorney wrote Fry demanding its return. There may have been some truth to these charges, although it is possible that "con" artists simply used the magic name of Baker to further their own schemes. For example, William H. Edsell, who posed as a Baker agent in Elmira, opened an office and extorted money from a number of people before he was exposed.[41]

The results of Lafayette Baker's labors were less significant than they would have been if he had been engaged for his task a year or so sooner. Nevertheless, he thoroughly disrupted many brokers' operations, put a large collection of swindlers behind bars, and preserved for posterity the story of a fantastic aspect of Civil War recruiting.

· 8 ·

The Enrolment Board.

THE PRESSURES ON CIVIL WAR enrolment boards were severe. The draft law of 1863 was much too vague, leaving wide discretionary powers in the hands of these officials. In addition, the looseness in the law's language opened the door to opportunities for fraud and favoritism. Unfortunately, many provost marshals, commissioners, and surgeons succumbed to pressures and bribes. Yet a far greater number of them firmly resisted all bribe attempts and carried out their duties honorably and efficiently. Some of these honest officials were bitterly attacked by those who had been unsuccessful in efforts to bribe them, and this has not simplified the historian's task of fairly evaluating their performances. However, it is our view that, while a few enrolment board members abused their trust, the great majority proved to be loyal and dedicated public servants. They performed a necessary and difficult task in commendable fashion and the few exceptions to the rule cannot be allowed to tarnish this fine record.

Still it is the few who failed to meet the test who provide the stories. One of them was George Clendon, Jr. of the 16th District on the shores of Lake Champlain. Clendon had been appointed provost marshal in April, 1863, when the Enrolment Act went into operation. His commissioner, A. P. Brand, was named to his post at the same time, while the original surgeon, George Page, was succeeded in December 1863 by J. Platt Foot. The board's two clerks were Hiram M. Cady and Edgar W. Pierce. Fraudulent enlistments in the district occurred in November 1863, but Clendon made a full report to Fry, showing that the exemptees had forged their affidavits of financial

149

stringency and had deluded their neighbors into testifying to the validity of the affidavits. Apparently these exemptions were a result of honest errors by the board.[1]

But in December 1864 Surgeon Foot and Commissioner Brand became suspicious of the behavior of Clendon and the two clerks, Cady and Pierce. The three men met in private frequently and the board members could not learn what was happening in those sessions. If they inquired they were told that it was none of their affair. They seldom had a chance to look at the mail. These suspicions were enhanced by public rumors of connivance between Clendon, the clerks, and bounty brokers.

At length, Brand and Foot came upon concrete evidence. They learned that Thomas Maguire, supervisor of the town of Minerva in Essex County, had deposited $3,000 in bonds with Clendon to procure five recruits at six hundred dollars per man. The provost marshal turned the matter over to his clerks, who found the required men at three hundred and fifty dollars a head for a total of $1,750. Clendon then turned over the $3,000 in bonds to Cady and Pierce, along with some other money that had been on deposit in the office to pay the recruits. Brand asked Clendon if it were not a violation of the Provost Marshal General's Regulations for officials of the enrolment board to supply a district's or subdistrict's quota. The provost marshal said no; an enrolment board could not supply substitutes, but it could supply recruits. Unconvinced, Brand went to Colonel Baker, whose investigations in New York City were now attracting attention, and early in February 1865 a Baker agent named Blood arrived in Plattsburgh to investigate.

Blood's findings strongly substantiated the doubts of Brand and Foot. With Clendon's knowledge and approval, Cady and Pierce had made agreements with district recruiting committees to fill quotas, and were usually paid one hundred dollars a man for the service. In some cases they "misrepresented the amount of local bounty provided by the towns thus saving to themselves . . . a larger margin as spoils for division." Occasionally when brokers brought recruits in for enlistment, the clerks would bargain directly with the men, and collect a good share of the bounties themselves. And in three specific cases

Cady credited men who had already been rejected for physical disability. Baker concluded his report to Fry saying that the evidence "demonstrates conclusively that the provost marshal and these favorite clerks constitute a ring within which private speculation is the rule, faithful discharge of duty the exception." Clendon, Cady and Pierce were dismissed on February 13, 1865.[2]

John Duffy, Provost Marshal of the 5th District, was dismissed in December 1863 for a multitude of reasons ranging from inefficiency to robbery. He was reported to have defrauded recruits of their bounty money by enlisting them while they were drunk. In one instance, he is supposed to have retained a recruit's bounty and confined the man in a cage in his office for several days. A recruiting officer who visited Duffy's office in November 1863 found the place so overrun with brokers, runners, loafers, thieves, and other undesirables that it was impossible to transact business there. The state of the office was "confused, disorganized, and demoralized," while the treatment which business visitors received was "shameful to behold and witness."

Whatever the truth of the accusations against Duffy it must be admitted that he labored under very adverse circumstances. Both his home and his headquarters were destroyed on July 13, 1863, the first day of the Draft Riots, and he found it difficult to rent another office. For some time he carried on from improvised headquarters on Governor's Island.

Over a year after the war ended Duffy wrote a plaintive note to Fry, requesting that his dismissal be converted into an honorable discharge. He was finding it almost impossible to reestablish himself in business with that black mark on his record and wanted it erased. Duffy insisted that he had never been informed of the charges against him, and that if he had been permitted an opportunity to defend himself he could easily have proven his innocence. He accused Orison J. Blunt of crucifying him because he had arrested and punished one of the supervisor's relatives for robbing a recruit. Blunt vowed revenge, said Duffy, and forwarded some trumped-up charges to Washington, which resulted in his dismissal.[3]

A sorry mess was uncovered in Brooklyn's 3rd District in the spring of 1864, where Provost Marshal Stephen B. Gregory held forth. Gregory's deputy provost marshal was B. L. Case, later described as "an individual widely-known for his rascality." The other two members of the enrolment board were Surgeon Nelson L. North and Commissioner Abner M. Beebe.

Surgeon North appears to have been an honorable man, but made the error of hiring a deputy surgeon named Anderson who was soon working hand in glove with Case in enlisting men unfit for service. These victims of fraud were taken into a back room without North's knowledge. North's name would be forged on the medical certificate, and the men presented to Gregory for muster when North was not around. Frequently men already rejected by North were taken secretly to Anderson and passed as physically sound.[4]

During the winter of 1863-64 complaints began filtering into Washington asserting that many physical wrecks enlisted in New York's 3rd District were serving in the Army of the Potomac. An examining commission, headed by Colonel George D. Ruggles, a member of Fry's staff, was set up to investigate, and on March 11 Ruggles submitted his report. Among the recruits enlisted at Gregory's office were the following:

> John B. Lane, aged 55, previously discharged from the army for old age and general disability.
>
> Thomas Doyle, aged 49, who had caires of tibia of left leg, variococele, deformed spine, old venereal disease, silver fork fracture of the radius of left forearm, and inability to close his hand. Although Doyle had dyed his hair and eyebrows before the examination, his numerous ailments were "apparent on a superficial inspection."
>
> Patrick Moran, aged 25, previously discharged from the service because of general disability, was found to have "secondary syphilis and broken down constitution."
>
> John Conway, aged 50, who was "drunk and stupid" at time of enlistment, had extensive variococele, old syphilitic disease, fracture of left leg, and "broken down constitution."
>
> James Spillane, aged 40, previously discharged from the service for phthisis pulmonalis, was found to have—phthisis pulmonalis.

Seamon Soper, aged 15, was found to be suffering from "mental imbecility and idiocy."

Augustus Brill, aged 60, had deformed chest and tuberculosis phthisis, and had been spitting blood for two years.[5]

The provost marshal insisted that he was unaware of any illegal procedures, but one of his accusers said flatly that Gregory split the proceeds of these fraudulent enlistments with Case, and was even living in Case's house. Gregory refused to discharge the deputy until an officer arrived from AAPMG Nugent's headquarters with explicit orders to let the man go. Even after his dismissal, Case continued to hang around the 3rd District office until arrested by the police for robbing substitutes.[6]

But what really finished off Gregory was the Ferdinand Schafer case. Schafer, recipient of a medical degree from the University of Breslau in 1856, arrived in New York City in the early fall of 1863. He hoped to resume the practice of medicine in a western state where German doctor friends of his had already settled. While in New York, however, he decided to get a job in a city military hospital to improve his skill in "surgical operations." His landlord, a German named Hellesget, took him to the 3rd District headquarters ostensibly to find him such a job, but really to enlist him in the army. Dr. North rejected Schafer because of a hernia, the same reason for which he had been rejected for Prussian military service. Since Schafer spoke no English he did not know what was happening and must have been puzzled that his infirmity should prevent him from performing medical duties.[7]

Hellesget then learned about the Case-Anderson arrangement and took Schafer to the little back room, where the usual procedure was followed. When Schafer saw the word "physician" on one of the documents he was asked to sign, he was sure he was entering the service as a medical man. Actually he was entering as an enlisted man.[8]

As he left the recruiting office, Schafer was hustled off by several armed soldiers to a dark cellar, where he found a number of other unhappy recruits. In about an hour he was taken to Riker's Island where he became ill with "inflammation of the lungs, erysipelas, inflammation of the testicles, and epileptic attacks." After lying sick for four weeks he was sent on an eight-day boat trip to South Carolina, and assigned to the 41st New York Regiment. The trip worsened his condition and upon arrival he had to be carried on a stretcher into the general hospital. The doctor who examined Schafer refused to discharge him, saying that the government would court-martial anyone who would release a patient in Schafer's shape. So there was poor Schafer, dying from disease and neglect in South Carolina, appealing to the Prussian ambassador in Washington for help.[9] Schafer did survive, although it took nearly two and one-half months from the time of his letter to the ambassador on January 22, 1864 to process his discharge. General Dix learned of the case in March and recommended that Schafer be released as long as he refunded the clothing he had received and whatever money he had left. On April 12 the discharge was formally approved, and Schafer went free. Four days later, on receipt of all the papers, Fry dismissed Gregory.[10]

The day Gregory learned of his dismissal he wrote Fry a letter expressing surprise at the news and defending his own policies. He claimed that he, like many other officers, had been enlisting all recruits approved by the surgeon, and it was not until mid-January 1864 that he learned certain unfit people had gotten through. He at once fired an "assistant surgeon" and the trouble ceased. "For the past three months," he concluded, "the reputation of my office for strict and close examination, has been such, that many recruiting agents have avoided it."[11]

Ira Harris, United States Senator from New York, wrote to Gregory demanding an explanation of the Schafer incident. The ex-provost marshal replied that he had no clear recollection of the matter since he had been very busy at the time of Schafer's enlistment. He did note, however, that all the papers were in proper order, and added that Gustav Leo, a reliable German clerk in the office, remembered that Schafer knew he was going as a private. "For his physical condition," Gregory reminded the Senator, "the surgeon is responsible. And I feel perfectly confident that no person connected with the office told him that he was enlisted other than as a private."[12] Apparently Fry felt otherwise.

During the summer of 1863 accusations of bribery were levelled at the enrolment board of the 27th District (Allegany, Steuben, and Chemung counties), with Samuel M. Harmon provost marshal, William T. Post commissioner, and Joshua B. Graves surgeon. A resident of Hornellsville in Steuben County told how the system worked for men that he knew. "The drafted man is told to come to the office of the examining surgeon some days or weeks in advance of the public examination. At this private interview the surgeon charges a fee of from twenty-five to fifty dollars, receives the money, and promises that the soldier shall be exempted, and which on the day of the public examination is done."[13]

Other victims of fraud were draftees from Angelica, a town of 1700 souls in the north-central part of Allegany County. It seems that these men, after travelling the eighty miles to Elmira for their examination, found that whether they were disabled or not, they had to pay up to one hundred and fifty dollars to be discharged. The question which led to an investigation conducted by State Supreme Court Judge Martin Grover, was who levied the illegal tribute, the enrolment board itself or outsiders who were acting without the board's knowledge?[14]

The board members, backed by the Elmira *Press* and Elmira *Advertiser*, conceded that men from Angelica had been robbed of thousands of dollars, but hotly denied that they had anything to do with it. They insisted that men outside checked the draftees, took money from them, and assured them that they would arrange everything with the board. Later at their examinations, disabled draftees were exempted, of course, and returned to Angelica convinced that the money had cleared them. When they learned it was unnecessary to purchase a legitimate exemption, they assumed that the board and its employees were responsible for the fraud. But the board insisted it was not a party to the plot.[15]

A somewhat different story emanated from Angelica. According to this version, many physically fit draftees gained exemptions by bribing board members. Others who were ignorant of the modus operandi the first time through, asked for a reexamination. The second time they had their money ready and were released. The Angelica *Reporter* flatly disputed the assertion that outside "strikers," unconnected with the board, were involved. One man inquired how to buy his way out, and was told to leave the money in the rear of the Brainard House. He did this and within a few minutes someone appeared and gave him his exemption certificate. Was this not collusion?[16]

A doctor in Angelica, W. S. Todd, wrote a letter to Lincoln on August 6, 1863, before the affair had attracted much attention, in which he endorsed the above charges. After advising the President that he would show him "something of the rottenness in Denmark," he proceeded as follows:

> Lawies, Doctors, and commertial politicians swarem around the provost marshal's office in Elmira, New York, like vultures around a dead carcass. And any man without any disability whatever can get clear by paying according to his Pile from $25 to $150 to some Loby for the benefit of the Board and Loby. . . . There were 33 conscripts from Angelica and 23 got clear and a more hale and hearty class of men rarily exhist than four-fifths of these are. . . .[17]

The people of Angelica were angry at the reaction of the board to the disclosures. Harmon demanded "a full investigation," and all those who were illegally freed had their exemptions annulled. But why take it out on the exemptees, inquired the Angelica *Reporter?* Instead of exposing the members of the board and the alleged "lobbyists" and "strikers," the board pounces upon those who bought their exemptions but then were so inconsiderate as to expose the bribe-takers. "Henceforth," the paper concluded, "there will be no fear of disclosures—lobbyists and strikers may reap their harvest—cheat and defraud the government of men and means—take their $150 per man fearless of exposure. The 'unanimous resolution' of the Board will be held in terror over the victims!" It was also revealed in Angelica that Harmon had privately informed a friend that he had incriminating evidence against Surgeon Graves, but preferred not to "blab."[18]

Major Diven, AAPMG for the Western Division, was at first inclined to minimize the charges against the 27th District Enrolment Board. Replying to Dr. Todd on August 17, he said he had found no evidence of corruption on the board and that the members had cooperated closely with him in correcting errors. He had known some of the members for a long time and he was convinced that they were honorable. Dr. Hollis S. Chubbock, he added, was serving as Graves' assistant and he was a highly reputed physician, which may have been a tacit admission that Graves was not. Fry urged Diven to wrap up the investigation as quickly as possible, so the AAPMG kept on digging. Graves' lawyer-son, he found, was "acting as a kind of agent for presenting the claims for exemption from drafted men . . . and many are influenced to pay him money on the supposition that he influences his father." Gradually enough other evidence came to light to call for Graves' dismissal, which was ordered on September 15. Commissioner Post resigned on August 8, 1863, on the eve of the disclosures, while Provost Marshal Harmon quit his position on July 18, 1864.[19]

Linden Eckert, who lived in Kingston, wrote Stanton in November 1863 asserting that at least fifty men in the 13th District had been exempted after bribing the surgeon and provost marshal with amounts varying from fifty to one hundred dollars. When Provost Marshal Joshua Fiero learned of the accusations he denied them and insisted that Eckert be punished. Nothing happened to Eckert, but three days later, Fiero resigned. Abram H. Knapp, Fiero's surgeon, stayed on and the fact that he was warmly praised by Fiero's successor for his honesty and dedication casts some doubt on Eckert's charges.[20] Nevertheless the fact remains that frauds were committed against ignorant recruits in the 13th District, which led to the Teall Investigation reported in Chapter Six. We saw there that the person most seriously implicated in these transactions, and the one whose immediate dismissal was urged by Teall, was George S. France, a deputy provost marshal acting under Fiero's authority.

Obviously some unsound men were passed by enrolment board surgeons by honest error, for it must be borne in mind that the pressures on the surgeons, just as the pressures on the provost marshals, were unrelenting. One overworked surgeon in New York City complained that he and other enrolment board members received but a fraction of what they might make in private business, yet they were doing the best they could under very difficult circumstances and getting nothing but abuse. The quality of men presented for examination was such that it would have taken half a day's careful study of each one to learn if he was a healthy, honest, and sincere volunteer. Yet the men had to be processed at the rate of one hundred and twenty per day—four minutes per man—which permitted only the most superficial scrutiny. No wonder unfit men got through. The problem would be greatly simplified, the surgeon concluded, by abolishing the bounty system entirely and instituting a general draft.[21]

The press in general seemed very reluctant to discuss the cases of dismissed provost marshals. Many times the matter was completely ignored, and the reader would be unaware of any change until he saw references to a new provost marshal. Occasionally a mild defense would be offered in behalf of such a discharged official, with the footnote that the ex-provost marshal was off in Washington demanding a full investigation. One case which received more than the usual publicity concerned Isaac Platt, who was dismissed as provost marshal of the 12th District in February 1864. Probably the only reason that anyone heard of Platt's discharge was because he also happened to be editor of the Poughkeepsie *Daily Eagle*. The paper referred to allegations that Platt and his surgeon, who was also fired, had enlisted unfit men but denied the charges.[22]

In the 30th District, Gustavus A. Scroggs, a Buffalo lawyer of good repute, was named provost marshal in April 1863, but resigned for personal reasons in February 1864. Wild charges of fraud were made against Scroggs in the fall of 1863, but these were proven groundless. Succeeding him was William F. Rogers, who had been serving as commissioner. Things got out of hand under Rogers, and Special Government Agent William W. Riley was ordered to Buffalo in October 1864 to investigate the operations of the 30th District office. Riley's report was typically obtuse, but it seemed to show that favoritism and the swindling of recruits of their bounties was practiced on a sizeable scale. It was not long before Rogers was out and Scroggs was reappointed provost marshal, the only person to serve two separate tours in that post.[23]

Enrolment board members who lacked executive and business experience, though perfectly honorable and dedicated, must have had difficulties trying to administer such an ambiguous law as the Enrolment Act. While only two cases of enrolment board members who left office for incompetence have been documented, many others must certainly have occurred.

The two cases about which we know something concern Abram L. Nanny, Provost Marshal of the 11th District, and Schuyler F. Judd, Commissioner of the 17th District. The political make-up of the 11th District, composed of Orange and Sullivan counties, was highly complex, and it would not have been easy for the most talented person to handle the draft without drawing criticism. And Abram L. Nanny was not a talented person. Although he devoted all of his time and energy to his job nothing seemed to work right, and as blunders piled on top of blunders, a wild chorus of complaint rose up against him. As was to be expected, his honest errors led to charges of dishonest errors, and he was soon being accused of inefficiency, extravagance, disloyalty, and corruption. Political cross-currents in the 11th District fed the mounting flame, and it was soon apparent that Nanny had lost whatever confidence the people of the district had once confided in him.[24]

In response to this criticism Northern Division AAPMG, Major Frederick Townsend in January 1864, sent his crack investigator, Captain Elisha H. Ludington, into the 11th District with instructions "not to return . . . until he had a thorough personal comprehension of the matters of dispute." Ludington visited the major towns of the district —Newburgh, Goshen, Middletown, and Monticello—talked with a number of distinguished citizens, and submitted a detailed report, which won Townsend's praise for its fairness, thoroughness, and useful recommendations. In speaking of Nanny, Ludington observed that the provost marshal was poorly prepared for his job, having had no business or administrative experience whatever. Furthermore, after eight months in office it was evident that he had learned little about being a provost marshal. Thus, although Nanny "labored zealously and faithfully . . . [there] arose delays and mistakes which are seized upon and magnified to the prejudice of the Board."[25]

Yet while the majority of the people in the district regarded Nanny as unqualified for the job because of "lack of business tact, quickness of apprehension and decision," he did have a loyal band of supporters.

His "close application to duty and his earnestness" had convinced other leading citizens of Orange County that the provost marshal had performed his duties satisfactorily. It was Ludington's conclusion, however, that in spite of Nanny's good intentions and honest efforts, he would have to go. "He is not deserving of censure," the report noted, "but it would certainly conduce to the interests of the government to place in his stead a thoroughly intelligent and experienced business man." While Nanny was not discharged, he was urged to resign, which he did on April 19, 1864.[26]

The Judd case grew out of an action by the Board of Supervisors of St. Lawrence County in November 1863. St. Lawrence, along with Franklin County, constituted the 17th District on the Canadian frontier. Meeting in Canton, the Supervisors recommended the twin ousters of Commissioner Judd for being overbearing, intemperate, and dishonest, and Surgeon Henry Hewitt for being old and a bungler. Upon learning of this, Townsend sent Ludington to see if the action was justified. After talking with reputable persons in the major towns, Ludington concluded that Judd, like Nanny, would have to go. No one appeared to like him and everyone who was consulted denounced his "offensive manner" and "gross intemperance." Even people Judd recommended as character witnesses told the same story. While no proof was furnished of partiality or dishonesty, Judd obviously lacked public confidence and was dismissed on December 16, 1863. As for Hewitt, Ludington found nothing objectionable about the surgeon except that he was an old man. Leading citizens, medical men, and Provost Marshal Thorndike all testified to his ability and honesty. Hewitt remained in office until he voluntarily resigned in December 1864.[27]

✿   ✿   ✿   ✿

While a small percentage of draft officials were corrupted by temptation, and while a number of others proved to be incompetent public servants, a great many more who were accused of corruption and incompetence were absolved of such charges after careful investigations. Most of the unfounded allegations stemmed from political jealousy. The draft act, by establishing some one hundred and seventy-eight boards, opened up a new field for political patronage, and the competition for jobs became most intense. The files are filled with earnest entreaties for office based exclusively on one's loyalty to party and Union. Losers often sought revenge against winners. Inter-party feuds were complicated by internal party feuds, and quite frequently in the attempt to settle old political scores, wild and savage accusations would be levelled against provost marshals, surgeons, commissioners, deputy provost marshals, clerks, recorders, and enrolling officers.

An excellent illustration of the pressures of these cross-currents is provided by Ludington in his report on the 11th District. In order to understand Nanny's predicament, Ludington first familiarized himself thoroughly with the political "power structure" of Sullivan and Orange counties. He learned that acute rivalry existed between the counties, Sullivan being Democratic, Orange Republican. County feelings were exacerbated by town rivalries, as Newburgh, Goshen, Middletown, and Monticello each wanted to be the location of district provost marshal headquarters.

Four political parties operated in the district: (1) *Union League Republicans,* or Radical Republicans, who strongly supported the Lincoln Administration, would have no truck with any Democrats, and felt entitled to all the patronage; (2) *Conservative Republicans,* who loyally supported the government, but who were willing to cooperate and share the jobs with "War Democrats"; (3) *Ultra Democrats,* or Copperheads, who firmly opposed the war and the Administration; (4) *War Democrats,* who retained their party ties, but still loyally supported the government and the war effort. The 11th District Enrolment Board was composed of Provost Marshal Nanny, Surgeon John C. Boyd, both Conservative Republicans, and Commissioner John C. Holley, a War Democrat. Since the Union League Republicans were unrepresented on the Board they took out their bitterness in attacking it. Most of the complaints against the Board, reported Ludington, came from that source. The Conservative Republicans and War Democrats were reasonably content with the makeup of the Board because they were both represented on it. The Ultra Democrats, on the other hand, while not happy with moderate control, feared that any change would result in a more radical complexion of the Board. "Each party," observed Ludington, "desires the Board of Enrolment to be turned into a political machine under its own control."[28]

In addition to the charge of incompetency lodged against Nanny, complaints were also made against the entire Board for extravagance, partiality, and disloyalty. While the Board had been occasionally extravagant, due to Nanny's errors, no foundations whatever were discovered for the accusations of partiality and disloyalty. It was stated in some of the grievance petitions, for example, that all the enrolling officers in Sullivan County were Democrats. Yet Ludington demonstrated that the enrolment board, in appointing enrolling officers, tried to be as fair as it could, naming Democrats in Sullivan where Democrats predominated, and Republicans in Orange where Republicans predominated. Accusations that Republican draftees were exempted to an unjustifiable degree, while practically all Democratic draftees were held to service, were proven false by a quick look at the board's official records. Ludington concluded that while Holley was a zealous Democrat, both he and Boyd were capable, loyal, and hard-working officials.[29]

Thurlow Weed, the influential state Republican leader, complained to Townsend in August 1864 that the surgeon of the 12th District, A. E. Van Dusen, was not trustworthy and requested an investigation. Townsend obliged by dispatching Captain J. B. Grimes to Poughkeepsie to make "a rigid examination." Grimes consulted with several "gentlemen" and the other members of the board and learned that Van Dusen's appointment had provoked dissatisfaction. His loyalty to the Administration was not only a "question of considerable doubt," but some people even thought him to be a Copperhead. As a kind of afterthought, Grimes noted that Van Dusen was not a very good doctor anyhow. His appointment was revoked on October 5, 1864.[30]

The Republican Union Club of the 7th District tried unsuccessfully to force out the Democratic provost marshal, Frederick C. Wagner, in October 1864. John J. Lee, club secretary, protested strongly that Copperheads controlled the board of enrolment and that no one could get a job unless he was a McClellan man. Wagner himself was not so bad, but he was the dupe of the real boss of the board, Barney P.

Woods, the chief clerk. Put Woods out, pleaded Lee, "and no matter who is in his place it will be a benefit . . . for Wagner is but a tool in his hands and all the influence of the office is exerted against the Administration." It did not matter who replaced Woods and Wagner, any "good Union men" would do, but it was imperative that a change be made. Of course, if they had trouble finding a good Union man for provost marshal, our own "D. W. Styles, who has contributed so much of his means to support our organization . . ." would make an excellent choice. But Wagner was retained and became one of eleven provost marshals who served the full time.[31]

General Isaac F. Quinby became provost marshal of the 28th District on January 21, 1865, but it was not long before he was under heavy attack. This prompted a crowd of Republican friends to draw up a petition urging his retention, which was sent on to Fry. The Provost Marshal General was assured that not only was there no just cause of dissatisfaction with Quinby, but he had, in fact, "honestly, faithfully and strictly discharged the duties of his office so as to promote the interests of the Government." It was pointed out that the move to oust him emanated from those "who have unworthy and selfish objects to promote by it." Quinby was not removed and received an honorable discharge in October 1865.[32]

* * * *

While political rivalries provoked numerous unsubstantiated charges against draft officials, other accusations were caused by jealous and vengeful feelings stemming from civilian relationships or alleged unfair practices by enrolment boards. In November 1863 George Tuthill and a man named Contrell, recorder and acting recorder for the 4th District were fired by Provost Marshal Joel B. Erhardt for "gross dereliction of duty." As a consequence, the irritated Tuthill preferred some fifteen charges against Erhardt and the rest of the district's enrolment board, which if authenticated would be sufficient for a mass dismissal. Erhardt was accused of altering enrolment lists, neglect of duty, appointing aliens and non-residents as enrolling officers and clerks, residing outside the district himself, illegally discharging substitutes from service, permitting his clerks to discount claims at "usurious interest rates," discouraging enlistments, imposing political assessments on the office staff, loaning out government money, compounding a felony, and retaining government property. For good measure, the provost marshal was charged with ungentlemanly conduct. In addition to this bill of particulars, Commissioner Daniel McFarland was accused of drunken drafting, and the whole board was catechized for allowing unjust exemptions and acting in an illegal manner.[33]

It would take a lengthy description of these charges to show their shallowness. Minor oversights were magnified, while normal behavior was distorted out of all reasonable proportion. Erhardt pointed out the animus of revenge which motivated Tuthill and Contrell, and observed that practically all of the witnesses' affidavits were based on hearsay evidence and often were in conflict with Tuthill's own statement. "These two men," he concluded, "glory in being called leading ward politicians, and presuming upon their supposed political influence, accepted bribes. Being detected, they endeavor to use their influence to make trouble. But being nothing of a 'politician' myself, I regarded their derelictions in the same light that I would those of any other persons."[34]

The provost marshal believed that Tuthill and Contrell hoped to make up in quantity what their accusations lacked in quality, trusting that the entire enrolment board would be quickly arrested. And then, even though the witnesses' charges would be quickly disproven, at least the stigma of wrongdoing would attach to the board. He insisted that his office was without a taint, a statement which the most exhaustive investigation would confirm.[35]

In the first few weeks of the draft Provost Marshal Samuel Gordon of the 19th District was accused of drunkenness and improper behavior. An investigator was sent to Norwich, and after observing Gordon in action for three weeks, declared the charges were unjustified. It was true that Gordon was a heavy drinker but never, except on one occasion, was he unable to execute his duties fairly and competently. Concerning improper behavior, it was discovered that one day a woman persisted in talking with Gordon after her business was finished and to convince her that she should leave, he clapped his hand down heavily on her knee. Soon the story got about that he had grabbed the woman "close between her thighs." However, according to the investigator's report, the charges made against Gordon were usually the work of lawyers who had prepared exemption cases for draftees, but whose requests the provost marshal had rejected. To get even with Gordon they accused him of drunkenness and vulgar behavior. It should be noted that Gordon and Erhardt were among the eleven provost marshals who served through the entire life of the Enrolment Act.[36]

Another excellent example of irresponsible criticism of a provost marshal concerns Gustavus A. Scroggs during his first tour of duty on the 30th Board in 1863. A letter from "John Williams" of Buffalo on September 21, 1863 asserted that draft examinations were a swindle on the government and that Scroggs was "notoriously dishonest, and has been so always." Colonel E. C. Brooks was ordered by Diven to go to Buffalo and investigate Williams' charges. Brooks spent several days in a vain effort to track Williams down and concluded that either there was no such person, or if there was, he was too ashamed to come forward to try and prove his statements. What Brooks did find out was that Scroggs was an honorable person who "at considerable personal sacrifice" worked hard to raise the troops for the government. The investigator concluded that Scroggs as provost marshal "has discharged the duties of that office to the satisfaction of the people of his district in a remarkable degree."[37]

Some accusations were too preposterous to merit serious consideration. For example, a New York broker named George Sitterly testified that he took a flock of rejected men to Owego in the 26th District where the surgeon passed them all while resting in Sitterly's hotel room. Later, after a drink and a session in a "billiard saloon," the surgeon returned with the commissioner and the men were sworn in.[38] This just does not make sense. For one thing, the enrolment board of the 26th District, consisting of Edward C. Kattell provost marshal, James N. Eldridge commissioner, and Samuel B. Foster surgeon, was one of the five boards in the state which experienced no personnel changes during the war. It is incredible that board members, who could survive all the pressures and criticism such people were daily subjected to, would conduct examinations in the sloppy, illegal way

Sitterly described. Maybe they did things that way, but it seems unlikely.[39]

Frequently accusations of fraud were based on false rumors or insufficient knowledge. Daniel E. Parks, an exemptee from Washington County, sent off a hot missive to Stanton in August 1863, which began with the words, "For God, and the nation's sake put a stop to the manner in which the draft is conducted in this district." Parks insisted that a dozen able-bodied men had been exempted, including one who was not held because his parents were supposed to be aged and infirm, although the father was a stonecutter who made two to three dollars per day. The letter was referred back to 15th District Provost Marshal Charles Hughes, who after a careful investigation, justified all exemptions mentioned including that of the stonecutter's son. He defended his surgeon and commissioner as honorable and dedicated public servants. Even well-meaning people complained, Hughes observed, but this was only because they were unfamiliar with the exemption provisions of the Enrolment Act.[40]

Hughes switched jobs with his commissioner, James Forsyth, in the summer of 1864, and it was not long before the now Provost Marshal Forsyth was in trouble. In order to check widespread bounty-jumping in his district he began to withhold the bounties of recruits being forwarded to the general rendezvous. By midwinter of 1864-65, Forsyth had collected on the average, three hundred and fifty to four hundred dollars from 323 recruits for a total of over $121,000, which he deposited in the Troy Savings Bank to the credit of the individual soldiers, but under his own control. Reports began to come back from Hart's Island and from the front that Forsyth had forcibly taken the bounty money from the men and would not send it forward. A thorough investigation was made in March 1865, and Forsyth was cleared of any wrongdoing.[41]

But even though his intentions may have been good, it was asserted that his system was fruitful of great fraud, which had indeed been practiced on many recruits. For one thing, although each soldier was given a deposit book certifying the amount of money waiting for him in the Troy bank, many deposit books were quickly lost in camp or battle and wound up in the wrong hands. Furthermore, the long delay

which transpired before a recruit could claim his deposit caused many
of them to sell their deposit books to "shysters and repulsive speculators" at large discounts. In fact, Forsyth's chief clerk quit his job,
"and joined the outside speculators—following the recruits from Troy
to Hart's Island and from Hart's Island to the front—denouncing the
Savings Bank as insolvent, and the deposits of little worth, thereby
buying up their claims for a trifling percentage."[42]

As far as the records go, the Forsyth case ends on a very inconclu-
sive note. The provost marshal was ordered to release the money,
but refused to do so and in April was arrested and taken to Washington. But the next thing we learn is that he was back in business in Troy
and the bounty money was still in the Troy Savings Bank. Matters
dragged on throughout the summer of 1865 with Forsyth paying out
some of the money to authorized recruits now home from the war. A
further problem resulted from the large sum of bounty money left
behind by deserters. No one seemed to know what to do with these
funds. Whatever happened, and the records provide us with no answer, Forsyth emerged unscathed, receiving an honorable discharge
on December 31, 1865.[43]

The only mass dismissal occurred in November 1863 when the entire enrolment board of the 6th District was fired on the same day.
Mutual incompatibility among the board members and divergent in-
terpretations of the law appear to have been at the root of the difficulty. Throughout the summer and fall of that first draft year, Provost
Marshal James W. Farr had clashed frequently with Commissioner
Charles A. Lamont and Surgeon James W. Powell over alienage exemptions. Farr thought a simple oath of alienage was sufficient to
merit exemption, while Powell and Lamont insisted on a more thorough check of the applicant's claim. Farr refused to order this. When
the roof finally fell in, the New York *Times* noted that "so far as the
commissioner and surgeon are concerned . . . there were no charges
preferred of either want of capacity for or neglect of duty." Incensed
at the implied insult, Farr wrote a letter to the editor blaming everything on Lamont and Powell. The problem, he said, was this:

> At the commencement of the enrolment, the Commissioner
> and Surgeon united together . . . to vote and act together in

making the appointments, etc., of their friends to positions, and
to drive me to retain them, after their services were not required. .... If I had consented to pension 15 or 20 of the Commissioner's friends on the Government at $3 per day, there
would have been no difficulty in the Board. To give you
an idea of the character of the Commissioner, I need only recite
a conversation which occurred on Friday last. When the Surgeon received the letter dismissing him from his positon, the
Commissioner remarked: "Well, Doctor, we have done what
we said we would—we have brought the house down with
us."[44]

Special Agent Riley made a free-wheeling assault on Diven and
several provost marshals in the Western Division in the fall of 1864.
Diven had already planned to quit his post to take a high level job
with the Erie Railroad when Riley let fly, so the AAPMG decided to
stay on, at least long enough to clear his name. The agent asserted
that Diven spent little time in his office and that his deputy, a Captain Low, was actually in charge. Low and a clerk made all endorsements and signed Diven's name. Communications to Fry and Stanton
which went through the Elmira office were illegally stopped, endorsed, and returned to the local provost marshal headquarters, on
the basis of which, it was alleged, men were improperly mustered out
of service. Under the erratic leadership of Diven, Riley went on, conditions in several provost marshal offices, notably the 24th, 28th, and
30th, were in a demoralized state. Soldiers were being released from
service without justification, desertions were numerous, nepotism was
widespread, provost marshals were growing suspiciously rich, and political activity among draft officials was hampering efficient administration.[45]

Riley noted that John A. Knapp, Provost Marshal of the 24th District, composed of Wayne, Cayuga, and Seneca counties, was a man
of modest means before he assumed his present post. Now, however,
he "sports a pair of fine horses and a carriage," and reputedly had
$200,000 in the bank. Furthermore, Knapp's father and a brother-in-
law appear to have been actively engaged in the brokerage business,
taking advantage of their inside connections with the provost marshal.

Riley insisted that even though the Cayuga Supervisors failed to un-
cover incriminating evidence, except on one occasion, against Knapp,
there were widespread doubts in the community about the integrity of
the 24th Enrolment Board. That one instance concerned David T.
Lynch, who was drafted in July 1863 and served in Knapp's Quartermaster Department until December, when he was allowed to commute. He was then enlisted by Knapp's father and received a bounty,
which he split with the elder Knapp.[46]

Riley did disclose an unusual situation in the 28th District, which
consisted of Monroe and Orleans counties and was presided over by
Provost Marshal Roswell Hart. In the fall of 1864, while Riley was
travelling around western New York, Hart was running for Congress
on the Republican ticket. This proved embarrassing, however, because Hart was swamped with requests from soldiers for furloughs,
requests which he could hardly refuse for fear of reprisals on election
day. Consequently, practically everyone who appealed to him got a
furlough. And many of them forgot to report back for duty after their
furlough was over. In one case, some twenty-two men came over from
Canada, enlisted in the 28th District and left three hundred dollars of
each of their bounties with Hart, who then gave them all furloughs.
They at once returned to Canada with the balance of their money.
Although these people could not legally have voted in the election,
Hart was not taking any chances. Riley concluded that the provost
marshals "are seeking political popularity more than the interests of
the Government and those men not running for Congress this year
expect to at some future day."[47]

When Fry received Riley's two reports of October 20 and November 12, 1864, he sent a confidential letter to Diven asking about the
accusations against him. The AAPMG, who was itching to become an
Erie Railroad executive, was understandably pained by the charges
and laboriously set out to answer them all. "I am," he began, "as I
always have been since this war commenced, ready to give my time
and money to the Government. Anything but my reputation—it can
do the Government no good to take that from me; to me it is inesti-
mable." He then proceeded to refute point by point everything alleged
by Riley, noting that the agent had never spoken with him person-

ally and had relied largely on hearsay testimony. The statement that he was rarely on duty in his office was "the last charge I ever expected to meet." He had neglected all of his private affairs, even necessary repairs to his house, and had worked so strenuously at his job that friends had protested that he was endangering his health. All this "at the sacrifice of a large private business to which my pay is a trifle."[48]

Diven insisted that he and he alone ran his office, and that no one but Captain Low ever endorsed any communication or signed his name, and only then with Diven's express authorization. It seems that the AAPMG had injured his right hand and could write only with great difficulty, so he permitted his deputy to sign his name more often than would normally have been the case. Furthermore, no documents which came through his office and were addressed to Stanton or Fry were ever stopped and returned, unless there was an obvious reason for not forwarding them. Finally, it was true men were mustered out of service without complete observance of all the technicalities, but these were exceptional cases. The only time something like this happened was when an enlisted man was elected by the men in his company to be an officer. In such circumstances Diven had to obtain approval of the commission by the Governor and then a confirmation of the discharge of the soldier as an enlisted man from General Dix in New York City. Because of the long delays entailed by this process, Diven did on several occasions discharge such men, who were waiting around to be commissioned, without Dix's official O.K.[49]

The Diven file ends at this point, but Fry, who knew Diven well, was undoubtedly reassured by this explanation. Diven resigned on December 9, 1864 to accept an $8,000 a year post as an Erie Railroad vice-president, with the promise of being advanced to the presidency at $10,000 within a year's time. His successor, Major John A. Haddock, got into all kinds of trouble almost at once, and became the central figure in the most celebrated court-martial case involving New York's Civil War draft officials, the subject of Chapter Ten.

In summing up this chapter, let it be reiterated that while some enrolment board members were corrupt, most of them acted honorably under very heavy pressure. Generally, the accusations against such officials were based on political or personal jealousies, and did not stand up under close scrutiny. All things considered, the country was lucky to get the fine service it received from its draft officers, all the way from Fry down to the lowest clerk.

· 9 ·

The Trial of Spinola.

A LTHOUGH MOST RECRUITING OFFICIALS were honest and conscientious, the press gave publicity to their alleged fraudulent behavior. Generally the charges were proved groundless, yet upon occasion they were found to be true. New York's two most famous recruiting fraud cases provide an example of each type. In the case of Brigadier General Francis B. Spinola, the charges were, for the most part, not confirmed, while those against Major John A. Haddock, to be considered in the next chapter, were convincingly substantiated.

❀ ❀ ❀ ❀

Authorized to raise a brigade of troops late in November 1863, Spinola opened a recruiting office on the second floor of Lafayette Hall, located on New York's lower Broadway. Almost at once, however, protests began to mount up from recruits and friends of recruits who claimed they had been enlisted at Lafayette Hall and defrauded of a sizeable portion of their three hundred dollar county bounty. General Dix called Spinola into his office, demanded to know what was going on, and was assured that even though brokers were permitted to operate there, no recruit was being defrauded. He went on to say that brokers were actually essential to the recruiting business and that few men could be obtained without them.[1]

However, the recruits' complaints continued until mid-January 1864, when Dix ordered the removal of Spinola and the arrests of broker Hawley Clapp, Lieutenant William N. Cole, one of Spinola's mustering officers, and Joseph A. Kerrigan, a surgeon. Cole was tried by court-martial, found guilty and dismissed from the service. Kerri-

172

gan, a civilian, was disqualified from future military service.[2] The record does not reveal what happened specifically to Clapp, although he did spend many months in jail. No action was taken against Spinola for a long while, but finally on July 14, 1864, a court-martial was convened in New York City to try him for encouraging, permitting, and participating in fraudulent practices against recruits during his tenure at Lafayette Hall. Many delays and interruptions developed during the trial, which was finally terminated on August 11. Another trial, however, commenced within a week and lasted until January 2, 1865.[3]

During the interval between Spinola's removal and the convening of the court-martial, the public had been led to believe the worst about the General's conduct of the recruiting office. Major Charles G. Halpine, Dix's Assistant Adjutant General, charged that the recruiting system was

> . . . one of organized pillage, resort being had to hocusing with
> narcotic poisons, threats, violence, false representations and
> kidnapping in order to furnish victims to the bounty brokers
> and fill up the army with discontented and unfit men. Cripples,
> old men, mere boys, men laboring under incurable diseases,
> and soldiers previously discharged for physical disability, form
> a great part of the recruits recently enlisted in this city.[4]

Dix reported angrily to Secretary of War Stanton that at Lafayette Hall only $200,000 of the bounty money went to the recruits, while $400,000 was "plundered" by the brokers. "It was," he wrote, "one of the most stupendous frauds ever committed in this country."[5]

In view of this publicity things looked black for Spinola, and the formal charges and specifications filed against him were not calculated to ease his mind. Of three charges, the first two accused him of "neglect of duty," and the third of "conduct unbecoming an officer and gentleman." Under charge one, Spinola was alleged to have (1) allowed brokers to defraud recruits at Lafayette Hall, (2) made no effort to restore money to defrauded recruits, (3) allowed a French sailor, Vincent Ruelland, to enlist without properly explaining to him the terms of his enlistment, and (4) when this fact was pointed out to him, Spinola cursed and said he did not care.

Under charge two, the General was said to have run his office so negligently that brokers could operate there with impunity, enlist intoxicated recruits, and defraud them regularly. He was also supposed to have remarked publicly that he did not care whether recruits got as much as one cent of their bounty money. As for the third charge, Spinola was accused of "conniving" with brokers in swindling recruits, of permitting them to use his office in consideration for their enlisting recruits in his brigade, and of falsifying the height of one volunteer so as to make him eligible for the army.[6]

*   *   *   *

To understand Spinola's predicament when he began to recruit, it is necessary to review the procedure adopted by the County Volunteer and Substitute Committee for paying the county bounty. In the summer of 1863 this Committee, under Blunt's chairmanship, set up a three hundred dollar bounty and agreed to allow brokers to disburse it. After a recruit was mustered in, he would receive from his broker the sum already agreed upon between them, in exchange for which he would assign his full bounty to the broker. The broker would then receive three hundred dollars from Blunt. To carry out this system Blunt prepared three printed forms: the statement of the volunteer, the certificate of the mustering officer, and the assignment of the bounty.

To clarify, let us consider the hypothetical case of a potential recruit, John Flynn. As soon as his desire to enlist became known, some broker would tell Flynn that he alone could arrange for Flynn's enlistment, and hold out to him the alluring promise of one hundred and fifty dollars county bounty money. That Flynn was entitled to three hundred dollars was not explained to him, and since Flynn was illiterate, he had not read about it in the newspapers.

The terms arranged, Flynn and broker next proceeded to Lafayette Hall where Flynn (with assistance) filled out his enlistment papers, was examined by the surgeon, and found fit to serve. Blunt's three forms—the volunteer's statement, the mustering certificate, and the assignment—were now made out, Flynn receiving one hundred and fifty dollars from the broker for assigning to the broker all rights to his three hundred dollar bounty. Flynn was then formally mustered into the army by an officer, who signed Blunt's mustering certificate. The broker now presented the three forms at Blunt's office, where, in exchange, the broker was given three hundred dollars.[7]

Spinola was not at all happy with this arrangement, and tried unsuccessfully to change it. He went himself to Blunt's office one day to see what could be done, only to be mistaken by one of the clerks for a broker and told to "go to hell." The system permitted many frauds, since Blunt gave the blank forms out to practically anyone who asked for them and since it was easy to forge the mustering officer's signature, the only one that had to be forged. The Committee itself was well aware of frauds perpetrated under the system, but insisted that as long as the three forms presented to it were correct on their face, the person presenting the forms was entitled to the three hundred dollar bounty. On one occasion, when Spinola told Blunt that frauds were being committed, Blunt answered that he

> ... did not care a damn or a God damn what bargains the men who brought the recruits there made with the recruits—they [the Committee] had made up their minds to carry out the bargains with those men—the parties bringing the recruits, and he did not care if they did not get but five dollars if they had made that bargain with them. . . .[8]

At the time when Spinola was relieved, Dix ordered Blunt to abandon his system of paying bounties, which was practically an admission that the trouble in Lafayette Hall was due more to Blunt than Spinola. Dix never saw the connection, however, and kept up the pressure on Spinola. The new plan of paying bounties called for the money to be sent directly to Lafayette Hall or to the several provost marshal offices where a recruiting officer would personally hand the three hundred dollars to the recruit upon muster. This plan, which Spinola himself had urged on Blunt, cut down the number of frauds, although it by no means ended them.[9]

Spinola's headquarters were located toward the front of the second story of Lafayette Hall. The stairway from the first floor entered into a large hall, divided into an outer office and an inner office. At the rear of the inner office was the surgeon's examining room and behind that were Spinola's own quarters. At the rear of the outer office on the other side of the stairway was a lounge for the 18th Cavalry and behind that a drill room. The 18th Cavalry's presence was to cause additional anguish for the hard-pressed Spinola.

The actual enlistment procedure at Lafayette Hall went something like this: the broker brought his recruit up the stairs and into the outer office, proceeding at once to the clerk's table where the enlistment forms were made out. Next, the recruit was passed through the turnstile into the inner office, a guard taking him into the surgeon's examining room. Occasionally, the broker was allowed inside the railing at this stage of proceedings, but more often than not he was told to stay in the outer office. When the surgeon had passed the recruit he signed the enlistment form, and summoned a guard who took the man back into the inner office, singing out "who brought this man?" The broker, now allowed inside the railing, took the recruit to Colonel Funk's desk. While Funk examined the enlistment papers, broker and recruit sat down at Clapp's table and filled out Blunt's three forms.

After Funk initialed the enlistment forms he handed them to one of the three mustering officers, Lieutenants Cole, Williams, or MacLean, at the front end of the room. The mustering officer then called the recruit to him, and asked him numerous questions, the purpose of which was to find out if the young man really knew he was going into the army for three years. Once that point was established the recruit was asked how much of his bounty he was assigning to the broker and did he know he was entitled to a full three hundred dollars. After the recruit assured the officer that he knew full well what he was doing with his bounty money, the broker, who had been made to stand back, was summoned forward and ordered to pay the recruit the previously agreed upon amount. The mustering officer then signed the enlistment papers as well as Blunt's forms. The broker now left for Blunt's office and the recruit was placed in the "pen," to await transportation to the rendezvous on Riker's Island.[10]

While little evidence was produced at the trial to substantiate Dix's and Halpine's charges that "mere Boys" were drugged and kidnapped, that men were enlisted while they were drunk, or that cripples or incurably ill persons were enlisted, a few cases did give a thin veneer of truth to such charges. The enlistment of the French sailor, Vincent Ruelland, for example, constituted the third and fourth specifications under the first charge against Spinola. After Dix had discharged Ruelland he sent an aide, Philip Marsh, to see Spinola and inquire why Ruelland had been enlisted. Marsh testified:

> I told him that the man had been fraudulently enlisted. . . .
> I asked him if it was not the duty of the mustering officer where
> the recruit could not read himself, that the enlistment papers
> should be read to him that he should know what he was
> signing. . . . The General remarked, "Damn it, if we did that
> we could not enlist twenty men a day." I then said, "General, in
> relation to this man . . . he could neither read, write, nor un-
> derstand a word of English—how is it in his case?" "Damn it,
> he signed his name," was his answer. . . .[11]

One recruit named George Smith, who was fraudulently enlisted, testified that he had been induced to come to Lafayette Hall by a broker for the purpose of signing up as a teamster. He was told repeatedly that he would be a teamster for only a six month period, driving between Washington and Alexandria, Virginia. When it came to signing the enlistment papers, Smith balked because the word "soldier" appeared on the papers. He was assured that this was a mere technicality and meant nothing; he would go as a teamster. So he went as a soldier and for three years. Smith was asked if the mustering officer heard the broker promising him he would go as a teamster. He answered that although the broker spoke in low tones, the mustering officer should have heard him unless he had "cotton in his ears."[12] While this was clearly a piece of brazen deceit, it was the only one uncovered in the 2,500 pages of trial testimony and does not justify the extravagant accusations that many other men and boys were so victimized.

Blunt testified that he was in Lafayette Hall one day when the surgeon passed a man with one eye and a set of weak legs. Blunt asked Spinola if he was going to accept the man, whereupon the General called the surgeon over.

"Doctor, did you pass that man?" inquired Spinola.

"Yes," was the reply.

"Doctor," interjected Blunt, "I would not take any such man as that."

"I may have been deceived in this man," conceded the doctor.

"In the first place," continued Blunt, "he has got but one eye, and in the next place he can hardly stand on his legs." Blunt then grasped the man's legs, felt them carefully, and prophesied that he would be in the hospital in less than two weeks after entering the service. Spinola then tore up the man's papers and ordered him out of the hall. The record does not tell us what happened to the doctor, although Blunt advised Spinola to fire him.[13]

A Brooklyn attorney named John Lomas, who apparently did considerable business at Lafayette Hall, testified that he frequently heard stories of men being brought in to enlist as teamsters and servants who afterwards went as soldiers. Brokers, said Lomas, regularly advised young recruits, when asked their age by clerks at the enlistment table, not to give their correct age but to say they were at least 20. Many recruits, according to Lomas, when put in the "pen" after muster, began to raise such a ruckus over not getting their bounty that they were taken downstairs. And to his knowledge no broker was ever arrested at Lafayette Hall for defrauding recruits. At the end of each day, Lomas reported that Spinola would meet in his quarters with the brokers, principally Clapp, and divide up the "spoils." Although he did not accuse Spinola directly of fraud, the inference seemed clear.[14]

Most of the evidence, however, pointed to fraud where recruits had already agreed with the broker to split the bounty. On many occasions, the recruits carried out their part of the bargain without complaint, although at other times, perhaps through misunderstanding or deceit, the recruit felt victimized and protested. But since Blunt's Committee recognized as valid all deals between brokers and recruits, Spinola and his men were put in a difficult position. For the most part they acquiesced in these arrangements which they heartily disliked. Spinola's frequent outbursts of profanity, when advised that recruits were not getting their three hundred dollars, well reflected his distaste for the whole business.

❖   ❖   ❖   ❖

In spite of the prosecution's case, much can be said in defense of Spinola. In the first place, when the General set up shop in Lafayette Hall he tried to enlist recruits without brokers. Initially he sent all new recruits, accompanied by a guard, to Blunt's office where each one was to collect his bounty. After waiting fruitlessly for several hours, recruits and guard would return empty-handed to Lafayette Hall. Next, Spinola urged Blunt's committee to send the bounty money to Lafayette Hall where it could be disbursed directly to the new enlistees. This request was rejected, although it was later adopted after Spinola had been relieved of his command.[15]

It must be admitted, however, that Spinola soon became a reluctant defender of the broker system. After a careful study of recruiting procedures in New York City and New England, he concluded that recruits simply could not be obtained except through the auspices of brokers. When he arrived at Lafayette Hall, recruiting in New York was at a halt because heavy pressure had been brought against broker operations. As a result the brokers were packing their recruits off to New England. Spinola reported, for example, that broker James Lee had three men rejected by the surgeon at Lafayette Hall, whereupon he took them to New England and sold them for a profit of $1,250. The General stated that New York City was losing from one hundred to one hundred and fifty recruits daily simply because brokers could make no money there and therefore took their recruits elsewhere.[16]

Since Spinola was under orders to raise a brigade as rapidly as possible, he decided that brokers must be allowed in Lafayette Hall. Halpine claimed Spinola told him that he felt two hundred dollars for the broker and one hundred dollars for the recruit was not an unreasonable split of the bounty money,[17] but later testimony at the trial cast some doubt on Halpine's statement.

Nevertheless, it appears that Spinola had made an uneasy peace with the broker system, though he fully recognized the opportunities for fraud. Even John Lomas, something of a hostile witness, conceded that Spinola did all he could to protect the rights of the recruits. When asked what reply the General made when Lomas spoke to him of fraudulent practices at Lafayette Hall, he answered, "General

Spinola seemed to regret that such things should be, almost necessary."

"Did he take any means to stop them?" Lomas was asked.

"I think he did all in his power," was the reply. "He certainly never
seemed to sanction . . . them."[18]

Colonel Funk and a Captain Thomas Smith of the 73rd New York
Regiment testified that all recruits were explicitly told how much
bounty they were entitled to and asked if they were agreeable to
assigning part of the bounty to their broker. The men were often advised to send their money to their wives and families, and special care
was taken to make sure the recruit was sober. If the mustering officer
had any doubts on this point he would make the man walk a straight
line. Both Funk and Smith had seen Spinola eject intoxicated men
from the office and deny the premises to brokers who were obviously
cheating recruits. Hawley Clapp flatly denied that brokers were permitted by Spinola to ply their trade illicitly in Lafayette Hall.[19]

Several witnesses testified that they had seen Spinola, on a number
of occasions, when a broker was caught defrauding a recruit in the
office, demand and enforce restitution of the money and then evict
the broker from the building. One Daniel Birdsall, a trouble-shooter
for Funk, recalled that a broker who got only twenty dollars from a
recruit went to Spinola and protested that the recruit had agreed to
give him one hundred and fifty dollars. The broker had brought the
man from "somewhere out West" and needed the large amount to
cover transportation expenses. Spinola summoned the recruit to him
and asked him where he met the broker and how much of his bounty
he had agreed to give the broker. The recruit said he met the man on
the boat coming down from Albany and had promised him no part
of his bounty. He had given him twenty dollars because he liked him
and for no other reason. Spinola turned on the broker and shouted,
"You have been lying to me in this matter," and ordered a guard to
throw him out into the street.[20]

Clapp told of a broker who had left Lafayette Hall without paying
a nickel to the recruit. Spinola sent out an order for the immediate arrest of the broker and then prepared new papers for the recruit, making sure he received the entire three hundred dollars this time. Another

witness reported that once Spinola even ejected a broker when the assignment was confirmed by the recruit. Although the recruit told Spinola quite frankly that he was to receive one hundred dollars and the broker two hundred dollars, the General was so angry at the broker's success in talking the boy into this arrangement that he threw him out anyhow.[21]

One of the difficulties was the determination of many recruits to accept only one hundred or one hundred and fifty dollars, even though it had been carefully explained to them that they were entitled to three hundred dollars. Broker James Lee testified he never took a man up to Lafayette Hall unless the man understood perfectly that he would get only a portion of his bounty. Blunt said it was not unusual to see men in the "pen" toss their money over the railing to the broker in the outer office. Apparently the brokers who had not yet received their "commissions" were not allowed inside on such occasions. The recruits would wrap the money up in tobacco paper and fling it across to the brokers as if it were a game of catch.[22]

Spinola told Halpine that every day there were recruits who resolutely refused to take more than one hundred or one hundred and fifty dollars even when strongly urged to accept the full amount. In one specific instance, a boy took one hundred dollars, assigning the other two hundred to the broker. After he was put in the "pen," however, he decided to give the broker fifty dollars more, leaving himself only fifty dollars. Several officers tried forcibly to restrain him, but he still managed to wad up a fifty dollar bill and fire it accurately to the broker. The boy, in Spinola's judgment, was perfectly sober.[23]

Like many modern readers, Judge Advocate General Joseph Holt found such behavior incomprehensible. In his report to Lincoln he largely absolved Spinola of much of the blame for fraud simply because many of the recruits preferred to be defrauded. He observed that

> . . . in consequence of secret bargains made between the recruits and brokers, the vast majority of the former, when told of the amount legally their due, persisted in stating their satisfaction with what they had received; and the cases were very numerous in which they would carry out their agreements, by throwing their money over the railing into the hands

of the brokers waiting to receive it. In fact the stupidity of
many of the recruits was so inconceivably great . . . that their
disposal of their bounties seems to have been something almost
beyond the control of the accused. . . . The willingness with
which recruits accepted and persisted in believing the statements made [to] them by the runners [i. e., brokers], in the
teeth of every assurance of their untruth, and the eagerness
with which they consented to their various exactions, and
handed over a fourth or a half part of their bounties in
fulfillment of their secret agreements previously made, showed
that they were far from being the reluctant victims of rapacity
and fraud which public opinion had insisted in thinking them.[24]

That Spinola was an honest man, anxious to see justice done to all
recruits within the limits of the broker system, and that he never
pocketed a dishonest dollar from his work at Lafayette Hall seems
clear from the trial testimony. Corrupt brokers were compelled to disgorge their fraudulent earnings and then expelled from the premises,
defrauded recruits were reimbursed, large signs posted all over the
recruiting hall advised recruits how much local, state, and federal
bounty money they were entitled to, and mustering officers made
sure all recruits were sober when they enlisted and that they knew
they did not have to surrender any part of their bounty to brokers.
Spinola obviously could not spend every minute in the inner office
supervising each enlistment and no doubt some regrettable things
occurred. But whenever fraud was brought to his attention he acted
promptly to redress the wrong. If the necessity for the broker system
with all its evils is admitted, Spinola can hardly be held criminally
responsible for the mistakes that occurred.

Another problem plagued Spinola constantly as he sought to keep
affairs at Lafayette Hall in order. The 18th Cavalry Regiment had
leased the room adjacent to the outer office sometime before Spinola
moved in. Just what this "lounge" was supposed to be used for is not
clear, but what is clear is that Spinola's recruiting efforts were badly
hampered by the cavalrymen's wild carousing. Heavy drinking, loud
noise, "skylarking," and general disorder prevailed in the room. Recruits on their way into the outer office would be detoured into the

"lounge," where they quickly lost interest in enlisting. Frequently the rowdyism would spill over into both the outer and inner offices, badly disrupting operations. Spinola tried to evict the 18th from Lafayette Hall, but Colonel Byrnes, the commanding officer, went to the higher-ups and was sustained. Since his lease predated Spinola's, the General could do nothing about the Colonel. Byrnes, in fact, was rarely present in Lafayette Hall and practically no restraints were imposed on his red-blooded boys. All this, a little extra burden for Spinola.[25]

❀　❀　❀　❀

The precise role of Hawley Clapp in the Lafayette Hall scandals is impossible to determine. Even more than Spinola, Clapp was a special target for Dix's investigations. Accused of defrauding recruits out of thousands of dollars, he was arrested and confined for months at Fort Lafayette. Clapp wrote a petition to the state legislature seeking relief and the Judiciary Committee of the Senate asked Dix why he was holding the man. In his reply Dix reported that Clapp was the "principal bounty broker" at Lafayette Hall, and "received from the Committee of the Supervisors the bounties for a large number of recruits . . . who . . . were cheated out of the greater part of it, by him, or the parties confederated with him in the business. As the money was paid into his hands, I consider him responsible for it. . . ."[26]

In this letter to the Senate Committee and in his report to Stanton, Dix is a little vague on what Clapp had exactly done. Dix does charge him with being the head broker at Lafayette Hall and states he received the bounty money from Blunt's committee, much of which he put in his own pocket. Dix also considers Clapp in league with other brokers in the game of fraud. However, none of these accusations are confirmed in the trial testimony. In fact, one gets the impression that Clapp's entire behavior was not only honorable, but also altruistic. He came to Lafayette Hall, it would seem, simply to help Spinola work around both the brokers and Blunt in behalf of recruits who desired to enlist directly and keep their entire bounty.

Clapp was a hotel proprietor during the 1850's with an establishment first at Fort Hamilton, and later owned the Everett House in New York City. He retired from business in 1859 and at the start of the war was a farmer in Westchester County. When Spinola found that it was impossible to enlist recruits directly, so that they might receive their full bounty, he decided to hire a "responsible citizen" who would facilitate direct enlistments. Clapp, an old friend of Spinola's, was approached by the General and asked to undertake this job, which he agreed to do. The arrangement subsequently worked out called for Clapp or his deputy, a man named Ellsworth, to be stationed at a table in the inner office a short distance from Colonel Funk's desk. Whenever a recruit came in without a broker and desired to enlist for the full three hundred dollars he would be taken to Clapp. Clapp was well supplied with Blunt's three forms and ample cash of his own, contained in a tin box on his table. The procedure was the same as if a regular broker was handling the enlistment, except that the recruit assigned the entire three hundred dollars to Clapp and the latter gave the recruit three hundred dollars in cash. Clapp, of course, would later be reimbursed at Blunt's office when he turned in the required forms. The only profit Clapp made on the transaction was from the fifteen dollars county "hand money" authorized by the bounty ordinance as payment to anyone bringing in a recruit to be enlisted. All brokers received the hand money, which was not subtracted from the three hundred dollars, but was above and beyond that amount.

No doubt Clapp did have a stack of Blunt's forms and was reimbursed by Blunt. This caused Dix to conclude he was operating like all brokers, and taking a good chunk out of each bounty for himself. However, both Clapp and Spinola indignantly denied that there was any profiteering in this effort to assist "un-brokered" recruits. Clapp, in fact, blew up when he was even called a "broker" by the judge advocate.

"Do you mean to class me with the brokers?" he thundered. "I am not a broker!"

"Make your own classification."

"I went there," he shouted, "as a friend of General Spinola for the purpose of cashing bounties to assist him in filling his brigade, an act of friendship on my part to him, and for this purpose—when a man came there and could not get his money I had a man there for the express purpose of paying the full amount. . . ."

Lieutenant Cole, one of the mustering officers, testified that whenever anyone came in to enlist voluntarily, or was brought in by friends or relatives rather than by a broker, "I always turned to Mr. Clapp." Cole added that "if it had not been for this assistance on the part of Mr. Clapp, we would have been scarcely able to carry on recruiting at all there." Although this last statement must have been an exaggeration, it seems evident that Clapp's presence helped resolve a troublesome problem. In answer to a question, Clapp stated that he made $1,825 while working for Spinola at Lafayette Hall. Assuming that his only income was from the fifteen dollar premium for each recruit, this would mean that he handled the enlistments for about one hundred and twenty men. Spinola reported that over 2,000 men were enlisted while he was at Lafayette Hall, so Clapp contributed about 6 per cent to the total number of recruits.[27]

After the conclusion of the trial, the court found Spinola guilty of all four specifications under the first charge, guilty of the first and third specifications under the second charge, and guilty of all three specifications under the third charge, and ordered him dismissed from the service. The only accusation of which he was fully cleared was the second specification under charge two, that he permitted drunken men to be enlisted. However, on every other specification, the court deleted the names of some of the alleged victims, and in numerous places it deleted adjectives and adverbs which implied negligent and corrupt administration of Lafayette Hall recruiting by Spinola. The court thus rejected any suggestion that Spinola (1) knowingly connived with brokers to defraud recruits, (2) allowed brokers to take part of the recruits' bounties without their consent, and (3) failed to make sure that the terms of their enlistments were explained to the recruits.[28]

Dix approved the court's findings and sent them, along with a covering letter, to the Judge Advocate General, Joseph Holt. Holt, however, could not agree with either the court or Dix, observing that "The findings of the court, under some . . . of the specifications, are unwarranted by the evidence, while others of those specifications are thought to be inherently unprovable, and indeed under the circumstances as developed in the testimony, impossible." Holt's main point was that, although great wrongs were committed at Lafayette Hall, these wrongs were the logical results of the broker system, Blunt's plan of disbursing bounties, and the fact that a great mass of the recruits who went through Lafayette Hall were either incredibly gullible or stupid. Spinola was trapped in a web of ruthless and unjust rules and customs; he bravely tried to protect the rights of all recruits, but there was a limit to what he could do. Dix's anger at the alleged frauds was a righteous one which all fair-minded people must share. But Spinola should not have been the victim. The real culprit was the broker system with all of its ramifications.[29]

Holt concluded his report to Lincoln on the Spinola case by saying that, although Spinola was the unfortunate scapegoat for the whole business, his future usefulness in the army had been impaired by the bad publicity he had received. In keeping with Holt's implied suggestion, therefore, the findings of the court and the sentence were never officially "promulgated," and Spinola was allowed to resign from the service.[30]

· 10 ·

The Haddock Affair.

WHILE THE SPINOLA CASE attracted a certain amount of attention in New York City, it never attained the publicity accompanying the arrest, trial, and conviction of Major John A. Haddock, AAPMG for New York's Western Division in the latter months of the war. Two factors set the cases apart. For one thing the crimes of Haddock far exceeded anything Spinola ever did; for another, the case had heavy political overtones which elevated it above the mere military. Haddock's chief offenses were committed against Utica and Oneida County—the 21st District—which was the home ground of Roscoe Conkling, the powerful Republican Congressman,[1] who took up the cause of Utica and resolved to destroy Haddock. In so doing he brought to a head his rivalry with James G. Blaine, which fascinated American political society for twenty years. But that is another story, told in Appendix C.

Conceivably one could blame Major A. S. Diven for all the trouble that ensued because had he not decided to resign as AAPMG for the Western Division to become a vice-president of the Erie Railroad, Haddock would never have gotten the job. However, Diven did resign on December 9, 1864, and Fry named Haddock his successor.[2] Undoubtedly this was Fry's worst appointment and he had a difficult time explaining why he made it, once Haddock had been exposed. Conkling would later label the AAPMG as Fry's "crony" and accuse the Provost Marshal General of protecting him long after he should have been court-martialed. Fry would deny these charges with some justice, although he probably should have moved more quickly in

187

prosecuting Haddock. Actually, Haddock's record was a good one before he went to Elmira. Something simply snapped in Haddock once
he was in office, and he became an unscrupulous money-mad fanatic.

Very little information is available on Haddock. Apparently
he was a Syracuse native, but later moved on to Ogdensburg and
then Watertown, owning newspapers in both places. When the war
broke out he was living in Watertown, where he organized a company
of volunteers, although nothing was said during his trial about actual
military service. That he did serve and was wounded is suggested
from his appointment to a commission in the Veteran Reserve Corps.
Haddock came to work for Fry in 1864 "highly recommended" by
AAPMG James Oakes of Illinois. Fry explains Haddock's rise to promi-
nence from that point on:

> He . . . served for a short time in a subordinate position in a
> branch of my office. . . . He was highly recommended by the
> officer under whom he served in my office, and was selected for
> a temporary provost marshalship in Pennsylvania, where he
> rendered efficient service, without his integrity or capacity
> being questioned. After serving for a short time with fidelity, so
> far as I know, as acting provost marshal at Buffalo, he was
> selected as acting assistant provost marshal general at Elmira
> for the reason . . . that I thought he was upright and suited to
> the position. . . .

When Haddock was at Buffalo, Fry wrote Diven that he was a "reliable officer," and a Buffalo newspaper commended him for his "energy, promptness, firmness, and honesty."[3]

In addition to Haddock, the principal figures in the events leading
up to the AAPMG's arrest and trial were Aaron Richardson, the well-
known broker, George W. Smith, a judge of Oneida County, and
Captain Peter B. Crandall, appointed provost marshal of the 21st District on January 14, 1865. Richardson and Smith worked closely with
Haddock for about two months, then as the heat of scandal began to
rise, Richardson fell out with his fellow conspirators and went over to
the state. At the trial, he was the chief government witness against
Haddock, while Smith, who served as the accused's counsel, sought

to impeach his testimony. Crandall was an unfortunate victim of the entire proceeding, as he attempted to evade Haddock's unreasonable orders and Richardson's unreasonable requests. Although Crandall committed no legal offense, Fry found him guilty of various "moral" errors and ordered his suspension, as well as the suspension of the rest of the enrolment board for the 21st District. And because all members of that board owed their appointments to Conkling, their dismissals were considered a personal affront by Conkling, and his enmity toward Fry was now beyond recall.

Even before he took office Haddock must have decided to exploit the post of AAPMG for all it was worth. He visited Judge Smith, who shared his Utica office with Richardson, and told him of the potential wealth that lay ahead if they only played their cards properly. They discussed for ten hours various ways of utilizing Haddock's advantageous post most profitably and concluded that Richardson was the man who could do more for them than anyone else. Smith saw Richardson later and found the broker receptive to the Smith-Haddock plans for plunder. Richardson said that if Smith could obtain "facilities" from Haddock for him, he would "compensate him [Smith] liberally."[4]

Richardson went to Elmira on January 7, 1865 and had his initial interview with Haddock that day. At first, the broker was hesitant about discussing the matter for fear of a trap, but Haddock assured him that he need have no fear and could speak freely. Richardson suggested that they could both benefit immensely if he could be given district credit and quota statistics before the provost marshals received such information. With this foreknowledge he could negotiate contracts for recruits with local committees based on quota figures far above the actual ones. Not knowing what the true figures were, the committees would accept Richardson's word and pay him the inflated amounts he asked. Of course, he would split all proceeds with Haddock.[5]

Richardson also asked Haddock for letters of introduction to all provost marshals in the Western Division of the state. These letters should speak highly of Richardson's reputation and urge favorable treatment of him in his business relations with the several boards.

On that very day Haddock gave Richardson such letters as were requested, but very soon would regret the deed. Within a month he was demanding the letters back, and Richardson's reluctance to part with them was a contributing factor to the cooling of their personal relations. Eventually, we are not told when or how, Haddock recovered all but one of the letters and destroyed them. Richardson retained the one with a probable view of using it against Haddock in the event of a trial. It read as follows:

Elmira, January 7, 1865.

Capt. Addison L. Scott,
Provost Marshal 22nd District, Oswego, N. Y.

This will be handed to you by a friend of mine named Aaron Richardson. He is a man of integrity and capacity, and will do as he agrees in all things. Any good you may be able to do him will be thankfully appreciated by

John A. Haddock,
Major, 12th V.R.C., AAPMG, Western
Division, New York.[6]

What was in all this for Haddock? Well, the final topic on the January 7 agenda was the gift of a horse to the AAPMG. Apparently Richardson owned a stable in Albany because Haddock knew that he had given a horse to someone else and wondered what the chances were for getting one of his own. Richardson replied that "if you will meet me at Canandaigua I will give you a horse." On January 16 the broker shipped a horse with saddle and accoutrements worth five hundred dollars to Canandaigua and then went to Elmira to advise Haddock that all was in readiness. The AAPMG met Richardson in Canandaigua on January 17 and the transaction was completed.[7]

In previous chapters it was reported that Richardson, early in January 1865, had offered to fill Oneida's quota under the December call for a lump sum payment of $750,000. This would have been before his first meeting with Haddock and before he had any inside quota information, but after he knew of Haddock's sympathetic attitude towards him. Apparently the $750,000 contract was never executed because in the court-martial record there is a reference to Board Commissioner Ivers Munroe's act of "saving the district" from the Richardson contract.[8] At any rate, Richardson went to Haddock's Elmira home on the night of January 29 and stayed until early the following morning, during which time the subject of credits and quotas was thoroughly reviewed.

The 21st District had a surplus of 210 credits from the July 1864 troop call which had never been reported to Washington. The books on that call were not yet closed when Diven resigned. If these credits were reported, and it was Haddock's duty to report them, the Provost Marshal General would subtract 210 from the district's quota under the new (December) call. But since Haddock had decided to conspire with Richardson for profit, and since no one except himself knew of these credits, he resolved not to report them, and to turn control of them over to Richardson instead. Thus, even though the 210 men were already enlisted and had received their bounties, the broker would be in a position to negotiate again for them with the Oneida Supervisors. Thinking that they were all brand new recruits, the Supervisors would pay the $725 bounty for each man, giving Richardson close to $150,000 which had to be split only with Haddock. Whether the two conspirators ever profited that extent from the arrangement is not revealed.[9]

At this same January 29 meeting Richardson offered Haddock a $1,000 Oneida County bond, which the AAPMG rejected, saying he "would not give four cents for it." He said that if his financial affairs were ever investigated and he was found with an Oneida bond in his possession he might be badly compromised. What Haddock wanted was cash and consequently a week later the broker sent his clerk, Collins, to Haddock with $2,000 in greenbacks. This proved highly embarrassing, as Collins approached the AAPMG in his outer office with his clerks gaping in stupefaction. The money was finally passed in Haddock's private office, but he was bitter at the clumsy manner in which Richardson handled the transfer. Haddock actually wrote the broker a letter, asking in feigned innocence, what the money was for. Since, however, he never pursued his query further and within four days sent the money to his wife, we can safely assume he knew what it was for.[10]

When Collins brought the money to Elmira on February 6 he also had a letter from Richardson which contained three more requests: first, post a guard detail to Utica; second, furlough three specific recruits at the Elmira draft rendezvous and send them to Richardson on a special assignment; third, allow credit for all men who have been mustered, but who deserted on the way to the rendezvous. Haddock was quick to oblige. That same day he wrote Crandall saying that he was sending a guard detail to Utica, and that credit was being allowed for every man who was enlisted and who deserted on the way to the rendezvous. The next day he induced Colonel B. F. Tracy, in command of the rendezvous, to furlough the three men for seven days, "for an investigation in Utica." At the trial it was shown that Haddock had lied when he spoke of an investigation in Utica, and that the men were simply old cronies of Richardson. No doubt they were veteran bounty-jumpers, too, because Tracy wrote Haddock a month later that they never reported back to him and were now listed as deserters.[11]

What were the objectives of Richardson's other two requests? He may have wanted a guard at the barracks in Utica to prevent the escape of new recruits before they left town. All Utica brokers were required by Crandall to deposit five hundred and fifty dollars with the provost marshal for each recruit supplied as a guarantee that the man would at least get to the rendezvous. If he deserted before that time the broker's bond would be forfeited. So perhaps Richardson did want a strong and reliable guard at the Utica Barracks to prevent desertion there. His second request—that credit be allowed for all men who deserted on the way to the rendezvous—was no doubt also tied up with his bonds. If credit was allowed for such a person then Oneida County had received its money's worth for the seven hundred and fifty dollar bounty and Richardson should get his bond back. If the county got credit on its quota, Richardson reasoned, who cared whether the man deserted? Since, at this time, Richardson had over $20,000 in bonds deposited with Crandall, we can well understand his concern.

A day or so after Collins' trip to Elmira, Haddock sent two non-commissioned officers to Crandall with the following word of introduction: "I send you Sergeant Sabine and Corporal Hanlon, both good men. You will place Sergeant Sabine in charge of the guard at your headquarters, as he appears to be a very trusty man." Haddock must have been joking, however, because before nine o'clock on the day of Sabine's arrival in Utica, eight men had deserted from the barracks, and Sabine was found in a downtown theatre with two other men, who had paid him ten dollars each to be allowed out. Other evidence suggests that all the men were allowed to leave simply by bribing Sabine. Furthermore, Sabine took the two men that stayed with him to Richardson's rooms in the Bagg's Hotel for possible re-enlistment purposes, although Richardson denied this and it cannot be proven. When Crandall learned of Sabine's escapade he ordered his immediate arrest and sent him to Elmira under guard. Haddock summoned Sabine, heard his story, and sent him back to his unit un-punished. Commissioner Munroe wrote Conkling that "in the selection of guard by Major Haddock, and by him detailed to these headquar-ters, he has been most unfortunate; out of eighteen sent in all, sixteen have been returned—two for ill health, and fourteen for incompetency, drunkenness or dishonesty."[12]

In the middle of February seeds of distrust between Haddock and Richardson began to germinate and by March it was all over between them. Perhaps an early clue to this break in relations appeared in the Utica *Herald* on February 13, when it was reported that Richardson and Collins were transferring operations to Auburn. Writing more truly than it knew, the *Herald* observed "we believe they have done very well here." The crux of the dispute were Haddock's letters and Richardson's bonds. Several meetings were arranged in various cities so that the two men could hammer out their disagreements in face-to-face talks, but these proved unsatisfactory. On February 20, amid rumors of governmental investigations, Haddock and Collins set up a late February "meet" in Rome. The AAPMG warned that in case of a government crackdown Richardson must remain mute at all costs.[13]

The Rome meeting never materialized because, although both men were in Rome for several hours, they stayed in different places. The mix-up infuriated Haddock, for when Collins again went to Elmira to seek and make explanations, the AAPMG screamed at him to "Tell Richardson to fire his biggest gun, and I'll fire mine!" He cooled down, however, and another meeting was scheduled in Rochester for March 4. Not much came out of this meeting at which Smith represented Haddock, who was now reluctant to be seen with Richardson. Smith transmitted the AAPMG's growing doubts about the broker's fidelity, while the judge returned to Elmira with seven more requests from Richardson to Haddock. The principal one, of course, was an order from Haddock to Crandall to turn over the $20,000 in bonds, but Haddock rejected all of them. He would do nothing for the broker until the letters were surrendered.[14]

On the morning of March 10, Haddock received an urgent telegram from Richardson and Smith advising him to meet them that night at the Osborne House in Rochester. Why a meeting was necessary at this time is unclear, but at this meeting Haddock demanded $5,000 which Richardson promised to raise. Smith went to Elmira on March 18 with $5,000 in bonds, but Haddock refused to accept them. By this time it was obvious the scandal was about to break and the AAPMG hoped to salvage something from his sorry situation. On March 13 the entire enrolment board of the 21st District was suspended, two days later Richardson was arrested (although he was released after Conkling intervened in his behalf), two days after that Major Ludington was ordered to Elmira and Utica, on April 1 Haddock was relieved, and on April 4 he was arrested.[15]

Before plunging into Haddock's trial let us examine several other illicit activities with which he was connected, but which were not related to Richardson or the 21st District. The most notorious of these was the release of a felon from jail, and his subsequent enlistment in the army with a partner of Smith receiving the entire bounty. On December 26, 1864, Henry T. Utley, Smith's associate, took from the Oneida County prison Charles E. Norton, "a desperado" who had been jailed for burglary and theft. Norton was apparently enlisted then and that night sent off to Elmira. He was not happy with the arrangements because while en route he tried to murder the agent who was accompanying him. The 21st Enrolment Board now had second thoughts about enlisting such a thug, and in some fashion which is not explained, caused his enlistment to be revoked and Norton was shipped back to jail.[16]

But on January 5, 1865, Smith ordered that Norton again be released from jail on bail with Utley supplying the bonds, and that he be permitted to enlist. With this order in hand, Utley took Norton and a deputy sheriff and reported to acting Provost Marshal D. C. Poole to enlist Norton. In support of his claim that Norton should be enlisted Utley gave Poole a letter from Smith to Haddock dated December 30, at the bottom of which was an endorsement from Haddock in the form of an order. Smith's letter contained an explanation of the case, with an urgent plea that Haddock approve Norton's enlistment. Norton would only get fifty dollars of the bounty, while Utley would receive the remaining five hundred and seventy-five dollars. Smith concluded:

> I do not see why the man cannot be mustered in. The government is to lose nothing even if the recruit should desert; and Utley will see to it personally that Norton is delivered at Elmira, and no credit need be given to the county until he is delivered. The whole arrangement is at the express desire of Norton, who fully understands his rights.

Haddock's endorsement at the bottom of the page read: "Colonel Poole will muster the man on showing him this note; but if the man deserts before reaching here the credit will not be allowed. Your letter fully explains the case. . . ."[17]

With this informal order from the AAPMG in his hand, Poole had little choice but to muster Norton, and on January 6 he was shipped off to Elmira in irons "fully understanding his rights," was credited to the Oneida town of Sangerfield, and the five hundred and seventy-five dollar bounty was given to Utley. Commissioner Munroe charged that Haddock knew Norton was a jailbird, and ignored all this just to put money in the pockets of Smith's partner. "The effect of this operation," he wrote, "was to give the men who had this matter and man in charge $575, and to add to the army (if he ever reached the front) a felon and desperado and to enable him thus to escape the punishment due his crimes. . . ."[18] Although this must be classed as one of the most brazen frauds committed by a government officer during the war, it was not listed in the specifications against Haddock at the court-martial.

Haddock was also in close collusion with certain Elmira brokers and was accused of giving valuable privileges to them in violation of orders, while denying such privileges to others. Most favored of all was the brokerage firm of Wildrick, Paine and Company, a partner of which was one George P. Morey, who also worked in Haddock's office and lived with Haddock. Frequently men brought in for enlistment by un-favored brokers would be rejected through Haddock's intervention, only to be accepted when supplied by Wildrick and Paine. Broker Peter La France, who was not on Haddock's privileged list, cited numerous instances of this sort where his men were turned down, but were told to go see Morey, Wildrick and Paine. Sure enough, within minutes, they would be accepted. One chap, Albert Easton, who had been rejected when brought in by La France, but later accepted when brought in by Wildrick, came back and told La France that other brokers had gotten him in, but that they had appropriated an unexpectedly large chunk of his bounty. When La France told him he had been swindled, Easton complained to Haddock, shortly after which the brokers came to Easton and gave him another one hundred dollars. Meanwhile Haddock denounced Easton and warned him that if he stepped out of line he would be in serious trouble.[19]

Furthermore, Haddock violated orders prohibiting the crediting of men who were enlisted in one district to another district. For example, if John Smith was enlisted in the 23d District he must be credited to that district alone. La France complained that when he refused, because it was illegal, to furnish five substitutes in the 27th District to the credit of the 25th District, Haddock permitted Morey to furnish the men. Similarly, on February 17, 1865, the AAPMG approved the mustering of seven men in Utica to the credit of a Herkimer County town in the 20th District. Six days later he ordered Crandall to muster fifty men to Schenectady's credit. When the AAPMG of the Northern Division informed the brokers in the above transactions that men mustered at Utica—in the Western Division— could not be credited in his division, Haddock sent an angry telegram to Crandall: "By what authority have you mustered seven men for the town of Schuyler, Herkimer County?"[20] Contradictory orders and statements such as these were characteristic of Haddock, and certainly caused the court to question anything he might say.[21]

Early in February 1865, according to Crandall, a Utica broker named Fiske appeared at the provost marshal's office with B. F. Secor, a Supervisor from Annsville in Oneida County, and seventeen sets of naval enlistment papers.[22] The provost marshal told Secor not to pay Fiske for the papers until word was received from Elmira that the men had been properly credited. Crandall claimed that Fiske then went to Haddock, who wrote Crandall on February 7 that the names on the enlistment papers *were already entered on his books*; hence Secor should settle with Fiske. Aware of a flagrant irregularity, Crandall still advised Secor not to pay. On the following day Fiske brought Crandall a telegram from Haddock saying that if Secor did not promptly pay Fiske, the seventeen recruits would be credited elsewhere.[23] Now, how could Haddock legally credit the men before their enlistments had been properly processed by Crandall, and how could he credit them to some other sub-district if they were already credited to Annsville?

The business of the bonds, while not involving Haddock too seriously, was a matter of deadly concern to Crandall and Richardson. During Crandall's incumbency five hundred and forty-four men were enlisted, forty-one of whom deserted before reaching the rendezvous, and of these forty-one, thirty-one were furnished by Richardson. By simple arithmetic this meant that Richardson paid five hundred and fifty dollars each in bonds to Crandall as security for thirty-one men who deserted, a total of $16,500 in bonds. All the discussion in the documents refers to $20,000 worth of Richardson's bonds held by Crandall, and I am not able to clear up this discrepancy. At any rate, Richardson insisted that the bonds be returned to him since Haddock was giving credit to all men who enlisted, even if they deserted before they reached their rendezvous. Haddock, however, wanted the bonds turned over to him for two reasons. In the first place he wanted them to bargain with Richardson for the incriminating letters; secondly, he was under orders from Fry, who was now apprised of the poor quality of troops enlisted at Utica, to confiscate the bonds in behalf of the Federal Government. Crandall, caught in the middle of this tug-of-war for the bonds, consulted with a prominent Utica attorney, Ward Hunt, and Hunt advised him to keep them until he was assured that the government would protect him in any civil suit that might follow.[24]

When Crandall refused to surrender the bonds to the government early in March 1865, Fry suspended him and the rest of his board. This and the fact that some of the men enlisted by Crandall deserted before they reached the front, were the principal "moral" wrongs committed by Crandall which led to his ouster. Because of the difficult position in which the board was placed, however, Crandall was eventually given a simple "discharge" from the service rather than being dismissed, while the other board members got honorable discharges. In the summer of 1865 Richardson brought a suit in replevin against Crandall for recovery of the bonds and Crandall wrote Fry asking that the federal government come to his assistance. Fry contended that the matter was no longer of government concern so he did not recommend any aid to Crandall. In the bond trial the court found against Richardson, and although the latter appealed the decision, no final ruling can be discovered. Before the appeal was made, however, arrangements were worked out which were no doubt carried through, that in case Richardson lost his appeal, Crandall would turn the bonds over to the Oneida County Supervisors and Richardson would be substantially indemnified for his losses. Just what this meant is left to our imagination.[25]

*   *   *   *

Conkling charged that Fry refused to move against Haddock until well after the AAPMG should have been dismissed. But since most of Conkling's criticism of Haddock at first appeared to be political, the Provost Marshal General decided to bide his time. He wrote that he befriended and sustained the AAPMG "until I had proper evidence of his being unworthy, and not a day longer; but on this point I required better testimony than Honorable Roscoe Conkling." Richardson probably began "singing" to Conkling early in March so that by the middle of the month Fry knew something was amiss in the Western Division. Consequently, on March 17, 1865, Major Ludington, the popular investigator, was ordered to Elmira and Utica "to make such inspections at those places as shall be indicated to him by the Provost Marshal General."[26]

Ludington, who reported to Fry on March 31, devoted most of his attention to Crandall's administration of the 21st District and only incidentally dealt with Haddock. While severely scoring Crandall, he did learn enough during his inspection of the 21st District to write that

> . . . facts in relation to the administration of Major John A.
> Haddock . . . were educed, which led me to the conviction that
> he is unfit for the position he holds. Men of undoubted char-
> acter charge him with being insolent and abusive in discharg-
> ing his duties and grossly immoral; that he is in collusion
> with bounty brokers, and prostitutes his official position to per-
> sonal ends. . . .[27]

Upon receipt of this report Fry at once recommended to Stanton that (1) Haddock be relieved and his conduct more fully studied, and (2) the appointments of all members of the 21st Enrolment Board be revoked. Haddock was arrested at Elmira on April 4 and Conkling was appointed by the Secretary of War to investigate any frauds in Haddock's division, with the proviso that he serve as special judge advocate in any proceedings the government might institute against the AAPMG.[28]

Conkling began his own inquiries at once and on April 14 forwarded to the War Department a list of charges and specifications against Haddock. He also urged that the trial not be held in Utica as that place might be "more harsh" on the AAPMG than some other place like Elmira or New York. About a month later the court-martial was ordered to convene at Elmira and on May 22 proceedings began. After four days the trial was suspended, reconvening on July 6 in Syracuse and ending early in August.[29] The charges were three in number: first, violation of the 99th Article of War, which covered any non-capital offense not included in the previous 98 Articles; second, violation of the 83rd Article, which covered "conduct unbecoming an officer and a gentleman"; and third, "fraud; malfeasance in office; abuse of official powers . . ."

Twenty-six identical specifications were listed under each of the three charges, including much of what has already been described. We have the horse bribe, the $2,000 cash bribe, the $5,000 bribe demand, the letters asking favored treatment for Richardson, his favoritism toward certain brokers at Elmira, the advance quota information, and the orders to muster men to the credit of other districts. All these and a few lesser deeds, which were but variations on the foregoing, were all carefully catalogued. As we have previously noted, Richardson was the chief witness for the government and consequently his testimony constituted a good portion of the more than fifteen hundred pages of transcript. A unique feature was Smith's role as both a witness and defense counsel, and his cross-examination by Conkling marked the most exciting moment of the trial. One witness recalled that at this point,

> Smith became very angry, menaced Mr. Conkling, who remained perfectly cool, though he became pale from suppressed anger and excitment; that kind that gave him that clear penetrating thrust, as clean as a rapier, when he spoke, and so violent did Smith become that the court, in view of the protection asked by Smith from the court from such questions, requested Mr. Conkling to tell the court what he expected to develop by his questions. Mr. Conkling arose as cool as could be and said, "May it please the honorable court: It is the province of the judge advocate to show the character of the witness, to break his evidence by showing him to be infamous, and if the court please, the judge advocate proposes to prove this witness to be infamous by his own testimony." Smith sprang to his feet and shouted, "I defy you!" and shook his fist at Mr. Conkling, whose eyes flashed and whose hand closed in a way to show that if he had the opportunity at a proper time and place, he would have made short work of Smith. . . .[30]

In his closing argument, Conkling tried to prove Haddock's involvement in these corrupt transactions by comparing his estimated wealth in December 1864 with that of April 1865. Giving Haddock the benefit of the doubt on all possible items of personal and real wealth, Conkling judged him to be worth $13,450.73 at the time he became AAPMG.

After his arrest, Haddock's holdings were valued at $57,729.39, a net gain of $44,278.66 in three and one-half months. In addition to this Haddock retained in his own possession, until compelled by government officers to disgorge it, $161,984.42 in bounty money taken from recruits who later deserted. Haddock made no attempt to convert these funds, although he was criticized for not turning the money in the moment he learned the men had deserted.[31]

Haddock's defense was weak since he obviously was guilty of most of the misdeeds with which he was charged. Smith's role must have been especially embarrassing as he was attempting to defend the man with whom he himself had consorted in crime. His strategy was simply to impeach Richardson's testimony, concede minor errors in judgment, ask what harm it had all done anyhow, assuming the accused did all the things charged, and appeal to the fair-mindedness and humanity of the court. It was a lame attempt, however, for it was not difficult for Conkling to show that Haddock's actions were more than "minor errors in judgment," that the favors granted Richardson and others had demoralized recruitment and brought considerable wealth illicitly to the conspirators, and that had Richardson's entire testimony been thrown out, Haddock would still have stood guilty of all charges by the corroborative words of other witnesses.[32]

The court found Haddock guilty as charged of ten of the specifications, guilty with some modification of ten more, and acquitted him of six. However, the twenty specifications where guilt was found were sufficient to convict him on all three charges. Several of the acquittal specifications are worth mentioning. Haddock was cleared of the accusation that he *ordered* Crandall to credit men mustered in Utica to other districts. The court evidently distinguished between insistence on such credits and mere approval of them. Also the 15th Specification which described Crandall's relations with broker Fiske was thrown out, from which we can only conclude that Crandall had not told the full story. Further, Specifications 22 and 23, which accused Haddock of using his official position to procure a job in the 22nd and 28th Districts for an unfit cousin of his, were dismissed. But in spite of these tiny scraps of vindication, Haddock was still guilty of the principal crimes.[33]

Haddock was sentenced to be dismissed from the army and barred from any future office in the federal service. He was ordered to pay a $10,000 fine and remanded to prison until such time as the fine was paid, although the term of imprisonment was not to exceed five years. Judge Advocate General Joseph Holt, in reviewing the court record, wrote to Stanton:

> The evidence fully sustains the findings of the court. The conduct of the accused, in his venality, in connection with the bounty and substitute brokers engaged in filing the respective quotas of men called for by the government, in his rapacity for the fraudulent accumulation of money, in the immorality of his domestic life, and in his utter abandonment of every principle of honor in the administration of his official duties, is almost without parallel in the criminal history of the war.

In view of the enormity of Haddock's offense, Holt was surprised at the leniency of the sentence, and urged that it be "enforced to the full extent." The president of the court-martial, General J. C. Robinson, said later that "the war has ended successfully and there is a general feeling toward pardon throughout the Government. I have partaken of that feeling. Did the war continue, Major Haddock's sentence would have been death."[34]

Haddock was sent to the state prison at Concord, New Hampshire, where he served a short term in October 1865, but upon paying the fine he was released. He then went to Washington and urged Fry to intercede for him in getting a revocation or modification of his sentence. He insisted that the whole proceedings were inspired by Conkling's political animus, an argument with which Fry must have sympathized. The Provost Marshal General refused to help Haddock, however, "because I thought he deserved punishment, not for all the crimes with which Mr. Conkling charged him, but for the offenses of which he was really guilty." Haddock then asked for a letter of "prior good behavior," that is good behavior prior to December 1864, but Fry refused him this too on the grounds that it might assist him in obtaining a pardon, which he did not deserve.[35]

In the Haddock court-martial packet is an undated letter from Haddock to President Andrew Johnson, wherein the cashiered major pleads for executive clemency. For over thirty legal-pad-sized pages he reviews his case and summarizes the charges, concluding that the sentence represented a grave miscarriage of justice. Haddock argues that Conkling was moved by personal enmity simply because certain friends of his had been removed by the AAPMG. The fact that Judge Smith, "an object of marked dislike of the . . . judge advocate," served as defense counsel, enhanced Conkling's determination to get a conviction. In such an atmosphere of partisan emotion justice could not be done. While we have no evidence that any action was ever taken on this appeal, we can safely accept both Haddock's guilt and Conkling's political motivation without doing violence to historical truth.[36]

Appendices.

A. Further Facts and Figures.

Some additional factual and statistical material, not suited for the text yet too important to be omitted entirely, is included in this appendix. The materials fall into three categories, namely, bounty expenditures, enrolment board personnel, and draft statistics.

Various bounty committees published interim reports on their progress in raising and spending money. An Albany aldermanic committee set up under the local draft exemption ordinance of 1863, stated that substitute fees totalling $47,785 had been paid to 177 men furnished by draftees, while commutation money to the amount of $50,626 had been paid for 180 more draftees. Supervisor Orison J. Blunt's New York committee announced in mid-March 1864 that under the present call it had paid out $2,398,500 in bounty money to new recruits, and $1,361,700 more to reenlisting veterans for a grand total of $3,760,200. During the same month the Buffalo bounty committee reported that since December 1863 it had paid three hundred dollar bounties to 1,387 men, one hundred and fifty dollar bounties to 291 men, and one hundred dollar bounties to 190 men. These expenditures plus the authorized payments of premiums to persons who had supplied the men, came to just over half a million dollars. The Utica committee said in December 1864 that it had spent $777,939.59 in bounty payments over the last year.[1]

Also reporting in December 1864 the Syracuse bounty committee stated that $1,529,625 had been paid out to 1,614 men under the July troop call, an average of $940 per man. Under the December call the same committee paid $473,300 to 793 men, an average of about six hundred dollars per man. This sizeable decline from the previous bounty average reflected the corrective influence of the state bounty

205

law. Ward committees were very popular during the fourth draft in March and April 1865. They sought to raise a ward bounty which would be tacked on to the county, state, and national bounties and thus make their own offers more appealing. New York, Buffalo, and Syracuse were the most active cities in the matter of ward bounties. Just at the close of the war, Syracuse's Seventh Ward Committee reported that $4,778 had been collected for bounty purposes. Contributions ranged from one dollar to two hundred dollars, with the average falling between five and ten dollars. The Third Ward Committee raised close to $3,500 and since all of it was not needed, the balance was prorated back to the contributors.[2]

Cayuga County, to take one final example, paid out $1,410,150 to 2,962 men during the four drafts, an average of $474 per man. Including bounty money spent during the 1862 Militia Draft, the county's indebtedness for the entire war increased by $2,206,786.47. This included both the principal and interest on bounty bonds for the several towns—$384,134.97—and the principal and interest on bounty bonds for the county—$1,822,651.48. This amount was paid for in part by direct taxation, $1,246,711.73, and in part by state bonds turned over to the county as reimbursement for bounty expenditures under the last draft.[3]

The total in *local* bounties paid out by citizens of all the states was $286,112,930. New York led with $86,801,128,[4] an amount twice as great as that of the second state, Pennsylvania, which paid out $43,-155,000. New Jersey spent $23,869,000, Ohio $23,557,000, and Massachusetts $22,965,500. At the bottom of the list was the District of Columbia with $134,000, but small Rhode Island and the border states of West Virginia and Kentucky were also below the one million dollar mark. Next lowest was Delaware and the frontier states of Missouri, Iowa, and Minnesota, all with two million dollars or less.[5]

In New York the Southern Division paid $23,000,000, the Northern Division $27,000,000 and the Western Division $36,000,000. The highest paying district in the state was the 26th, consisting of Broome, Tioga, Schuyler, and Tompkins Counties, which spent over $4,800,000. Next came the 14th District of Albany and Schoharie Counties with $4,300,000, and the 10th—Westchester, Putnam, and Rockland Counties—with $4,100,000, and the 20th—Herkimer, Lewis, and Jefferson Counties—with four million dollars even. Excluding the six Manhattan districts, where bounty figures were not fully broken down, the Second

District in Brooklyn paid the smallest amount of bounty money in the state, $1,469,325. Other districts which paid less than two million dollars were the 11th, 16th, and 17th. The Western Divison not only possessed the highest paying district of all, but every district in the Division spent over $2,100,000 in bounties. Bounty payments by draft reveal that $4,100,000 was spent in the first draft, $19,000,000 in the second, $36,500,000 in the third, and $16,400,000 in the fourth. Table 1 shows total bounty expenditures by district and division.

Eleven districts had only one provost marshal, sixteen had two, two had three, and two had four. Twenty-two districts had one commissioner, six had two, one had three, and two had four. Eighteen districts had one surgeon, nine had two, and four had three. The length of service for the office of district provost marshal was thirty months, while the average term in office for the fifty-seven provost marshals was 15.8 months. Table 2 shows the turnover in personnel of all enrolment boards.[6] Table 3 reveals how each district fared during the four drafts. As the table indicates, twelve districts were drafted all four times, six districts three times, eight districts two times, and five districts were drafted only in 1863.[7]

The final statistics on the draft in the thirty-one districts are contained in Table 4. The column "drawn" refers to the total number of names of enrolled men taken out of the draft wheel. "Did not report" means the number of men who received their official notice to report, but did not do so and were subsequently classed as deserters. The next column gives the figures on those who answered their notices, reported to the provost marshal's office and were examined, while the following column gives the statistics on those who were examined but exempted. "Held to service" means the men who were examined and found qualified to serve. The figures in the "held to service" and "exempted" columns, when added together equal the figures in the "examined" column. The last three categories all apply to men who were held to service. If such men could not commute or furnish a substitute, they would have to serve as draftees. Hence the figures for the men in the last three columns when added together equals the number of those "held to service."[8]

TABLE I: *Bounty Expenditures in New York State*

Southern Division		Northern Division		Western Division	
1.	$ 2,983,208.45	11.	$ 1,532,045.00	21.	$ 2,955,562.00
2.	1,469,325.00	12.	3,341,159.60	22.	2,703,800.00
3.	2,141,550.00	13.	3,686,113.62	23.	3,505,760.00
4.	143,200.00	14.	4,295,065.45	24.	3,996,592.93
5.	583,100.00	15.	. . . .	25.	3,860,900.00
6.	464,800.00	16.	1,728,538.78	26.	4,827,475.00
7.	406,500.00	17.	1,952,954.00	27.	3,284,262.00
8.	323,600.00	18.	3,497,478.00	28.	3,924,480.00
9.	261,100.00	19.	3,046,476.64	29.	2,239,640.00
10.	4,139,600.00	20.	4,078,800.00	30.	2,174,000.00
				31.	2,659,650.00

$12,915,983.45	$27,158,631.09	$36,132,121.93
10,594,391.68°		

$23,510,375.13

°Add this amount
paid out by Blunt
in Districts 4-9.

Totals by Division

Southern	$23,510,375.13
Northern	27,158,631.09
Western	36,132,121.93
	$86,801,128.15

TABLE II: *Enrolment Board Turnover for New York State*

District	PM	Com.	Surg.	Total	District	PM	Com.	Surg.	Total
1	2	1	3	6	16	2	1	2	5
2	2	1	1	4	17	1	2	2	5
3	2	1	3	6	18	1	1	2	4
4	1	1	1	3	19	1	1	2	4
5	2	2	2	6	20	1	1	1	3
6	3	3	2	8	21	2	1	1	4
7	1	2	1	4	22	1	1	1	3
8	1	1	2	4	23	4	1	1	6
9	2	1	1	4	24	2	1	1	4
10	2	1	2	5	25	1	1	1	3
11	2	2	1	5	26	1	1	1	3
12	2	1	3	6	27	4	4	2	10
13	2	1	1	4	28	3	1	1	5
14	2	1	1	4	29	1	1	3	5
15	2	2	1	5	30	2	4	1	7
					31	2	2	1	5

TABLE III: *Frequency of Drafting by District in New York State*

District	1st	2nd	3rd	4th	District	1st	2nd	3rd	4th
1	*	*	*	*	17	*	*	*	*
2	*	*	–	*	18	*	*	*	*
3	*	*	–	*	19	*	*	*	–
4	*	–	–	*	20	*	*	*	–
5	*	–	–	*	21	*	–	–	–
6	*	–	–	–	22	*	–	–	*
7	*	–	–	*	23	*	*	–	–
8	*	–	–	–	24	*	–	–	*
9	*	–	–	*	25	*	–	*	*
10	*	*	*	*	26	*	–	–	–
11	*	*	*	*	27	*	*	*	*
12	*	*	*	*	28	*	–	–	*
13	*	*	*	*	29	*	*	*	*
14	*	*	–	*	30	*	*	–	*
15	*	–	–	–	31	*	*	*	*
16	*	*	*	*		31	18	14	24

(The asterisks indicate which districts were drafted in the first, second, third, and fourth drafts.)

TABLE IV: *Draft Statistics by District for New York State*

District	Population	Drawn	Did Not Report	Examined	Exempted	Held to Service	Commuted	Furnished Substitutes	Drafted
1	126,142	6,914	1,138	3,990	2,665	1,325	723	498	104
2	146,950	9,269	3,237	5,607	4,120	1,487	188	1,200	99
3	132,172	8,381	2,541	5,789	4,229	1,560	367	1,135	58
4	134,766	4,949	2,374	1,958	1,554	404	87	315	2
5	129,983	5,893	3,453	2,440	1,994	446	19	417	10
6	117,148	3,075	712	2,363	1,912	451	91	354	6
7	132,524	4,394	836	2,550	2,193	357	25	331	1
8	173,998	3,075	878	2,197	1,710	487	100	380	7
9	124,569	7,336	1,363	2,468	1,855	613	29	579	5
10	135,991	8,852	2,233	5,922	3,528	2,394	815	1,481	98
11	94,076	4,346	942	3,119	1,899	1,220	653	375	192
12	112,113	4,652	403	3,160	2,013	1,147	927	157	63
13	108,311	10,468	3,455	5,676	3,375	2,301	560	1,641	100
14	148,385	4,466	681	3,448	1,774	1,674	1,161	464	49
15	132,227	1,911	204	1,705	1,284	421	344	70	7
16	95,383	3,045	487	2,205	1,489	716	401	176	139
17	114,524	3,219	628	2,534	1,637	897	599	203	95
18	129,778	3,723	385	3,305	2,145	1,160	889	79	192
19	133,556	4,781	365	4,233	2,350	1,883	1,638	107	138
20	138,960	3,354	590	2,752	1,592	1,160	1,019	78	63
21	105,201	2,531	303	2,228	1,395	833	685	91	57
22	119,418	4,394	334	2,994	1,917	1,077	768	217	92
23	116,980	2,382	191	2,191	1,332	859	731	74	54
24	131,664	4,937	398	3,767	2,241	1,526	914	276	336
25	104,399	4,103	219	2,703	1,665	1,038	807	126	105
26	114,902	3,227	273	2,951	1,601	1,350	982	100	268
27	135,487	4,985	391	3,932	2,689	1,243	721	211	311
28	129,365	4,799	578	3,274	2,367	907	440	395	72
29	114,553	4,192	553	3,590	2,401	1,189	609	447	133
30	141,971	5,809	1,134	4,139	3,091	1,048	280	674	94
31	102,304	4,026	354	3,455	1,889	1,566	625	681	260
Totals	3,877,800	151,488	31,633	102,645	67,906	34,739	18,197	13,332	3,210

B. Was It a "Poor Man's Fight"?

Most controversial of all features of the Enrolment Act was the commutation clause. Commutation was defended because it kept the price of substitutes down and raised a reservoir of funds which might be used to pay federal bounties. On the other hand, it was denounced because it raised money rather than troops and favored the rich while penalizing the poor. Since the $300 commutation fee constituted a sizeable chunk of a workingman's annual wage, a widespread protest arose that it was "a rich man's war, but a poor man's fight." So loud did this cry become that the clause was repealed in July 1864.

Professor Hugh Earnhart has shown that this popular phrase was not fully justified. In his study of Ohio districts he found that low income groups commuted almost as much as high income groups. He did concede, however, that after the commutation clause was repealed the low income people could not pay the high substitute prices.[1] An examination of the situation in New York State also suggests that no clear correlation between economic status and commutation payments existed. In other words, there was just as much paying of commutation money to avoid the draft in poor districts as there was in wealthy districts. Before analyzing the evidence, let us set forth a few guidelines used in making this study.[2]

First, in determining the wealth of a provost marshal district we have taken the total personal and real property valuation for each county in each district as of 1858, added these figures together, and then divided the sum by the 1860 population of the district. This has given us a "per capita valuation" for each district, which provides a

211

yardstick for determining rich, poor, and intermediate districts. Admittedly, (1) there are other means of determining wealth in a district, and (2) this method may not be the most accurate one for establishing the wealth of a district. But all things considered, this method does give us a rough approximation of a district's wealth, adequate enough to make some comparisons on the questions of commutation, substitution, and the draft.

Second, the two Brooklyn districts (numbers 2 and 3) and the six New York City districts (numbers 4, 5, 6, 7, 8, and 9) have no per capita valuation because the property valuations of each ward of the two cities are unavailable. Furthermore, so many abnormal factors operated in New York and Brooklyn that a normal rich-poor pattern would not be too meaningful.

Of the 23 districts for which property valuation data is available, ten have a per capita valuation of over $300, ten more have a per capita valuation of from $200 to $300, and only three fall below $200. The ten $300-plus districts are concentrated in two areas: one along the Hudson River valley, just north of New York City, and the other in the northwestern part of the state, extending from Lake Cayuga to Buffalo. The ten $200-$300 districts are located along the Pennsylvania border and in the central upstate region. The three sub-$200 districts are along the Canadian border, down Lake Champlain, and in Oneida County (Utica).

The highest percentage of commutation among those draftees held to service is found in the 20th District, a rural upstate area, comprising Herkimer, Lewis, and Jefferson counties. In this district, where the per capita valuation was $221, 88% of those held to service commuted. Close behind the 20th, was the 19th District (Otsego, Chenango, and Delaware Counties), with a per capita valuation of $239, where 87% of those held to service commuted. Next was the 23d District (Onondaga and Cortland Counties) with a per capita valuation of $290, where 85% commuted. And most astonishing, the fourth highest commuting district was the 21st (Oneida County), one of the three sub-$200 districts. In fact, not until we move on to fifth place do we finally reach a $300-plus district, the 15th (Rensselaer and Washington Counties), located along the upper Hudson.

At the lower end of the list, not counting the New York and Brooklyn districts, a relatively poor district, the 13th (Greene and Ulster Counties), with a $211 per capita valuation, had a commutation percentage of 24.3. And of the six districts just above the 13th in lowest percentage of commutation rates, five of them had a $300-plus per capita valuation. Obviously, from this table one can find little to sustain the argument that the rich districts commuted more than poor districts. There seems to be no pattern at all, with some poor and some rich districts commuting at a high rate, and some rich and some poor districts commuting at a low rate. Whatever factors explain commutation, wealth does not appear to be one of them.

While it might also be assumed that districts which furnished the most substitutes would be the wealthier districts, the statistics refute this assumption too. It is true that there is a closer correlation between wealth and substitution than between wealth and commutation, but still many discrepancies occur. Of the 23 districts for which data is available, the 13th, with a $211 per capita valuation, led the state, 71.3% of those held to service furnishing substitutes. Of the next eight districts, six are $300-plus, one high in the $200-plus category, and one low in the $200-plus bracket. The poorest district in the state, the 16th (Clinton, Essex, and Warren Counties), located along Lake Champlain, was tenth in the list, 37.5% furnishing substitutes. At the bottom of the list are $100-plus and $200-plus districts, but not too far from the bottom may be found several $300-plus districts, including the two wealthiest in the state, the 12th and the 25th.

In considering the percentages of people actually drafted, it has always been assumed that the poorest districts would have the highest draft rates. This would follow logically since poor people would be unable to commute, or furnish substitutes, and had no choice but to be drafted. Yet here again the pattern is unclear with both poor and rich districts scattered throughout the whole list in confusing fashion. Hence in none of the three matters, commutation, substitution, and the actual draft, is there any correlation with the wealth of the particular district.

Manhattan and Brooklyn constitute a special case. We know that those metropolitan districts were at the bottom of the commutation and the draft lists, while at the top of the substitution list. It might also be noted that those districts led the field in percentage of persons whose names were drawn, but who did not report. All of this is tied in with the Draft Riots, the widespread recruiting frauds in the military and naval service in New York City, revised and rigged enrolment lists, and so many other matters that it is not easy to piece together the full story.

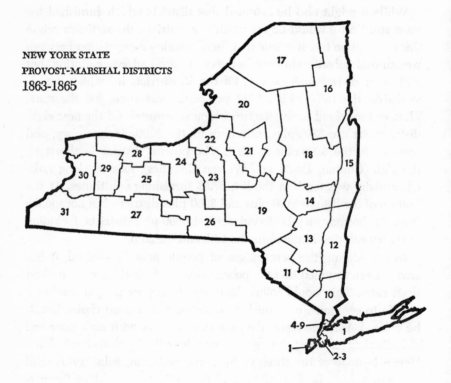

NEW YORK STATE
PROVOST-MARSHAL DISTRICTS
1863-1865

District Number	Counties in District	Percent Commuting	Percent Substitution	Percent Drafted
1	Richmond, Suffolk	54.5	37.5	8.0
2	Brooklyn	12.6	80.8	6.6
3	Brooklyn	23.6	72.7	3.7
4	Manhattan	21.5	78.0	0.5
5	Manhattan	4.3	93.5	2.2
6	Manhattan	20.1	78.5	1.4
7	Manhattan	7.0	92.7	0.3
8	Manhattan	20.5	78.0	1.5
9	Manhattan	4.7	94.5	0.8
10	Westchester, Putnam, Rockland	33.0	62.9	4.1
11	Orange, Sullivan	53.5	30.7	15.8
12	Dutchess, Columbia	81.0	13.5	5.5
13	Ulster, Greene	24.3	71.3	4.4
14	Scoharie, Albany	69.4	27.7	2.9
15	Rensselaer, Washington	82.0	16.5	1.5
16	Warren, Essex, Clinton	56.0	24.6	19.4
17	Franklin, St. Lawrence	66.8	22.6	10.6
18	Hamilton, Saratoga, Fulton Montgomery, Schenectady	76.0	7.5	16.5
19	Otsego, Delaware, Chenango	87.0	5.7	7.3
20	Herkimer, Lewis, Jefferson	88.0	6.7	5.3
21	Oneida	82.5	10.7	6.8
22	Oswego, Madison	71.3	20.2	8.5
23	Onondaga, Cortland	85.0	8.6	6.4
24	Cayuga, Seneca, Wayne	60.0	18.0	22.0
25	Ontario, Yates, Livingston	77.8	12.1	10.1
26	Schuyler, Tompkins, Tioga, Broome	72.7	7.4	19.9
27	Allegany, Steuben, Chemung	58.0	17.0	25.0
28	Orleans, Monroe	48.5	43.5	8.0
29	Genesee, Wyoming, Niagara	51.0	37.6	11.4
30	Erie	26.7	64.3	9.0
31	Chautauqua, Cattaraugus	40.0	43.5	16.5

C. The Conkling and Blaine-Fry Controversy.

During the spring and summer of 1866, the Haddock court-martial escalated into one of the great political rivalries of American history, that between James G. Blaine and Roscoe Conkling. The roots of the dispute only went back a year or so, but once the trouble erupted even Father Time could not patch over the ill feelings. In later years Blaine apparently was willing to make up, but Conkling was not. Asked late in life if it was not time to shake hands with Blaine, Conkling snapped back, "Never!"[1]

Early in 1866 the Joint Committee on Reconstruction brought before the House of Representatives a measure to revise the basis for congressional representation. By this plan the number of eligible voters rather than the total population would constitute the basis. Conkling, a member of the Committee, read the report, but Blaine spoke up against it, arguing that it was unfair to New England. The bill died in the Senate,[2] but a seed of dislike between the men had been planted. Some weeks later Conkling chided Blaine over a factual error in a speech dealing with the presidential appointing power, and Blaine began to seethe. Then at a formal dinner Blaine and Conkling squared off over the authorship of a couplet one of the guests jokingly tossed off:

No pent-up Utica contracts our powers,
But the whole boundless continent is ours.

It was Addison, said Conkling. No, countered Blaine, it was Sewell's "Epilogue to Cato." A bottle of champagne was bet, and when Blaine was declared the winner the angry Conkling refused to attend the party Blaine hosted to uncork the prize.[3]

These were small clues, but important ones. On April 24, 1866, the hatred burst forth on the floor of the House. Earlier General Robert Schenck, as chairman of the Military Affairs Committee, had brought forth a bill to reorganize the army, Section 20 of which would transform the Provost Marshal General's office into a permanent bureau. Conkling now objected to the bill, moved to strike out Section 20, and then mounted a lengthy attack on Fry. He had not forgiven Fry for what he considered a defense of Haddock and for discriminatory treatment of two Utica provost marshals. Now was his chance to get even and he did not hesitate. Fry, said Conkling, had caused the people of western New York to suffer "beyond the capacity of any man adequately to state in the time allotted to me." His constituents remembered, he continued, "wrongs done them too great for forgetfulness and almost for belief by the creatures of this bureau and by its head." Conkling charged that Haddock and his henchmen, all friends of Fry whom the Provost Marshal General had sent to rule over western New York, had "turned the business of recruiting and drafting into one carnival of corrupt disorder, into a paradise of coxcombs and thieves." False quotas had been given out, $438,000 was "wrongfully wrung" from the people, honorable public servants were discharged without notice or cause, and "never was the 'insolence of office' more offensively portrayed." Why elevate and enrich an officer, queried Conkling, "whose administration during the war has had in it so little to commend and so much to condemn?"[4]

When Conkling objected to Section 20 and launched his assault on Fry, Blaine was in the diplomatic gallery chatting with a friend. But grasping the character of the speech on the floor, he quickly excused himself, hastened to his seat, and gained the Speaker's eye when Conkling sat down. Why Blaine chose to defend Fry is not entirely clear. The Provost Marshal General states that the two had been on good terms for about three years, and that Blaine "was moved by a sense of justice and fair play."[5] This no doubt was true. But one can hardly avoid the conclusion that the occasion afforded Blaine an opportunity to strike a few verbal blows against a man who seemed to

enjoy striking blows against him. Certainly, he never suspected the
matter would get out of bounds the way it quickly did, but probably
the combined desire to defend Fry against unfair charges and to put
Roscoe Conkling in his place caused him to speak out.

Conkling, in his remarks, had introduced a letter from General
U. S. Grant to a United States senator, wherein Grant said he thought
the Provost Marshal General's Bureau ought to be abolished. The
purpose of producing the letter was to imply that Grant, in opposing
continuation of the Bureau, was indirectly denouncing Fry. The first
thing Blaine did when he obtained the floor was to introduce another
letter from Grant, which had been placed before the Military Affairs
Committee when it was drafting the army reorganization bill. In it,
the General submitted a favorable opinion of Fry and urged that all
recruiting be placed in his hands.[6] Blaine next observed that he was
aware of Conkling's quarrels with Fry in which, he noted, the Utica
congressman had come out "second best." Furthermore, the member
from Maine eulogized Fry as a fine gentleman, officer, and public
servant and thought it not very honorable for Conkling to attack a
man who had no opportunity to defend himself. With respect to Fry's
handling of the Haddock scandal, Blaine concluded with these words:

> . . . when I hear the gentleman from New York rehearse in this
> House, as an impeachment of General Fry, all the details of the
> recruiting frauds in New York, which General Fry used his
> best energies to repress with iron hand, a sense of indignation
> carries me beyond my personal strength and impels me to
> denounce such a course of proceeding.[7]

Conkling took up the challenge, disputing the statement that he
came out "second best" in quarrels with Fry, and reiterating that Fry
was an incompetent who had done far more harm than good. On this
last point Conkling commented that if his remarks offended anyone,
he would answer for them "not here but elsewhere" if necessary.
Blaine retorted that on his best authority Fry had won out over Conkling in their official disagreements, and that such talk of being responsible for one's statements "here and elsewhere" was the "cheap
swagger" of the duelist, and strongly reminiscent of the ante-bellum

aristocracy. Several other members—Schenck and Spalding of Ohio and Farquhar of Indiana—then submitted their personal testimony as to Fry's honesty, integrity, and diligence as Provost Marshal General, while one member—Mercur of Pennsylvania—opined that most of the confusion in the draft machinery was due to Fry's quota juggling. Thaddeus Stevens then proposed a substitute amendment for Section 20, which was subsequently adopted. By this proposal the Provost Marshal General's Bureau would continue only as long as the Secretary of War thought necessary to close out its business, but for not more than six months after passage of the act.[8]

Had Fry been content to suffer Conkling's calumnies in silence no more would have been heard of this phase of the Blaine-Conkling rivalry. But Fry understandably felt insulted by the New Yorker's remarks, and decided to defend himself in the best fashion available to one denied access to the exalted chambers of Congress. He drafted a letter, in whose composition he was aided by several friends including Blaine, and sent it off to the latter on April 27. The purpose of the document was to thank Blaine for defending him and to supply Blaine with some facts which would refute Conkling's accusations. Fry did not know what specific use Blaine would make of the letter, but he did hope that he might employ it so as to publicly vindicate himself of "Mr. Conkling's unexpected, unjust and violent attack upon me personally and officially."[9]

Fry's first point was that Conkling had unlawfully received pay both as a member of Congress and judge advocate in the Haddock court-martial simultaneously. The Provost Marshal General also hinted that Conkling solicited the judge advocate job for the purpose of "getting" Haddock—Fry's crony—and thereby evening the score with Fry for his discriminatory treatment of the 21st District. The Provost Marshal General had dismissed two successive provost marshals in that district —Joseph P. Richardson in December 1864 and Peter B. Crandall in March 1865. Conkling had sought to have both men reinstated, but Fry refused to oblige, and Conkling was naturally aggrieved. This, it appeared, was the motive for the New Yorker's assault on the Provost Marshal General. As for the Haddock appointment, Fry defended his choice on the grounds that Haddock came to him with good credentials. However, when it became clear that Haddock had abused his trust, he was dismissed, arrested, and court-martialed. While Conkling "was as zealous in preventing prosecutions at Utica, as he was in making them at Elmira," the Provost Marshal General said he personally preferred "exposure at both places." Fry did not deny that frauds had been committed in the recruiting service, but stoutly insisted that he had done all humanly possible to punish them; he welcomed an investigation of his Bureau which Conkling or anyone else might instigate. Since Fry was subject to military law, Conkling "was guilty of grave public wrong," if he had evidence of improper behavior by Fry and did not file charges with the Secretary of War.[10]

Blaine decided that the best way to handle the Fry letter was to have it read by the Clerk of the House. Had he read it himself it would have been a breach of the privileges of the chamber since it was written by an outsider and contained charges against a member. However, when the clerk read the letter, Blaine evaded technical responsibility for its contents. The House could have refused to permit the reading, but surprisingly, it was unanimously agreed that it be read. Still, when the letter had been read, an uproar broke out in the House which led to a lengthy investigation, and caused the Blaine-Conkling dispute to pass the bounds of all convention.

Conkling took the floor and laboriously denied all of Fry's contenions. He had been requested to serve as judge advocate and had received a $3,000 counsel's fee only at the suggestion of the War Department, and there was nothing unusual about a member of Congress receiving a fee from the government for professional services. He had no quarrel with Fry—"that distinguished mathematician and warrior," "a clerk in the War Department"—but naturally Fry was irked because Haddock, "his assistant and friend," had been prosecuted by Conkling. After a bit of quibbling, Blaine arose and delivered the most celebrated parcel of sarcasm ever heard in the House, "all the more remarkable," notes Stanwood, "for having been uttered on the spur of the moment."[11]

> As to the gentleman's cruel sarcasm, I hope he will not be too
> severe. The contempt of that large-minded gentleman is so

wilting; his haughty disdain, his grandiloquent swell, his majestic, supereminent, overpowering, turkey-gobbler strut has been so crushing to myself and all the members of this House that I know it was an act of the greatest temerity for me to venture upon a controversy with him. But, sir, I know who is responsible for all this. I know that within the last five weeks, as members of the House will recollect, an extra strut has characterized the gentleman's bearing. It is not his fault. It is the fault of another. That gifted and satirical writer, Theodore Tilton, of the *New York Independent,* spent some weeks recently in this city. His letters published in that paper embraced, with many serious statements, a little jocose satire, a part of which was the statement that the mantle of the late Winter Davis had fallen upon the member from New York. The gentleman took it seriously, and it has given his strut additional pomposity. The resemblance is great. It is striking. Hyperion to a satyr, Thersites to Hercules, mud to marble, dunghill to diamond, a singed cat to a Bengal tiger, a whining puppy to a roaring lion. Shade of the mighty Davis, forgive the almost profanation of that jocose satire![12]

Conkling could neither forgive nor forget, and never spoke to Blaine again. And thus Fry became the accidental instrument of the Blaine-Conkling break. It was an unhappy business, prompted by Conkling's resolve for revenge and his wild attack on Fry.

When the tumult had abated the following resolution was adopted:

> That a select committee of five members of this House be appointed to investigate the statements and charges made by Honorable Roscoe Conkling in his place last week against Provost Marshal General Fry: whether any frauds have been perpetrated in his office in connection with the recruiting service; also, to examine into the statements made by General Fry in his communication to Hon. Mr. Blaine, read in the House this day; with power to send for persons and papers.[13]

In due course, the select committee, chairmaned by Samuel Shellabarger (Republican of Ohio), and including William Windom (Republican of Minnesota), Benjamin M. Boyer (Democrat of Pennsylvania), Burton C. Cook (Republican of Illinois), and Samuel L. Warner (Republican of Connecticut) was created. Hearings commenced on May 7, 1866, and were concluded on June 26, and the committee's report (*HR Report 93*) was printed on July 14. The report was presented to the full House on July 19, and following a short debate was adopted, with 96 members voting in the affirmative, four in the negative, and 82 not voting at all. The four negative notes came from Illinois, Fry's home state. All committee members voted for the report except Cook of Illinois, who abstained.[14]

To anyone conversant with the congressional practice of launching free-wheeling investigations which whitewash favorite persons, yet assassinate disliked persons, Shellabarger's select committee provides no surprises. Before its first session convened, it had already decided that Fry had violated the privileges of the House and had brutally insulted Conkling. It then went resolutely to work to prove its prefabricated conclusion. It forgot all about Conkling's accusations against Fry, and concentrated its energies solely on vindicating Conkling from Fry's charges. The tone of the entire document is venomous; phrases attacking Fry's character, honesty, and integrity, occur repeatedly. While the Provost Marshal General was a cad who never did anything right or honorable, Conkling emerges a golden warrior, whose behavior through the whole messy business was above reproach. Passages referring to the dignity of Congress, and the impudent invasion of that dignity by a "clerk" in the War Department reappear ad nauseam. Amid the repetitious denunciations of Fry's "libelous attack," it never entered anyone's head that it was Conkling's own libelous remarks, delivered under circumstances which allowed no rebuttal, which sparked the controversy.

Turning to the charges in Fry's letter to Blaine, the Committee took them up one by one. First of all, Conkling had not solicited the judge advocate post, but had been urged to accept it by Stanton. And as for receiving pay for a second office while being a member of Congress, this statement was simply not true. The Committee devoted nearly one half of its report to this one subject, and reviewed the six federal laws and a number of court rulings which bore upon it.

The odd conclusion was that even though Conkling had been elected to Congress in 1864 and his term began March 4, 1865, he was not really a member of Congress until he was sworn in and actually took his seat, which was not until December 1865. Since he had relinquished his duties as judge advocate some months before December there obviously was no dual federal employment. But even admitting that Conkling was in Congress as of March 4, the Committee continued, there still was no problem. This opinion was arrived at by deciding that a temporary post, such as judge advocate in a special court-martial, was not an "office" in the meaning of the 1853 law, which Fry appeared to have in mind when he wrote his letter. Furthermore, an 1864 law which prohibited Congressmen from appearing as defense counsel in a court-martial was not contravened because Conkling represented the government and not the defendant.[15]

The charge that Conkling opposed investigations in Utica while pushing them in Elmira was flatly rejected. Moreover, there was nothing at all improper in Conkling's urging the reinstatement of provost marshals Richardson and Crandall. Not only was there nothing improper about such requests, but it was also hinted that Fry's firing the two men was done in collusion with Haddock and was indefensible in itself. The Committee could find no "moral frauds" by Crandall, which Fry mentioned in justifying the provost marshal's dismissal. That Conkling might have been sticking his nose in other people's business when he interceded for Aaron Richardson and obtained his release from custody, was denied by the Committee because the broker had made disclosures to the Government. The Committee devoted about one-fourth of its report to the Hoboken entrapment scheme in order to set forth testimony by Theodore Allen that Fry posted him to Utica to get incriminating evidence against Crandall.[16]

The one remark which got the Committee's back up more than anything else was Fry's suggestion that Conkling might have gotten $5,000 from people in Utica for prosecuting Haddock, and "additional fees from guilty parties for opposing proceedings at Utica." At this point in the report the Committee read a lengthy lecture on the irresponsibility and immorality of such false insinuations, and was unable to contain its contempt for Fry:

That such a charge should, without any shadow of cause, be
made *in any way*, seems almost incredible. But that it should
be carefully couched in the forms of insinuation, showing
timidity and solicitude in the author to avoid responsibility,
and should then be written out and sent into Congress, to be
read, in the presence of the nation, and preserved against the
accused and his children in the history of Congress, presents, as
a libel, a case almost new—certainly singular—for its bad
eminence as a wanton and inexcusable violation of the rights
of a citizen and member of the government.[17]

One would almost think that Congressmen like Conkling never made
insinuations.

The question of Richardson's bonds which Crandall refused to surrender when ordered to do so by Fry, and which was one of the
chief reasons for Crandall's dismissal, was also considered by the
Committee. The Committee denounced Fry for insisting that Crandall
turn over the bonds to his agents, and for not providing Crandall
with government counsel when Richardson sued him.[18] Although the
evidence is not plentiful on this matter, it does seem that Fry was
wrong on the bonds, and that his antagonism toward Crandall, which
Conkling's behavior must have heightened, was the reason for his
refusal to help him in his legal suit. Crandall did about the only thing
he could do with the bonds, or so it appears from this "disadvantage
point," and Fry should have recognized this. That the Provost Marshal General may have erred here, however, by no means justifies the
partisan, lopsided character of the rest of the Committee's report.

During the debate on the report prior to the vote, a number of representatives rose up to cast further imputations upon Fry. When
Thomas T. Davis, a Republican from Syracuse, discoursed on the need
for congressmen to be able to say anything they wished on the floor
and not be harassed by outsiders, he was asked if it was proper for a
public official to be insulted in the House when he had no chance to
defend himself. It certainly was, shot back Davis. If Fry was hurt, let
him ask the War Department for an investigation. Thaddeus Stevens
practically said that Fry belonged in prison, which struck no one as a
"libelous" remark. Shellabarger simply could not insult Fry enough:

I repeat what has been said in the report, that a more careful
and more malicious and wanton violation of the privileges
of the House and of its members has not been brought to the
notice of any member of the committee. There is not to be
found any more hurtful libel upon any member of this body in
the history of its proceedings.

Giles Hotchkiss, a Republican from Binghamton, who served as one
of the Committee's counsel during the hearings, became hysterical:

We have been lectured here this session from all quarters, until
finally clerks in the Departments come here and read lectures
to us, or use members of this House for that purpose. Next
come in bullies and attack us, and attack the officers of this
House. When will the dogs be set upon us?

To Hotchkiss, Fry's Provost Marshal General's office was "a bureau
reeking with corruption, a stench in the nostrils of the people."[19]
Blaine, Fry's only defender, was away sick in Maine, so the assault
on the Provost Marshal General proceeded without interruption.

How did Fry react to the Committee report? He circulated a pamphlet to all the members of Congress, reaffirming the accuracy of his
charges, on July 19, the very day the report was submitted to the
House. Of course, this was another "breach of privileges," and was
the cause for the further anti-Fry fulminations during the debate.
Aside from this, however, he decided to bide his time, certain of the
vindication which "time would bring." It was suggested that he apply
for a military Court of Inquiry, to safeguard himself against adverse
Senate action when future promotions or appointments were pending.
He decided against this, however, and never suffered from punitive
Senate action. Following his retirement in 1881, Fry turned to literary
pursuits, and in time his interest in the Conkling affair revived. Several
newspaper articles in the New York press, and the Alfred R. Conkling
biography of Roscoe Conkling in 1889, all reported that Conkling had
demolished both Fry and Blaine. These accounts stirred Fry to action
and one of his last acts was to put together "a plain and public account of a public matter in which I was misjudged and wronged."
Consequently, in 1893 appeared *The Conkling and Blaine-Fry Con-*

troversy in 1866, in which the Provost Marshal General presented his version of the dispute.[20]

The privately-printed volume, 341 pages in length, includes the debates in the *Globe* of April 24, 30, and July 19, 1866, the Committee's report, Fry's point-by-point rebuttal to the report, and several other miscellaneous items. A little over half the book is devoted to appendixes covering the *Globe* debates, while the main portion of the text is the 103-page rebuttal. In the rebuttal, Fry makes a strong case, exposing the Committee for the partisan, unfair, and vindictive body it was. The Committee was stacked against Fry; the Committee did not investigate Conkling's charges against Fry which it was instructed to do, but only Fry's countercharges against Conkling, which was the secondary section of the instructions; the Committee refused to include any of Fry's documents in the report, thus suggesting that his charges had no foundation; the Committee deliberately misinterpreted and distorted Fry's words in the Blaine letter and consequently drew dishonest and unfair conclusions based on those misinterpretations and distortions; dual employment was illegal, in spite of the Committee's findings; and lastly, no breach of House privileges had been committed by either Fry or Blaine.

It would require far too much space to detail Fry's defense in full, but several examples of the Committee's failure to act fairly and observe judicial correctness will demonstrate the Provost Marshal General's point. For one thing, the Committee stated flatly that Conkling had had nothing to do with Crandall's appointment, which was proven false by Crandall himself and in writing. The Committee also reported quite baldly that Conkling had secured Aaron Richardson's release from custody because he had made important "disclosures" to the government, when in fact the Secretary of War was never officially informed of such disclosures until two weeks later. Conkling actually had no authority to receive any disclosures until his appointment as judge advocate on April 3. Moreover, the Committee asserted that Crandall's good character was vouched "generally" by the people of the 21st District, when the evidence revealed that only Conkling testified to the effect. Not that Crandall's character was not good; but the Committee made statements not supported by the testimony,[21]

Fry was irked about the raising of the Hoboken affair and the introduction of Theodore Allen as a witness. Fry never mentioned the matter in his letter, which was the only subject the Committee had decided to investigate, so why should the Hoboken matter be brought
up? The Committee observed strict rules of evidence when Fry wished
to submit some material, but relaxed those rules when it suited its
own purpose. Of course, the reason the Hoboken affair was brought
into the hearing was to get Theodore Allen on the stand, because
Allen could testify to a "deal" which Fry allegedly made with him.
This deal, mentioned in the Baker chapter, had Fry asking Allen to
go to Utica in order to dig up some incriminating evidence on Crandall. As far as Allen's testimony before the Committee was concerned,
Fry was justfiably astounded that the Committee should accept without challenge Allen's statement that Fry collaborated with him to "get"
Crandall. It accepted his word in spite of the fact that he was a convicted thief, and that several police officials stated unequivocally that
he was a liar. None of this evidence derogatory to Allen was included
in the report, only his recollections about the "deal." Furthermore,
nothing Fry submitted to the Committee to rebut Allen was used in
the report. Thus the word of a soldier with 40 years of unblemished
service was allowed to stand contradicted in the pages of the *Globe*
by a thug like Theodore Allen.[22]

The Committee asserted that "detailed reports of specific acts of
official dishonesty committed by Haddock had been made to General
Fry in writing" on February 3 by Edward Meloy, a crony of Allen,
and Peter La France, the Elmira broker, on February 28. This was
completely untrue. Meloy's letter was directed to Baker and did not
even mention Haddock, while La France's letter referred to Haddock's
favoritism toward certain brokers, which was not one of the acts for
which he was convicted. La France's letter never reached Fry, but
even if it had, it would have had no bearing on the case at hand.[23]

We turn finally to the question of whether Fry's letter to Blaine and
Blaine's having it read from the clerk's desk was a "breach of the
privileges" of the House of Representatives. Clearly it was not. In the
first place the entire House, and Conkling in particular, wanted to have
it read.[24] How could a breach have been committed when the reading

was unanimously agreed to? Secondly, Fry closed his narrative with a discussion of every previous breach in the House of Representatives' 77-year history, and found no instance "where the reading of a letter by a member or the Clerk of the House has been adjudged by the House a breach of privilege by the writer of the letter, or by the member introducing it."[25]

A document such as *HR Report 93* scarcely requires comment. The Committee was composed of Conkling's friends and was determined both to exonerate him and convict Fry. It used evidence favorable to Conkling and did not use that which was unfavorable to him. It not only distorted Fry's words and meanings, but indulged in outright falsehoods. It abandoned rules of evidence whenever it was convenient to do so. And when it had completed its exercise in partisan, one-sided vindictiveness, it concluded that a calamitous breach of the House privileges had occurred, even though the House itself had invited the "breach." The immediate judgment certainly was against Fry, but reading the record over today, Fry was the real winner, and the Committee has simply provided us with another example of an irresponsible, unproductive congressional investigation.

Notes to the Text.

CHAPTER 1.

1 See Lawrence Lader, "New York's Bloodiest Week," *American Heritage* X (June 1959), 44-49, 95-98, for a recent, popular account of the Draft Riots.

2 Albany *Atlas and Argus*, Feb. 3, 1864. (Hereafter cited as *Argus*.)

3 New York *Times*, March 1, 1865.

4 See Walter Millis, *Arms and Men* (New York, 1958), pp. 11-63, for a discussion of "the democratization of war."

5 Frederick M. Cutler, *The History of Military Conscription With Special Reference to United States* (Unpublished Clark University Doctoral Dissertation, 1922), pp. 37-42. Emory Upton, *The Military Policy of the United States* (Washington, 1904), is a bitter attack on the futility of trying to wage war with untrained, undisciplined, and poorly-led militia.

6 Upton, pp. 221-22.

7 Jack Franklin Leach, *Conscription in the United States: Historical Background* (Tokyo, 1952), pp. 132-34, 136-39. *Final Report Made to the Secretary of War, by the Provost Marshal General, House Exec. Docs.*, 39 Cong., 1 Sess., IV, pt. 1 (Serial 1252), p. 102. (Hereafter cited as PMG, *Final Report*.) Fred Albert Shannon, in *The Organization and Administration of the Union Army, 1861-1865* (2 vols., Cleveland, 1928), criticizes the government for its failure to exploit the early enthusiasm for volunteering. See vol. 1, pp. 31-32. In the wake of Lincoln's call for seventy-five thousand troops, enough young men rushed forward in Ohio alone to supply the entire country's quota. Governor William Dennison, however, was compelled to send them all home because he did not know what to do with them. Whitelaw Reid, *Ohio in the War: Her Statesmen, Her Generals and Soldiers* (2 vols., Cincinnati, 1868), I, pp. 42-43.

8 Leach, pp. 156, 158-59.

9 *Ibid.*, pp. 28-30, 52-97, 121-22; Shannon, I, pp. 47-48.

10 U. S. *Statutes at Large*, XII, 2 Sess., pp. 597-600. Shannon, I, pp. 275-80; Leach, pp. 138-41. PMG, *Final Report*, II, pp. 105-07.

[11] Leach, pp. 143-52; Shannon, I, pp. 286-89. PMG, *Final Report*, II, p. 217.

[12] Shannon, I, pp. 289-92.

[13] *Ibid.*, pp. 295-302; Leach, pp. 157-58; Upton, p. 443.

[14] *U. S. Statutes at Large*, XII, 3 Sess., pp. 731-37. Leach supplies his readers with a blow-by-blow account of the debates, pp. 162-216, while Shannon's narration is more concise, I, pp. 302-23.

[15] Leach, pp. 251-56; Shannon, I, pp. 305-08. See Edward A. Fitzpatrick, *Conscription and America* (Milwaukee, 1940), pp. 22-24, for a criticism of the clause making provost marshals responsible for the apprehension of spies and deserters.

[16] Fry was made Brevet Brigadier General in 1864, and Brevet Major General in 1865.

[17] PMG, *Final Report*, I, p. 14. Detailed regulations for the operations of the Provost Marshal General's Bureau were published on April 21, 1863. See *The War of the Rebellion: A Compilation of the Official Records of the Union and Confederate Armies* (128 vols., Washington, 1880-1901), Series III, Vol. III, pp. 125-46. (Hereafter cited as *OR*. All references, unless otherwise noted, are to Series III.)

[18] In other words, it would become a "rich man's war, but a poor man's fight." No other feature of this unpopular law quite incensed the general public as much as the commutation clause. However, a study based on property values and rates of commutation in all but the New York City districts suggests that draftees in poor districts paid the commutation fee just as frequently as draftees in rich districts. See Appendix B. Hugh Earnhart has confirmed this finding in a detailed examination of draftees by occupation in four Ohio districts. "Commutation: Democratic or Undemocratic?" *Civil War History* XII (June 1966), 132-42.

[19] Leach, p. 169. It was also permissible for militiamen to furnish substitutes in the early days of our history.

[20] There was no provision in the original law to exempt conscientious objectors, but any people whose teachings forbade them from bearing arms could find refuge in either furnishing substitutes or paying commutation. However, a number of groups, such as the Quakers, refused to do this because both substitutes and commutation money helped promote the war, which they felt was just as objectionable as personal service. See Edward Needles Wright, *Conscientious Objectors in the Civil War*, rep. (New York, 1961), pp. 65-90.

[21] PMG, *Final Report*, I, pp. 26-29. Shannon, II, pp. 112-15.

[22] PMG, *Final Report*, I, pp. 29, 174-75.

[23] *U. S. Statutes at Large*, XIII, 1 Sess., Appendix, pp. vi-vii.

[24] Shannon, II, pp. 127-29. PMG, *Final Report*, I, pp. 39-42.

[25] *Ibid.*, pp. 184-85.

[26] Shannon, II, p. 129.

[27] *U. S. Statutes at Large*, XIII, 1 Sess., Appendix, pp. xvii-xviii.

28 PMG, *Final Report*, I, pp. 198-99. Shannon, II, pp. 131-32. Enrolled men were permitted to furnish substitutes in advance of a draft by Section Four of the February 24, 1864 amendment to the Enrolment Act.

29 U. S. *Statutes at Large*, XIII, 2 Sess., Appendix, pp. iii-iv.

30 PMG, *Final Report*, I, pp. 211-12. Shannon, II, pp. 132-35.

31 PMG, *Final Report*, I, pp. 175, 185, 199, 212. Unfortunately, serious discrepancies appear in the Provost Marshal General's final figures for the fourth draft. I have relied upon the numbers supplied in the state-by-state tables, pp. 211-12, rather than on the earlier figures on page 46.

32 U. S. *Statutes at Large*, XIII, 1 Sess., pp. 6-11. Shannon, II, pp. 28-34; Leach, pp. 395-400.

33 U. S. *Statutes at Large*, XIII, 1 Sess., pp. 379-80. Shannon, II, pp. 35-42; Leach, pp. 409-15. A provision to prohibit substitution was deleted before final passage.

34 U. S. *Statutes at Large*, XIII, 2 Sess., pp. 487-91. Shannon, II, pp. 44-46; Leach, pp. 441-42. In view of the sharp limitations placed upon the brokerage business, it seems strange that Shannon should characterize the law as "a coalition with substitute brokers," II, p. 46.

35 Interview with General Lewis B. Hershey, September 2, 1964.

CHAPTER 2.

1 Upton, pp. 21-22, 35, 40.

2 *Ibid.*, pp. 28, 29, 35, 41-42, 48, 67.

3 *Ibid.*, pp. 79, 92, 107, 122-23.

4 *Ibid.*, pp. 205-06.

5 Shannon, II, pp. 50-53, 57.

6 Eugene C. Murdock, *Ohio's Bounty System in the Civil War* (Columbus, 1963), p. 11.

7 PMG, *Final Report*, I, pp. 84-87, 213, 744-45. Shannon, II, pp. 53, 62-66.

8 *Laws of the State of New York* (1863), pp. 18, 320-22; (1865), pp. 39-46. See Silas W. Burt, *My Memoirs of the Military History of the State of New York During the War for the Union 1861-65* (Albany, 1903), pp. 97-98, for the background on Morgan's decision to offer the fifty dollar bounty.

9 *Historical Report*, 20th District, Record Group 110 (National Archives). All *Historical Reports* are in Record Group 110.

10 Syracuse *Journal*, Sept. 1, 1862; Shannon, II, pp. 57-59.

11 See Leach, pp. 314-16, for a discussion of exemption ordinances.

12 *Argus*, July 21, Aug. 10, 1863; New York *Times*, July 26, 22, 28, 1863; Syracuse *Standard*, July 23, 25, 31, Aug. 6, 1863; Buffalo *Morning Express*, Aug. 11, 18, 1863.

13 Jamestown *Journal*, Aug. 21, 1863; Utica *Herald*, Sept. 4, 5, 12, 1863; *Argus*, Sept. 7, 11, 19, Oct. 8, 1863.

14 New York *Times*, July 28, 1863; Leach, pp. 311-12.

15 New York *Times*, Aug. 14, 17, 26, 28, 29, 30, Sept. 2, 3, 1863. The temporary chairman of the committee was Orison J. Blunt, who would become chairman of the permanent County Volunteer and Substitute Committee which came into being in November 1863.

16 New York *Times*, Aug. 8, 1863; *Argus*, Sept. 7, 1863; Syracuse *Standard*, July 23, 25, 31, 1863.

17 New York *Times*, July 28, Aug. 3, Sept. 7, 1863. The *Times* here had a pretty good "book" on New York City government. In the summer of 1865, just as the Tweed Ring was sinking its fangs into the city exchequer, *Harpers Weekly*, Aug. 12, 1865, reported:

> The City of New York undoubtedly pays more money for a worse government than any city in the world. Its local administration is a vast and notorious swindle. Its taxes are doubtless three times as large as they need be. Its chief officers are, with a few exceptions, the most venal of politicians. Neither honesty nor ability, as a rule, are to be found in any department of its civic affairs. . . . Every necessary public work is a mercenary job, for which the taxpayers are enormously fleeced. The "city" is a jest and a by-word at home and a disgrace abroad.

18 New York *Times*, Sept. 16, 21, 29, Oct. 8, 16, 31, 1863.

19 *Argus*, Nov. 30, Dec. 2, 1863.

20 New York *Times*, Oct. 21, Nov. 12, 1863.

21 Syracuse *Journal*, Nov. 27, 1863; Jamestown *Journal*, Nov. 27, 1863; Glens Falls *Republican*, Dec. 1, 15, 29, 1863; Poughkeepsie *Daily Eagle*, Dec. 5, 9, 1863; Utica *Herald*, Dec. 7, 1863.

22 Syracuse *Journal*, Nov. 30, 1863; Syracuse *Standard*, Dec. 9, 10, 11, 14, 1863. Among other towns and counties which in December 1863 decided to pay bounties were Buffalo, Albany, Rensselaer County, Westfield, and Otsego. Buffalo *Morning Express*, Dec. 7, 1863; *Argus*, Dec. 8, 9, 1863; Jamestown *Journal*, Dec. 18, 1863; Cooperstown *Freeman's Journal*, Dec. 25, 1863. (Hereafter cited as *Freeman's Journal*.)

23 Utica *Herald*, Feb. 3, 1864; Syracuse *Standard*, Feb. 5, 10, 15, 1864; *Argus*, Feb. 10, 1864; Glens Falls *Republican*, Jan. 19, 1864; New York *Times*, Jan. 26, 1864; Jamestown *Journal*, Feb. 12, 1864.

24 Buffalo *Morning Express*, June 21, 1864; New York *Times*, June 23, 1864; Saratoga *Republican*, July 8, 1864; *Argus*, July 8, 19, 1864; Utica *Herald*, July 25, 1864; Poughkeepsie *Daily Eagle*, July 21, 1864; Elmira *Daily Advertiser*, July 28, 1864.

25 One two-year veteran from New Scotland, Garrit Bradt, was anxious to re-enter the army, but not because of the bounty. It seems that a warrant was out for Bradt's arrest on the charge of raping his sixteen-year old daughter. By re-enlisting he hoped to avoid prosecution, but he was arrested while undergoing his physical examination. *Argus*, July 30, 1864.

26 Poughkeepsie *Daily Eagle,* Aug. 16, 1864; Utica *Herald,* Aug. 24, 27, 29, 30, 31, 1864; *Argus,* Aug. 25, 26, 30, 1864.

27 Glens Falls *Republican,* Aug. 30, Sept. 6, 1864; *Freeman's Journal,* Aug. 26, Sept. 2, 1864; *Argus,* Sept. 10, 1864; Syracuse *Journal,* Aug. 31, Sept. 1, 1864.

28 When the *Poughkeepsian* in a typographical fluff, reported that Dutchess County Supervisors had agreed to pay $250,000 bounties, the rival *Eagle* remarked that at such a price no one could afford to stay home. *Eagle,* Dec. 9, 1863.

29 Syracuse *Standard,* Nov. 21, 1863; Syracuse *Journal,* Nov. 27, 1863; Poughkeepsie *Daily Eagle,* Dec. 5, 1863; *Freeman's Journal,* Jan. 1, 8, 15, 1864.

30 Utica *Herald,* July 26, 1864; Elmira *Daily Advertiser,* July 30, Aug. 10, 1864.

31 *Freeman's Journal,* Aug. 26, Sept. 2, 9, 1864; Syracuse *Journal,* Sept. 5, 1864; Saratoga *Republican,* Aug. 19, 1864.

32 *Laws of the State of New York* (1865), pp. 39-46. The adjutant-general issued "General Order Number 6" to implement the law on February 28, 1865, and the paymaster-general issued "General Order Number 1" to implement "General Order Number 6" on March 1. New York *Times,* March 5, 1865; Buffalo *Morning Express,* March 7, 1865.

33 *Laws of the State of New York* (1863), pp. 28-29.

34 Syracuse *Journal,* Nov. 27, 1863; Syracuse *Standard,* Dec. 2, 1863; *Laws of the State of New York* (1864), pp. 7-11, 12-25, 79, 237-39, 350-52.

35 PMG, *Final Report,* I, pp. 216-17; Syracuse *Journal,* Nov. 11, 1864; Glens Falls *Republican,* Sept. 20, Oct. 18, 1864. These surplus men were applied to the district's quota for the fourth draft, and thus made both additional recruiting and drafting unnecessary then. There was something a bit ironical in all this because a compilation of personal and real property values across the state reveals that the 16th District was the poorest one in New York. See Appendix B.

36 *Argus,* July 28, Sept. 7, 26, 1863; Syracuse *Standard,* Oct. 17, 1863; Poughkeepsie *Daily Eagle,* Oct. 30, 1863. Unconfirmed reports had it that Secretary of War Stanton was using commutation money to liberate slaves of loyal masters in Maryland. *Argus,* Sept. 28, 1863. A drafted priest whose parishioners desired to pay his commutation turned the offer down, saying "I cannot permit this." Syracuse *Standard,* Oct. 12, 1864. Among other objections to commutation, was the erroneous belief of some people in Glens Falls that the Commissioner of Internal Revenue pocketed a commission on the money turned into him. Glens Falls *Republican,* Aug. 25, 1863.

37 *Argus,* June 22, Sept. 5, 1864; Syracuse *Standard,* July 22, 1864, quoting Watertown *Reformer;* Poughkeepsie *Daily Eagle,* July 27, 1864.

38 *Argus,* Aug. 5, Oct. 10, 1863, Aug. 22, 1864, quoting Hudson *Gazette.* A Seneca Falls draftee advertised for a substitute, not to serve for him in the army, but to run his office and pay his bills. *Ibid.,* July 30, 1863, quoting Seneca Falls *Reveille.*

39 Poughkeepsie *Daily Eagle,* Aug. 3, 18, 1864.

40 Jamestown *Journal,* March 24, 1865, quoting Dunkirk *Journal.*

41 Murdock, pp. 13-15, 17-18.

[42] Syracuse *Standard*, March 4, 1865; Skaneateles *Democrat*, Sept. 1, 1864; Jamestown *Journal*, Sept. 9, 1864; Glens Falls *Republican*, March 14, 1865; Elmira *Daily Advertiser*, March 11, 1865.

[43] See below, footnote 51.

[44] Syracuse *Journal*, Aug. 7, 1863; Syracuse *Standard*, Jan. 1, 1864; Jamestown *Journal*, Feb. 19, 1864.

[45] Glens Falls *Republican*, July 12, 1864; Poughkeepsie *Daily Eagle*, July 18, 19, 21, 1864; Elmira *Daily Advertiser*, July 21, 1864.

[46] Utica *Herald*, July 28, 29, Aug. 11, 15, 27, 29, 30, 1864.

[47] *Argus*, Dec. 8, 1863; Feb. 10, March 3, Sept. 10, 1864; Jan. 24, 1865. The *Argus* noted with alarm the rising rate of indebtedness in town, city, and county throughout the state. *Ibid.*, Sept. 10, 1864.

[48] New York *Times*, March 9, 1864; April 3, 1865; *Freeman's Journal*, Aug. 12, 1864; Elmira *Daily Advertiser*, Aug. 25, 1864; Buffalo *Morning Express*, Oct. 7, 1864; March 28, 1865.

[49] Syracuse *Standard*, Feb. 10, 15, Aug. 15, 1864; Jan. 2, Feb. 2, 1865; *Argus*, June 1, 1864; Utica *Herald*, Aug. 31, 1864.

[50] Glens Falls *Republican*, Nov. 1, 1864; *Argus*, Jan. 20, 1865.

[51] Thomas M. Cooley, *Constitutional Limitations*, (Boston, 1874 3rd ed.), pp. 252-62. One case which attracted attention in New York developed in the spring of 1865 and involved a suit against one Truair, the Syracuse City Treasurer and Tax Receiver. An injunction was issued ordering Truair to desist from collecting a special bounty tax authorized by the supervisors of Onondaga County. In July the case was argued before State Supreme Court Justice Foster, who upheld the tax. An appeal was carried to the general term of the Supreme Court, which in October, also sustained the tax. Syracuse *Journal*, Sept. 25, Oct. 5, 1865. See Murdock, p. 18, for a discussion of Ohio's two most important bounty tax cases.

[52] *Historical Report*, 28th District.

[53] PMG, *Final Report*, I, p. 87.

[54] Poughkeepsie *Daily Eagle*, Jan. 11, 1864; Buffalo *Morning Express*, April 22, 1864.

[55] New York *Times*, July 3, 1864. An attempt by Oneida Supervisors to limit local bounties to three hundred dollars was defeated in August 1864. Utica *Herald*, Aug. 24, 1864. Andrew D. White, later President of Cornell University, was a member of the New York State Senate in 1864 when bounty legislation was introduced. He supported such legislation. *Autobiography of Andrew Dickson White* (2 vols., New York, 1905), I, p. 112.

[56] New York *Times*, Jan. 1, 1865. *Harpers Weekly* virtually ignored the bounty system for almost three solid years. The only time it spoke with an unmuted voice, was when it attacked the *Times* for opposing the Philadelphia petition. *Harpers Weekly*, Jan. 14, 1865.

[57] *Historical Reports*, 14th, 20th, 27th Districts.

58 *Historical Reports,* 20th, 24th, 27th, 28th Districts; Western Division.

59 *Historical Reports,* 14th, 20th, 24th Districts.

60 *Historical Reports,* 24th, 28th Districts; Western Division.

61 *Historical Reports,* 17th, 25th Districts.

CHAPTER 3.

1 PMG, *Final Report,* II, p. 132. The following table lists the eight Acting Assistant Provost Marshal Generals who served in New York during the war:

Division	AAPMG	Date of Service
Southern	Colonel Robert Nugent	4-18-63—10-28-63
	Brigadier General Williams Hays	10-27-63— 1-31-65
	Brigadier General E. W. Hinks	1-31-65— 2-27-65
	Major R. I. Dodge	2-27-65— 2- 1-66
Northern	Major Frederick Townsend	4-23-63— 2- 1-66
Western	Major A. S. Diven	5-15-63—12- 9-64
	Major John A. Haddock	12- 9-64— 4-10-65
	Major Samuel B. Hayman	4-10-65— 2- 1-66

2 *Ibid.,* pp. 136-39.

3 *OR,* III, p. 127.

4 *Historical Reports,* 17th, 19th Districts.

5 *Historical Report,* 24th District.

6 *Historical Report,* 19th District.

7 *OR,* III, pp. 133-34. Leach, pp. 256-58.

8 *Historical Report,* 17th District.

9 PMG, *Final Report,* I, p. 17; *OR,* III, p. 245. The exemption matter will be discussed later. A minor frustration developed in New York City in mid-June when the supply of enrolment blanks was temporarily exhausted. *Ibid.,* p. 360. Provost Marshal John Duffy of the 5th District who was later dismissed from office, complained to Fry in August that he could not enroll anyone because his headquarters had been destroyed in the Draft Riots and no one would rent him another one. *Ibid.,* pp. 628-29.

10 New York experienced little violence in enrolment resistance compared to such states as Pennsylvania, Indiana, and Illinois. When it came to draft resistance, however, New York stood alone as the worst state.

11 New York *Times,* May 31, June 14, 1863; *OR,* III, p. 490.

12 New York *Times,* Sept. 2, 1863; Syracuse *Standard,* Sept. 14, 1863; *Argus,* Sept. 22, 1863.

13 *OR,* III, pp. 347-49, 368-69. About a year later the same commissioner who freed Briody released four men who had been arrested for resisting the enrolment in the 7th District. The men had not been at the rooming house when the EO called and the proprietor knew only their last names. Enrolling blanks with the last name printed in were left, to be filled out by the men when they returned. When the EO came back the next day the men were still absent and

the blanks still blank, so their arrest was ordered. The commissioner, however, held that there was no evidence that they had refused to give their names or had resisted the enrolment, so he turned them loose. New York *Times*, June 5, 1864.

14 *OR*, III, pp. 595-96.

15 *Freeman's Journal*, July 31, Aug. 21, 1863. Nothing can be found as to the fate of the two Waldos.

16 *Argus*, Sept. 30, 1863.

17 *OR*, IV, p. 108. See also Diven's letter to Fry, Feb. 6, 1865, for another account of the difficulties which beset the enrolment process. *Ibid.*, pp. 1146-49.

18 PMG, *Final Report*, I, pp. 18-19; *OR*, III, pp. 700-01.

19 PMG, *Final Report*, II, pp. 113-14. We must keep in mind the distinction between the case where a name is removed from the enrolment list thereby making that person ineligible for the draft, and the case where a person properly enrolled is drafted but pleads exemption from service.

20 *Historical Report*, 24th District; Buffalo *Morning Express*, May 24, 1864; *Argus*, June 20, 1864; Jamestown *Journal*, July 29, 1864; Glens Falls *Republican*, Aug. 9, 1864.

21 *OR*, IV, pp. 935-36.

22 Elmira *Daily Advertiser*, Jan. 19, 1865; *Argus*, Nov. 22, Dec. 28, 1864; Jan. 10, 12, 14, 16, 17, 18, 20, 21, 23, 24, Feb. 21, 1865. Yet, as several provost marshals pointed out, enrolment revision generally meant removing very many names and adding very few names. It was a one-way proposition. In the 24th District, Snow noted that in January 1865, 596 were added, but 2,894 were deleted. Thorndike, in his report, observed that the supervisors at times "were overzealous in getting names dropped and underzealous in getting names added." *Historical Reports*, 24th, 17th Districts.

23 *OR*, III, pp. 478-79.

24 Buffalo *Morning Express*, July 14, Aug. 3, 1863; *Argus*, July 14, Sept. 29, 1863. Fry did advise Nugent and other AAPMG's, on the eve of the New York Draft Riots, that the draft should "be entirely public." *OR*, III, pp. 484-85.

25 *Historical Report*, 24th District.

26 Utica *Herald*, Aug. 26, 1863.

27 *Historical Reports*, 17th, 19th, 24th Districts.

28 Jamestown *Journal*, Aug. 21, 1863; Skaneateles *Democrat*, Aug. 27, 1863.

29 *Argus*, Aug. 14 (quoting Utica *Telegraph*), Sept. 30, 1863; Utica *Herald*, Aug. 26, 1863; Poughkeepsie *Daily Eagle*, Sept. 6, 1864.

30 *OR*, III, pp. 490, 496-97, 515-17, 528-30. One can almost hear a sigh of relief as Townsend reported "I have got through with Oswego without difficulty." *Ibid.*, p. 633. Provost Marshal Gordon wrote that the draft could not have been carried out in his district without the suspension of the writ of habeas corpus. *Historical Report*, 19th District.

31 *Annual Report of the Secretary of War* (1864), p. 56; Murdock, p. 25.

32 Hulburd to Stanton, May 6, 1865, "Fraud File," Record Group 110 (National Archives).

33 *OR*, IV, p. 580. See also the *Argus*, Aug. 25, 1864, for more examples of draft-flight at this time.

34 *Argus*, July 25, 1863; Dec. 14, 1864. The *Argus*, which had little use either for the draft or for Republicans, told the story of the man who said, "If I am drafted I shall go." He was drafted, and when last seen he was going—to Canada! No doubt he was a Republican. July 28, 1863. Similarly, a Negro barber in Ogdensburg was drafted, accepted, and given a short furlough to close out his affairs. Soon afterwards he left for Canada. The *Argus*, which liked Negro equality slightly less than it liked Republicans, moaned, "Oh, let my people go!" *Ibid.*, Aug. 18, 1863, quoting Ogdensburg *Advance*. About a year later the anti-Administration Glens Falls *Republican* reported that "a large number of 'sufferers' liable to the conscription, residing in this county, have lately skedaddled to Canada, the climate of which is considered peculiarly adapted to the cure of draft disease. We are informed that 18 young and robust gentlemen, 17 of whom were 'War Republicans,' left the vicinity of Luzerne Mountain last week for the land of the Kennucks." Aug. 30, 1864.

35 *OR*, III, p. 137.

36 Saratoga *Republican*, Aug. 12, 1864, quoting Lyons *Republican*; Buffalo *Morning Express*, Sept. 7, 1864; Murdock, p. 22.

37 New York *Times*, Aug. 4, 1863. Whether Ebner ever served in the army is not revealed. An Ohioan named Flannigan hanged himself to avoid a draft which never occurred. Murdock, p. 22.

38 Buffalo *Morning Express*, Aug. 10, 1863, quoting Rochester *Union*.

39 *Argus*, Aug. 15, 1863, quoting the Troy *Times*.

40 *Argus*, Feb. 6, 1864, quoting Kinderhook *Rough Notes*; Jamestown *Journal*, March 11, 1864, quoting Hornellsville *Tribune*.

41 The Oswego *Times*, after looking over the technical names on the list of disqualifying afflictions, wanted to know if a man who "has torticolls, anchylossis of the radius, paralyzation of the iter adertio ad quartem ventriculum, obliteratum of the lavater labii superiosis alequinasi, and besides, does not feel very well," would be exempt? Jamestown *Journal*, Sept. 18, 1863.

42 Shannon, II, p. 181.

43 Syracuse *Standard*, Oct. 3, 1863; New York *Times*, Oct. 6, 1863.

44 New York *Times*, July 31, 1863. Dr. Nelson E. Jones, surgeon for the 12th District in Ohio, discusses affidavits prepared by exemption agents in PMG, *Final Report*, II, pp. 93-94.

45 It should be remembered that the provost marshals were responsible for all voluntary enlistments which were to be charged against a district's quota, as well as for all draftee enlistments. The examination procedure for volunteers was similar to that for draftees, but since this chapter is devoted to the draft, I have referred only to draftee-recruits rather than volunteer-recruits.

46 *Historical Reports*, 17th, 19th, 24th Districts.

47 *Historical Report,* 19th District; Moon to Fry, Sept. 22, 1863, "Fraud File," Parsons, in the 14th District, described at great length his very rigid acceptance policy, yet he was accused by the Troy *Times* of taking anyone, especially Troy rejects. *Historical Report,* 14th District; *Argus,* Dec. 28, 1863. This was unfair, because in July 1864 a man turned down by Parsons for being too short was accepted a few hours later in Troy. *Ibid.,* July 21, 1864.

48 Utica *Herald,* Aug. 15, 1863. Larey Affidavit, Feb. 16, 1865; Stauchfield Affidavit, Feb. 16, 1865, "Baker File," Record Group 110 (National Archives).

49 Provost Marshal Isaac F. Quinby of the 28th District urged that the obvious physical exempts not be enrolled. It was a waste of time and money to transport them to the headquarters, examine them, and ship them back home. *Historical Report,* 28th District.

50 Syracuse *Standard,* Aug. 17, 1863, quoting Auburn *Advertiser.*

51 *Freeman's Journal,* Aug. 21, 1863, quoting Bangor *Times.*

52 New York *Times,* Aug. 12, 1863, quoting Providence *Journal; Argus,* Aug. 26, 1863, quoting Providence *Journal.* In similar fashion a Poughkeepsie exemption claimant soberly advised the enrolment board that he already had two brothers in state service at Sing Sing, and that he was the only son and support of a widowed mother now serving a jail sentence. *Ibid.,* Sept. 19, 1863.

53 *Argus,* Oct. 1, 1863, quoting Troy *Whig;* Utica *Herald,* June 20, 1864.

54 *Argus,* June 17, 1864; *Freeman's Journal,* July 31, 1863.

55 *Argus,* Sept. 19, 1863.

56 *Ibid.,* quoting New York *Sun.* A discussion of corrupt surgeons will be found below in Chapter Eight.

57 The name varied from place to place. In Ohio, for example, such an organization was called a "Mutual Protective Association." New Yorkers, however, preferred Draft Insurance Society.

58 Utica *Herald,* Sept. 28, 1863; Syracuse *Standard,* Aug. 15, 1864; Syracuse *Journal,* March 29, 1865.

59 Jamestown *Journal,* July 31, 1863; *Argus,* Aug. 6, 1863; July 12, 1864; Saratoga *Republican,* Aug. 26, 1864; Glens Falls *Republican,* April 4, 1865. Certainly many communities organized DIS's which were never reported in the press.

60 New York *Times,* July 24, 1863; Buffalo *Morning Express,* Aug. 19, 1863; Aug. 9, 1864.

61 *Ibid.,* Aug. 6, 1863.

62 New York *Times,* July 24, 1863; *Argus,* July 12, 21, Aug. 13, 16, 31, 1864; Jan. 30, 1865. The recruiting committees of Utica's First and Third Wards arbitrarily assessed each enrolled man twenty dollars in August 1864, the money to be used in securing volunteers. This, however, was dissimilar to the DIS, where the enrollees organized their own society and raised and disbursed the money themselves. Utica *Herald,* Aug. 11, 15, 1864.

63 *OR,* IV, pp. 1042-44, 1253-54.

CHAPTER 4.

[1] See above, p. 45.

[2] The substance of this chapter originally appeared as "Horatio Seymour and the 1863 Draft," *Civil War History*, XI (June 1965), 117-41. The first revisionist writings on Seymour, aside from Howard Carroll's brief chapter in 1883, were by Alexander J. Wall, one-time librarian for the New York State Historical Society. He wrote "The Administration of Governor Horatio Seymour During the War of the Rebellion and the Draft Riots in New York City, July 13-17, 1863, With the Events Leading up to Them," *Quarterly Bulletin of the New York Historical Society* (Oct. 1928), 79-115, the basis for a short book which appeared the following year, *A Sketch of the Life of Horatio Seymour, 1810-1886* (New York, 1929). Much more comprehensive, and the subject of considerable comment in this chapter, is the volume by Stewart Mitchell, *Horatio Seymour of New York* (Cambridge, 1938). The Carroll sketch of Seymour appeared in *Twelve Americans* (New York, 1883), pp. 1-47. A good traditional account of the matter can be found in William B. Weeden, *War Government: Federal and State in Massachusetts, New York, Pennsylvania, and Indiana* (Boston, 1906), pp. 284-307.

[3] *OR*, III, pp. 613-19, 636, 639-51.

[4] *OR*, III, pp. 640, 646, 649. In the nine New York City districts 175,430 men were enrolled, while the total quota was 33,729. In the nineteen upstate districts where the enrolment had been completed, 211,445 persons were enrolled, while the total quota was 39,626. *Ibid.*, p. 642; New York *Times*, Aug. 13, 1863. The nineteen upstate, pro-Lincoln districts had a total vote in 1860 of 457,257, while the nine metropolitan, anti-Lincoln districts had a total 1860 vote of 151,243. *OR*, III, p. 648. Seymour made much of the fact that though the upstate vote was three times that of the City, the respective quotas were about the same.

[5] *Ibid.*, pp. 635-36, 666-67. We do not propose to get bogged down in a discussion of the correctness of the quota system. Many problems existed and no doubt errors occurred. It seems apparent, however, that the government sought to administer the law in as impartial a manner as it could, and that any attempt to analyze the many reasons advanced for quota discrepencies would serve no purpose and lead us far afield.

[6] John G. Nicolay and John Hay, *Abraham Lincoln, A History*, rep. (10 vols., New York, 1904), VII, pp. 12-15; James B. Fry, *New York and the Conscription of 1863* (New York, 1885), pp. 12-15. In Albany, the pro-Administration *Journal* lost five of its staff to the draft, while the anti-Administration *Argus* lost only two to the draft. *Argus*, Sept. 30, 1863.

[7] Fry, *Conscription*, pp. 18, 32; James F. Rhodes, *History of the United States From the Compromise of 1850*, rep. (7 vols., New York, 1913), IV, p. 330; Sidney D. Brummer, *Political History of New York State During the Period of the Civil War* (New York, 1911), pp. 331-32.

[8] Morgan Dix, *Memoirs of John Adams Dix* (2 vols., New York, 1883), II, p. 83; *OR*, III, pp. 703-05; Carroll, p. 32.

[9] Fry, *Conscription*, pp. 14-15.

[10] *OR*, III, pp. 166, 169.

[11] *Ibid.*, pp. 167-68, 210, 217-18; Fry, *Conscription*, p. 17.

[12] *Ibid.*, pp. 22-23; *OR*, III, p. 471. Fry's account in *Conscription* is not in complete accord on this point with the correspondence published in the *Official Records*. Despite these discrepancies, however, it cannot be disputed that Seymour was definitely told by Fry that the draft had been ordered in the 8th and 9th Districts, those districts where the riots broke out, fully five days before the draft actually began.

[13] Dix, II, p. 84.

[14] *OR*, III, pp. 657-63, 728-29; Fry, *Conscription*, pp. 27-28.

[15] *Ibid.*, pp. 23-24.

[16] Carroll, p. 33; John B. McMaster, *A History of the People of the United States During Lincoln's Administration* (New York, 1927), p. 407; Mitchell, p. 307; Shannon, II, p. 208. To begin proceedings on Saturday, July 11, was particularly unfortunate, it was argued, because this permitted the Irish working-class elements, those most heavily hit by the draft, to read their names in the Sunday papers, to brood on that day of idleness, and resolve to do something about it when the draft would resume on Monday, July 13. Even sympathetic Morgan Dix commented that the time was "the most unfortunate that could possibly have been chosen." Dix, II, p. 72. Fry, on the other hand, dismissed this criticism of the Sunday "break." "It is true," he said, "that as Sunday intervened . . . a day was thus afforded for the operation of bad influences. But the same length of time was afforded for the operation of good influences, and perhaps it was admissible in this Christian land and in the loyal State of New York to hope for as much effect on Sunday from the latter as from the former." *Conscription*, pp. 30-31.

[17] Nicolay and Hay, VII, p. 18; *New York Times*, July 11, 1863; Rhodes, IV, p. 321; Shannon, II, p. 210; William Hesseltine, *Lincoln and the War Governors* (New York, 1955), p. 298.

[18] "The questions were," Fry wrote, "should the draft go on in New York City, as elsewhere, should it be abandoned or postponed there, or should resistance be assumed and military force presumably large enough to overawe or overcome a formidable uprising be concentrated in the city before trying to execute the law without such threatening preparations? These questions were carefully weighed by the President and by the War Department. The conclusions were that no exception in the application of the law should be made in New York. . . ." *Conscription*, pp. 28-30.

[19] It is not our purpose here to review the events of that infamous affair; our concern is with Seymour and his relations with Fry, Lincoln, and the government. For those who wish to read about the riots, dramatic accounts may be found in many places: Nicolay and Hay, VII, pp. 18-25; *Appleton's American Annual Cyclopedia*, 1863, pp. 811-16; Rhodes, IV, pp. 321-28; McMaster, pp. 407-13; and David M. Barnes, *The Draft Riots in New York* (New York, 1863). See

also Lawrence Lader's article in the *American Heritage* cited in footnote 1, Chapter 1.

20 Carroll, pp. 32-33; Mitchell, pp. 321-22.

21 Mitchell is right in revising the traditional interpretation of the "My Friends" speech, pp. 323-29. It was absurd to conclude that Seymour was condoning the monstrous acts of the rioters because he happened to address them as "friends." Under the pressure of the moment such a salutation was justified.

22 *OR*, Series I, XXVII, Part 2, pp. 895, 898, 901. Correspondence relating to the Draft Riots can be found in *ibid.*, pp. 875-940.

23 *OR*, III, pp. 494, 495, 496-97, 553.

24 Brummer, p. 220; James G. Randall, *Lincoln the President: Midstream* (New York, 1952), p. 305; Dix, II, p. 85; Mitchell, p. 340.

25 Dix, II, p. 85; Randall, p. 305. Mitchell not only denounces the Dix appointment, but he also fails even to mention the attempts to force the appointment of Butler, and the probable consequences of such an appointment.

26 Dix, II, p. 85. Dix, of course, was aware of the hardship to the Army of the Potomac which would follow the withdrawal of troops from the front for service in New York. *OR*, III, p. 592.

27 Dix, II, pp. 76-77; *OR*, III, p. 690.

28 *Ibid.*, III, pp. 592, 652-54; Dix, II, p. 78.

29 *OR*, III, pp. 552-53, 608-09, 665; Fry, *Conscription*, p. 77.

30 *OR*, III, pp. 671-72, 672-74, 677, 685-86, 693; Fry, *Conscription*, pp. 82-84; Dix, II, pp. 81-83; Randall, pp. 307-08.

31 Dix, II, p. 82.

32 From the hostile tone of the Seymour letter Fry concluded that the Governor would not have helped enforce the July draft "if he had known the very moment when the first name was to be drawn from the wheel by the Provost Marshal at the corner of Forty-sixth Street and Third Avenue, where the riot began." Fry, *Conscription*, pp. 43-44. Mitchell had a golden opportunity to discuss the letter on page 345, but could not bring himself to do it.

33 Randall, p. 308; Nicolay and Hay, VII, pp. 37-38; Brummer, p. 336; Fry, *Conscription*, pp. 44-45. On the progress of the draft resumption in New York City, see New York *Times*, Aug. 20, 1863, and *Harpers Weekly*, Sept. 5, 1863.

34 "Running recruits" was a legitimate object of complaint, but it was a practice by no means peculiar to New York City or New York state.

35 *OR*, III, pp. 635-36, 666-67, 703-05, 720-21, 727, 728-29; Dix, II, pp. 83-84; Brummer, pp. 329-30. In Seymour's letter to Lincoln of August 21, he included a number of enclosures, one of which was a copy of a letter Seymour purportedly sent to Fry on August 12. When Fry saw the August 21 letter he searched his office carefully, but found no trace of the "original" of the August 12 letter. *OR*, III, p. 729.

36 Mitchell, p. 344.

37 Brummer, pp. 329-30; Hesseltine, p. 302; Randall, pp. 311-12; *Harpers Weekly*,

Aug. 8, 1863. Only Brummer and Hesseltine mention this provocative phrase.

38 *OR*, III, pp. 650, 699-700.

39 Nicolay and Hay, VII, pp. 9, 40-42; Fry, *Conscription*, pp. 49-57; Mitchell, pp. 346-47. *OR*, IV, pp. 103-18.

40 Mitchell, pp. 341-44.

41 Rhodes, IV, p. 329; Jacob D. Cox, *Military Reminiscences of the Civil War* (2 vols., New York, 1900), I, p. 447; William H. H. Terrell, *Indiana in the War of the Rebellion*, rep. (Indianapolis, 1960), p. 66.

42 Nicolay and Hay, VII, p. 6; Fry, *The Conkling and Blaine-Fry Controversy in 1866* (New York, 1893), p. 18; Buffalo *Morning Express*, Aug. 4, 1863.

43 Shannon agrees that Seymour must "share . . . in the blame," II, p. 208.

CHAPTER 5.

1 PMG, *Final Report*, I, pp. 84-90. See Murdock, pages 26-34, for a general account of bounty-jumping in Ohio. The state's most famous case is described in E. C. Murdock, "The Bounty System in Cincinnati," *Bulletin, Cincinnati Historical Society*, XXIV (Oct. 1966), 278-84.

2 Poughkeepsie *Daily Eagle*, May 4, 1864.

3 John McElroy, *Andersonville: A Story of Rebel Prisons* (Philip Van Doren Stern edited this modern abridgment published in the Premier Civil War Classics Series, Greenwich, Conn., 1962), pp. 39, 53, 61-62, 102-03, 108-27.

4 Frank Wilkeson, *Recollections of a Private Soldier in the Army of the Potomac* (New York, 1887).

5 That Wilkeson received no bounty when he enlisted in the winter of 1863-64, is scarcely credible. It is difficult to see how anyone, no matter how patriotic he might be, could get into the army at that time without receiving some bounty. This fact compels one to read Wilkeson's entire narrative with some caution. While prone to occasional exaggeration and contradiction, he provides us with a vivid personal account of the bounty-jumper in barracks and camp and shows us what the private in the army thought of him.

6 Wilkeson, pp. 2-5.

7 *Ibid.*, pp. 2-3.

8 *Ibid.*, pp. 9-19.

9 *Argus*, Jan. 7, Nov. 29, 30, 1864; Buffalo *Morning Express*, June 2, 1864.

10 *Argus*, Dec. 5, 1864.

11 *Ibid.*, March 30, 1865. During the Utica bounty frauds of January 1865, Colonel N. G. Axtell, commanding officer of the 192nd, protested to Townsend against the quality of recruits then being assigned to that outfit. He wrote: "The men who have been received . . . from that city are, without doubt, 'bounty-jumpers,' and should not have been mustered by any intelligent mustering officer." Fry, *Conkling and Blaine-Fry Controversy*, p. 201.

12 *Argus*, Feb. 5, 1864; Poughkeepsie *Daily Eagle*, Feb. 6, March 11, 16, 1864.

13 Forsyth to Townsend, Dec. 10, 1864, "Fraud File"; Buffalo *Morning Express*, April 2, 1864. One paper complained that not more than forty men in one hundred ever reached the front, and demanded corrective action. So notorious were the security precautions at Camp Distribution near Washington, where newcomers were processed, that many recruits returned home on the very same train which had brought them south. Elmira *Daily Advertiser*, July 28, 1864. So accustomed did this writer become to epithets directed at bounty-jumpers that when he saw a headline, "The Rats Leaving Rochester," he was certain it was about jumpers. Actually the story dealt with another kind of rat—real ones.

14 Poughkeepsie *Daily Eagle*, Jan. 27, 1864; *Argus*, Jan. 25, 1864; New York *Times*, Sept. 25, 1863.

15 Buffalo *Morning Express*, Aug. 24, Sept. 15, 1863.

16 *Argus*, Oct. 10, Dec. 21, 1863.

17 *Ibid.*, Aug. 15, 1864, quoting the Troy *Whig*.

18 *Ibid.*, Jan. 21, 1865; Syracuse *Daily Journal*, July 20, 21, 1865; Glens Falls *Republican*, Jan. 26, 1864.

19 *Argus*, June 24, 25, 1864; March 16, 21, 1865.

20 *Ibid.*, June 9, 10, 11, 1864; (Columbus)*Ohio State Journal*, June 17, 1864, quoting Hartford *Times*.

21 *Argus*, June 9, 13, 1864.

22 *Ibid.*, June 9, 1864.

23 Utica *Herald*, Jan. 31, 1865; *Argus*, Jan. 30, 1865.

24 Utica *Herald*, Feb. 4, 1865, quoting Albany *Evening Journal*.

25 See Chapter Ten below.

26 New York *Times*, Aug. 9, 1863.

27 *Argus* Aug. 10, 1863; July 20, 1864.

28 *Ibid.*, July 31, 1863; April 18, 1864; March 14, 1865.

29Syracuse *Daily Standard*, Sept. 25, 1863; Jamestown *Journal*, Oct. 2, 1863, quoting Dunkirk *Union*; Buffalo *Morning Express*, Aug. 23, 1864.

30 *Argus*, Sept. 17, 1863; April 11, June 22, Aug. 24, Oct. 7, 1864; Feb. 16, 17, 20, March 29, 1865; Jamestown *Journal*, Feb. 19, 1864, quoting Dunkirk *Union*; Poughkeepsie *Daily Eagle*, Feb. 27, 1864; Syracuse *Daily Standard*, March 2, 1864; Elmira *Daily Advertiser*, Sept. 19, 1864.

31 *Argus*, July 13, 1864; March 4, 1865; Elmira *Daily Advertiser*, Sept. 23, 1864. The New York *Times*, July 29, 1863, quoting New Bedford (Mass.) *Mercury*, discusses another blanket-rope escape.

32 *Argus*, Aug. 15, 1864; March 9, 20, 1865.

33 *Ibid.*, Jan. 16, 1865.

34 Buffalo *Morning Express*, Aug. 21, 1863; May 6, 1864.

35 Report of Special Board of Inquiry, "Fraud File"; Buffalo *Morning Express*, Dec. 30, 1864.

36 *Ibid.*, March 30, 1865.

[37] Syracuse *Daily Standard*, Feb. 1, 1864; *Argus*, Feb. 8, 1865.

[38] *Ibid.*, March 16, 21, 29, 1865.

[39] Utica *Herald*, April 13, 1864; *Argus*, June 15, 1864; Buffalo *Morning Express*, April 30, 1864.

[40] *Argus*, June 27, 1864; Glens Falls *Republican*, March 21, 1865; Buffalo *Morning Express*, May 30, 1864.

[41] Poughkeepsie *Daily Eagle*, Sept. 16, 1863.

[42] Buffalo *Morning Express*, March 30, 1864; *Argus*, May 11, 18, Aug. 3, 1864.

[43] Syracuse *Daily Standard*, Aug. 6, 1863.

[44] *Ibid.*, Aug. 31, 1864.

[45] Poughkeepsie *Daily Eagle*, Sept. 2, 1863; Buffalo *Morning Express*, Sept. 1, 1863, quoting the Elmira *Press*.

[46] Elmira *Daily Advertiser*, July 27, 1864. Yet it was not long after this that the *Daily Advertiser* strangely observed, "Never before, perhaps, was a better class of human material being secured for our armies. . . ." Sept. 14, 1864.

[47] New York *Times*, Aug. 11, 1864.

[48] Poughkeepsie *Daily Eagle*, Feb. 4, 1864; Jamestown *Journal*, Feb. 26, 1864, quoting Dunkirk *Union*.

[49] Syracuse *Daily Standard*, Sept. 26, 1864; Poughkeepsie *Daily Eagle*, Feb. 16, 1864; Elmira *Daily Advertiser*, Feb. 13, 1865. See Murdock, p. 30, for an amusing incident, somewhat comparable to that which occurred in downtown Elmira.

[50] New York *Times*, Aug. 31, 1863; Utica *Herald*, Sept. 8, 1863.

[51] *Argus*, April 26, 27, 1864. A substitute, who had not yet jumped any bounty, was executed at the Elmira Barracks in February 1864 for poisoning a guard and several fellow soldiers. Since he appears to have been made of the proper stuff for bounty-jumping, we thought we should mention him here. Syracuse *Daily Standard*, Feb. 25, 1864.

[52] *Argus*, Aug. 17, Sept. 24, Oct. 27, 1864. A desperado from Utica named Thomas Baker, who killed a man at Oriskany in the winter of 1863-64, escaped and enlisted in the army. After deserting a few times, he was recognized as a bounty-jumper-murderer, while at New Bern, North Carolina. Tried and convicted, he was executed at New Bern in August 1864. Utica *Herald*, April 2, 1864; Syracuse *Daily Standard*, Aug. 24, 1864.

[53] A. P. Smith, *History of the 76th Regiment New York Volunteers* (Cortland, N. Y., 1867), pp. 260-62.

[54] New York *Times*, Feb. 4, 1865.

[55] *Argus*, Aug. 30, 1864; Elmira *Daily Advertiser*, Dec. 28, 1864; Harry M. Caudill, *Night Comes to the Cumberland* (Boston, 1963), p. 48. A deserter from the 95th Regiment who was caught at Hudson in September 1864, bore the surprising name of Abram Rockefeller. Poughkeepsie *Daily Eagle*, Sept. 6, 1864.

[56] *Argus*, April 12, 13, 1864; Syracuse *Daily Standard*, April 13, 1864.

[57] *Argus*, Dec. 16, 1863; Syracuse *Daily Standard*, Dec. 19, 1863.

⁵⁸ Poughkeepsie *Daily Eagle*, April 27, 1864. It was only three days later that the *Eagle* reported that bounty-jumpers could make good soldiers.

⁵⁹ *Ibid.*, April 30, May 3, 24, 1864.

⁶⁰ *Argus*, July 29, 1864.

⁶¹ Poughkeepsie *Daily Eagle*, Aug. 4, 6, 1864.

⁶² William F. Raney, "Recruiting and Crimping in Canada for the Northern Forces, 1861-1865," *Mississippi Valley Historical Review*, X (June 1923), 21.

⁶³ Buffalo *Morning Express*, March 12, 1864; Elmira *Daily Advertiser*, July 26, 1864; *Argus*, Aug. 1, 1864.

⁶⁴ *Argus*, March 30, 1864; Feb. 4, 1865.

⁶⁵ Elmira *Daily Advertiser*, Sept. 21, 1864; Murdock, p. 27.

⁶⁶ *Ibid.*, p. 31; Elmira *Daily Advertiser*, Dec. 8, 1864.

⁶⁷ *Argus*, Aug. 15, Sept. 17, 18, 20, 21, 23, 24, Oct. 4, 7, 1864.

⁶⁸ Elmira *Daily Advertiser*, July 28, 1864; Buffalo *Morning Express*, March 8, 1865.

⁶⁹ *Ibid.*, Feb. 14, 1865.

⁷⁰ Elmira *Daily Advertiser*, Feb. 8, 1865.

CHAPTER 6.

¹ The substance of this chapter originally appeared as "New York's Civil War Bounty Brokers," *Journal of American History*, LIII (Sept. 1966), 259-78. See Murdock, pages 34-52, for an account of the broker system in Ohio.

² General Winfield S. Hancock asserted that brokers dominated five-sixths of the recruiting business. *OR*, IV, p. 1089. See the New York *Times*, Aug. 25, 27, 1864, for specific cases where it was next to impossible to enlist without broker participation.

³ Syracuse *Daily Standard*, Jan. 16, 1865; Elmira *Advertiser*, Dec. 2, 1864; New York *Times*, July 30, 1863; Utica *Herald*, Aug. 29, 1864; Buffalo *Morning Express*, Aug. 18, 1863; Jan. 18, 1865; Syracuse *Journal*, Feb. 18, 1865.

⁴ Elmira *Daily Advertiser*, July 21, 1864; Buffalo *Morning Express*, Aug. 13, 1863.

⁵ Syracuse *Daily Standard*, July 19, 1864. A bill was introduced in the New York State legislature in February 1872 to appropriate $1,000 for back pay for Maynard and Griswold. Syracuse *Journal*, Feb. 23, 1872.

⁶ The details of Blunt's system may be found in the "Spinola Court-Martial," MM 1527, Record Group 153 (National Archives). It is summarized below, pp. 174-75.

⁷ *Historical Report*, 14th District; *Argus*, Aug. 6, 1864.

⁸ Mosher to Dalton, Dec. 6, 1864, "Baker File."

⁹ MM 2612, "Haddock Court-Martial," Record Group 153, (National Archives).

¹⁰ New York *Times*, Aug. 7, 1864, quoting Troy *Times*; Glens Falls *Republican*, Jan. 12, 1864, quoting Scoharie *Republican*.

11 *Argus*, Dec. 12, 1863; Feb. 22, 1865, quoting Elmira *Advertiser*; Elmira *Advertiser*, Jan. 31, 1865.

12 John Parnall to Baker, March 7, 1865, "Baker File"; New York *Times*, Dec. 28, 1863.

13 *Argus*, Feb. 9, 1865; Jamestown *Journal*, Sept. 9, 1864, quoting Dunkirk *Journal*; Poughkeepsie *Daily Eagle*, Feb. 28, 1865.

14 Syracuse *Journal*, March 23, Dec. 19, 1864.

15 *Argus*, July 14, 1864, quoting Troy *Press*.

16 Elmira *Daily Advertiser*, July 4, 1864.

17 *Argus*, Sept. 1 (quoting Rochester *Democrat*), 18, 1863.

18 East to Archbold, Nov. 1, 1863; Archbold to Lyons, Nov. 12, 1863; Lyons to Seward, Nov. 19, 1863; Seward to Stanton, Nov. 21, 1863, "Fraud File"; New York *Times*, Nov. 9, 1863. A son of the famous African explorer David Livingstone arrived in the United States sometime in 1864, was enlisted by a broker in the 30th New Hampshire Volunteer Regiment, and was listed as missing after a skirmish at Richmond in October of that year. *Harpers Weekly*, April 8, 1865.

19 Ella Lonn, *Foreigners in the Union Army and Navy* (Baton Rouge, 1951), pp. 455, 456, 457.

20 *Ibid.*, pp. 451, 452, 469.

21 Matthew H. Stein to Baker, March 1, 1865; Edward Bourke to Baker, May 21, 1865, "Baker File."

22 U. S. *Statutes at Large*, XIII, 1 Sess. pp. 385-87.

23 New York *Times*, Aug. 19 (quoting Springfield *Republican*), 26, Sept. 15, 17, 1864. Gunther, a Democrat, was elected mayor in the fall of 1863.

24 New York *Times*, Aug. 26, 1864 (quoting Quebec *Chronicle*, Aug. 18, 1864). It is safe to say that Teft was on his own and that his behavior did not reflect official government policy.

25 Marguerite B. Hamer, "Luring Canadian Soldiers into Union Lines During the War Between the States," *Canadian Historical Review*, XXVII (June 1946), 151-52; Raney, 28.

26 *Ibid.*, 28-30.

27 Hamer, 152, 155; Robin W. Winks, *Canada and the United States: The Civil War Years* (Baltimore, 1960), pp. 197-98.

28 *Argus*, Nov. 9, 1863. See Murdock, pp. 39-41, for an account of Ohio brokers who regularly ran recruits to Detroit and Buffalo.

29 New York *Times*, July 31, 1863 (quoting Philadelphia *Enquirer*), Aug. 18, 1863, quoting Providence *Journal*.

30 Not to be confused with Samuel Gordon, provost marshal of the 19th District.

31 Utica *Herald*, April 16, 18, 19, 1864; Syracuse *Standard*, April 16, 1864; Syracuse *Journal*, April 16, 18, 19, 1864.

32 Utica *Herald*, Dec. 22, 1864; Syracuse *Standard*, Dec. 23, 1864.

[33] Teall to Townsend, Jan. 8, 1864, "Fraud File."

[34] New York *Times*, March 12, 1864.

[35] Buffalo *Morning Express*, March 14, 1865; New York *Times*, Aug. 27, 1864, quoting Detroit *Advertiser*. See Murdock, p. 40, an for account of Ohio's most celebrated "doper-broker," Joe Fitzpatrick of Toledo. *Harpers Weekly*, Jan. 23, 1864, carries a cartoon showing a broker bringing a decrepit old man into a barber shop for preliminary doping.

[36] *Argus*, Aug. 4, 1864, quoting St. Louis *Democrat*.

[37] Syracuse *Journal*, Sept. 16, 1864, quoting Rochester *Democrat*.

[38] *Argus*, June 29, 1864; Utica *Herald*, Sept. 3, 1864.

[39] Certain Poughkeepsie operators were alleged to have made at least $10,000 apiece during the second draft, while James Cook who robbed John Robinson, reportedly amassed a "fortune." Franklin Krum of Scoharie, accumulated $15,000 in broker activities before he was drafted in June 1864. Needless to say, he had little trouble in furnishing a substitute. Probably the most affluent broker, however, was Theodore Allen of New York City, who purportedly made over $100,000 in his interstate operations. Poughkeepsie *Daily Eagle*, Aug. 24, 1864; New York *Times*, March 12, May 21, 1864; *Argus*, June 25, 1864.

[40] Syracuse *Standard*, Aug. 22, Nov. 19, 1863. Similarly, William Ketcheson was prosecuted in Utica in the fall of 1864 for enticing a soldier to desert and go as a substitute; broker James Riley was also guilty of this practice in both Buffalo and Rochester. Utica *Herald*, Sept. 1, 1864; Buffalo *Morning Express*, Nov. 19 (quoting Oswego *Times*), 23, 1863.

[41] Col. N. P. Chipman to Fry, June 14, 1865, "Fraud File"; Lafayette C. Baker, *History of the United States Secret Service*, (Philadelphia, 1867), pp. 427-28.

[42] New York *Times*, Dec. 5, 1863; Poughkeepsie *Daily Eagle*, Feb. 28, 1865; *Argus*, June 2, 1864, quoting Rochester *Union*.

[43] New York *Times*, Feb. 28, March 5, 1864.

[44] *Ibid.*, Jan. 24, Feb. 5, 6, 28, March 26, 1864.

[45] Syracuse *Standard*, Aug. 15, 1864, quoting Buffalo *Courier*; Buffalo *Morning Express*, Jan. 11, 1865.

[46] Poughkeepsie *Daily Eagle*, Jan. 13, Feb. 18, 1864; Jan. 8, 1865; Buffalo *Morning Express*, Feb. 16, 1864, quoting Albany *Knickerbocker*.

[47] Poughkeepsie *Daily Eagle*, July 27, 1864; January 23, 1865.

[48] Buffalo *Morning Express*, Sept. 3, 1864; *Argus*, Dec. 12, 1863 (quoting Goshen *Democrat*); Feb. 9, 1865.

[49] *Harpers Weekly*, Sept. 24, 1864.

[50] Poughkeepsie *Daily Eagle*, Aug. 10, 1864, quoting Poughkeepsie *Press*. An improbable story appeared in a midwestern paper about a jokester who told a broker he would sell him an Indian for one hundred dollars. The broker raced off to the address given him only to find that the Indian was wooden. Still the disappointed broker philosophized, "He is better than some live men

248   *Patriotism Limited.*

that have gone as substitutes." Saratoga *Republican,* March 3, 1865, quoting Detroit *Advertiser.*

51 Elmira *Daily Advertiser,* July 30, 1864; Syracuse *Journal,* Feb. 21, 1865.

52 *Argus,* Jan. 25, 1864.

53 MM 1527: "Report of Special Committee on Volunteering"; "Trial Transcript." See below, p. 175.

54 New York *Times,* Dec. 13, 16, 1863; *Argus,* Dec. 14, 1863. The *Argus,* however, quickly retreated to its "necessary evil" position. Admitting that the brokerage system had many faults, it added that "the success that has attended recruiting the past Fall is, to a great extent, attributable to these [broker] agencies." *Ibid.,* Dec. 15, 1863.

55 New York *Times,* Dec. 16, 22, 1863. The point that the *Times,* Dec. 16, 1863, makes here may seem valid on its face, but the truth was that brokers were not interested only in "expenses" as the paper implies. Brokers generally wanted as much of the bounty money as they could possibly obtain. No reasonable relationship whatever existed between broker expenses and broker profits.

56 New York *Times,* Dec. 22, 1863.

57 *Ibid.,* Dec. 16, 1863; New York *Tribune,* Feb. 16, 1864.

58 New York *Times,* Jan. 27, Feb. 4, 1865. Of course, many of these upstate quotas were being filled with fraudulent enlistments, which, after Colonel Baker's investigation, were all invalidated.

59 *Argus,* June 30, July 27, 28, 1864. Parsons defended his tough policy toward substitutes and brokers in his final report to Fry. Bounty crimes, he said, had grown to such alarming proportions that unless checked, they would "have resulted in the theft of all the money without the furnishing of a single recruit." In the absence of any safeguard, he continued,

> I found the only remedy to be to reject every recruit that by the best judgment I could give in the matter, I believed to be dishonest. . . . I based my action . . . upon the conviction that my duty to the government as a mustering officer was not simply to fill the quota of my district on paper but to furnish to the service *men*—men not simply able physically to perform the duties of a soldier but men who would not desert the service . . . men who would be true to their enlistment, to their oath, and to their country. *Historical Report,* 14th District.

60 *Argus,* July 26, 27, 29, 1864.

61 Syracuse *Standard,* Aug. 15, 1864, quoting Rochester *Express.*

62 New York *Times,* Aug. 28, 1864.

63 Murdock. p. 48.

64 Saratoga *Republican,* July 15, 1864; *Argus,* March 15, 16, 1865.

65 *Annual Report of the Adjutant-General of the State of New York for 1863* (Albany, 1864), p. 32; *Laws of the State of New York* (1864), p. 2.

66 OR, IV, pp. 203-04; Elmira *Daily Advertiser,* Dec. 30, 1864; Syracuse *Standard,* Dec. 29, 1864.

67 *Argus,* Aug. 8, 1864; Poughkeepsie *Daily Eagle,* Aug. 3, 1864. Nothing more was heard of the income tax suggestion.

68 *Argus,* March 18, 1865.

69 Murdock, p. 50.

70 *Laws of the State of New York* (1865), pp. 41-42; *U.S. Statutes at Large,* XIII, 2 Sess. pp. 489-90. It is pleasant to contemplate the possibilities had these laws been on the books two years earlier.

71 *Historical Reports,* 14th, 27th Districts; AAPMG, Western Division; PMG, *Final Report,* I, pp. 86-87.

CHAPTER 7.

1 Baker, pp. 398-99; PMG, *Final Report,* I, p. 87.

2 A major problem in writing this chapter has been the unreliability of Baker himself as an historical source. Many of his contemporaries and most later scholars insist that he was a fraud and dismiss his book, *History of the United States Secret Service,* as practically worthless. A House of Representatives committee charged him with "deliberate perjury." In spite of this body of opinion, however, Baker's role in the annals of the New York bounty system cannot be omitted. He did investigate and break up broker operations in New York City, and he did organize the fantastic Hoboken entrapment, which netted one hundred and eighty-three jumpers and twenty-seven brokers. His work was warmly praised by Fry. Since these matters were fully reported in the daily press and in the case of the Hoboken raids, in a congressional report as well, we do have a little more to rely on than only Baker's account. Consequently, even though errors might creep into the story, that story is accurate in its essentials and is sufficiently important to be included in this study.

3 Jacob H. Mogolever, *Death to Traitors* (New York, 1960), pp. 30, 31, 35-36, 39-40, 86-88.

4 *Ibid.,* pp. 100, 107-08, 109-10, 111, 117-27, 279-80.

5 Baker, p. 399.

6 Baker commented that practically all the brokers were illiterate.

7 He was really still a colonel.

8 Baker, pp. 399-401, 431-33.

9 This is no doubt one of Baker's improbable stories. What a notary public had to do with recruitment is not easy to determine.

10 Baker, pp. 400-01, 404-05.

11 *Ibid.,* pp. 408-10.

12 New York *Times,* Feb. 8, 1865.

13 *Ibid.,* Feb. 10, 11, 14, 1865.

14 *Ibid.,* Feb. 14, 1865.

15 *Ibid.,* Feb. 10, 11, 14, 1865; MM 2598, Record Group 153 (National Archives); MM 2612.

16 New York *Times*, Feb. 8, 1865.

17 Baker, p. 406; New York *Times*, Feb. 8, 1865.

18 *Ibid.*, Feb. 11, 1865.

19 Baker, p. 406; New York *Times*, Feb. 8, 11, 1865.

20 *Ibid.*, Feb. 12, 1865.

21 Baker, pp. 438-41. This might be another instance where Baker's veracity could be questioned. This triple-enlistment seems incredible, but then the bounty system itself was incredible and maybe it did happen the way Baker reported it.

22 *Ibid.*, pp. 441-43.

23 *Ibid.* pp. 444-45.

24 *Ibid.*, pp. 411-12; New York *Times*, March 12, 1865.

25 Baker, pp. 412-13; New York *Times*, March 12, 1865.

26 Baker, pp. 411, 434; New York *Times*, March 12, 1865.

27 House of Representatives, *Reports of the Committees*, 39 Cong., 1 Sess., vol. 1, no. 93, pp. 169, 332. (Hereafter cited as HR Report 93.) New York *Times*, May 21, 1864.

28 HR Report 93, pp. 160-62, 170, 171, 332. Baker had first contacted Allen at the office of Marcus Stanly, a friend of Allen's, at 86 Nassaau Street, late in January 1865, and enlisted his services in the fraudulent enlistment investigation. *Ibid.*, p. 170.

29 *Ibid.*, p. 25; New York *Times*, March 12, 13, 1865. Allen testified that the brokers usually got two hundred dollars and the jumpers four hundred dollars, while he kept from twenty-five to fifty dollars on each man. If the recruit came without a broker, Allen said the recruit got the full amount and he [Allen] retained nothing, which seems hard to believe. HR Report 93, p. 163.

30 *Ibid.*, pp. 163-64; New York *Times*, March 12, 13, 1865; Baker, pp. 434-35.

31 *Ibid.*, p. 435; New York *Times*, March 12, 1865.

32 *Ibid.*

33 HR Report 93, p. 181.

34 Baker, p. 414; HR Report 93, pp. 25-26, 236, 333.

35 Baker, pp. 415-16; HR Report 93, pp. 236, 333-34; New York *Times*, March 26, 1865.

36 HR Report 93, pp. 164-66. See Appendix C for the Fry-Conkling dispute.

37 HR Report 93, pp. 32, 237-38, 334-35; Baker, pp. 416-17; New York *Times*, March, 26, 1865.

38 Baker, pp. 417-24; HR Report 93, pp. 32, 174-75, 335. Following Fry's order to arrest Allen, Henry Raymond, editor of the New York *Times* and member of Congress from the Sixth Congressional District, where Allen lived, wrote Fry asking that the broker be treated fairly. Raymond later saw both Fry and Stanton, requesting that the Hoboken credits be allowed and that Allen not be persecuted. *Ibid.*, 249-54. There was a touch of irony in this because the *Times* was one of Allen's most outspoken critics. Allen stayed in Canada for four of five months before returning home. By that time the credits had been

allowed and he was in the clear. During his exile he traveled four times to Boston "to get my tea." *Ibid.*, p. 174.

39 Mogolever, pp. 330-31.

40 Baker, pp. 424-26.

41 Wall Affidavit, March 30, 1865; Williams Affidavit, April 21, 1865; John H. Bergen to Fry, July 11, 1865, "Fraud File"; Elmira *Daily Advertiser*, April 17, 1865, quoting New York *World*.

CHAPTER 8.

1 PMG, *Final Report*, II, pp. 137-38; Clendon to Fry, Nov. 19, 1863, "Fraud File." The resignation of Surgeon George Page in November 1863 appears to have been unrelated to the fraudulent exemption cases, which broke at the same time.

2 Baker to Fry, Feb. 8, 1865; Foot to Gen. C. McKeever, Feb. 22, 1865; Brand to McKeever, Feb. 20, 1865, "Fraud File." Baker must have hinted that Foot and Brand also knew about the frauds, but both denied such knowledge and attributed the charges to persons who had been damaged by their exposure of the illegal transactions. These accusations were apparently considered false, and Foot and Brand received honorable discharges when the war was over. PMG, *Final Report*, II, pp. 137-38.

3 The charges against Duffy are contained in an undated document, "Fraud File." John Kink (Recruiting officer, 16th New York Artillery) to Hays, Nov. 30, 1863; Duffy to Fry, July 24, 1866, *Ibid.*; OR, III, pp. 628-29.

4 Charles Goddard to Fry, May 19, 1864, "Fraud File."

5 Ruggles to Fry, March 11, 1864, "Fraud File."

6 Goddard to Fry.

7 *Ibid.*; Schafer to Prussian Ambassador, Jan. 22, 1864, "Fraud File."

8 *Ibid.*

9 *Ibid.*

10 Endorsements on Goddard letter include Fry's dismissal statement. There must have been some re-transcribing of these endorsements, however, because they were actually written almost a month before the Goddard letter.

11 Gregory to Fry, April 23, 1864, "Fraud File."

12 Gregory to Harris, May 14, 1864, "Fraud File."

13 W. M. Hawley to some general, whose name is illegible, Aug. 1, 1863, "Fraud File."

14 Grover had been an Anti-Mason, Whig, Free Soiler, and Republican, voting for Lincoln in 1860, but after the war broke out he became a Copperhead. He denounced Greenbacks, the President, and the use of Negro troops, while defending the Ft. Pillow massacre and describing Union troops as "Bull Runners." Fry was not happy with Grover's handling of this investigation, but conceded that he had "persons who indorse him on general principles." *Harpers Weekly*, Nov. 11, 1865; OR, III, p. 708.

[15] New York *Times*, Aug. 18, 1863, quoting Elmira *Press*; *Argus*, Aug. 19, 1863, quoting Angelica *Reporter*.

[16] *Argus*, Aug. 15, 19, 1863, quoting Angelica *Reporter*.

[17] Todd to Lincoln, Aug. 6, 1863, "Fraud File."

[18] *Argus*, Aug. 19, 1863, quoting Angelica *Reporter*.

[19] Diven to Todd, Aug. 17, 1863, "Fraud File." Diven's comment on Graves' son is contained in an endorsement on an affidavit concerning private physical fitness examinations given by Graves, Sept. 11, 1863, *Ibid*; *OR*, III, p. 708; PMG, *Final Report*, II, pp. 138-39. It should be recalled that the 27th District had the largest turnover in enrolment board personnel in the state, with four provost marshals, four commissioners, and two surgeons. See above, p. 42. As for Harmon, a month after his resignation, he established himself as a recruiting agent in Elmira, offering to pay large bounties to volunteers and substitutes. Business may not have been too good because in March 1865 he enlisted in the army as a substitute and was on Riker's Island awaiting shipment south. Elmira *Advertiser*, Aug. 26, 1864; March 7, 1865.

[20] Eckert to Stanton, Nov. 12, 1863, "Fraud File." Townsend transmitted Eckert's letter to Fiero, who replied on Dec. 1. *Ibid.*; *Historical Report*, 13th District.

[21] New York *Times*, Jan. 22, 1865. *Harpers Weekly* noted that some bad surgeons had been appointed and that the people blamed the Federal Government. This was unfair, however, because all such appointments were based on local character testimonials, and consequently the people themselves in a given community were responsible for all appointments. They should be more careful whom they recommended. Jan. 21, 1865.

[22] Poughkeepsie *Daily Eagle*, Feb. 18, 27, 1864. No reference to the Platt case can be found in the "Fraud File."

[23] Col. C. E. Brooks to Diven, Nov. 9, 1863; Riley to Fry, Oct. 8, 1864, "Fraud File"; PMG, *Final Report*, II, p. 139.

[24] Ludington to Townsend, Jan. 29, 1864, "Fraud File."

[25] *Ibid.*

[26] *Ibid*; PMG, *Final Report*, II, p. 137.

[27] Ludington to Townsend, Dec. 9, 1863, "Fraud File." Provost Marshal Thorndike reported that Judd performed his duties acceptably until the day the supervisors recommended his ouster, after which he was guilty of regular intemperance, thereby disqualifying himself for office. Thorndike to Townsend, Dec. 4, 1863, *Ibid*. In his final report, Thorndike wrote that much of the board's success was due to the diligent and untiring efforts of William Stephenson, Judd's successor. *Historical Report*, 17th District.

[28] Ludington to Townsend, Jan. 29, 1864, "Fraud File."

[29] *Ibid*. The criticism of Holley for his Democratic Party allegiance apparently became too strong to resist, because his appointment was revoked in December 1864. PMG, *Final Report*, II, p. 137.

[30] Townsend to Grimes Aug. 20, 1864; Grimes to Townsend, Aug. 25, 1864,

"Fraud File"; PMG, *Final Report,* II, p. 137. Van Dusen was the second surgeon in the 12th District to have his appointment revoked. William M. Pitcher, who first held the post was dismissed on Feb. 13, 1864. Van Dusen's successor, T. C. Payne, managed to hang on and received an honorable discharge. *Ibid.*

31 Lee to C. T. Dana, Oct. 12, 1864, "Fraud File"; PMG, *Final Report,* II, p. 137.

32 H. Clarke to Fry, March 31, 1865, "Fraud File"; PMG, *Final Report,* II, p. 139. The petitioners had sent their request to Clarke, Comptroller of the Currency, who forwarded it to Fry along with a cover letter from which the quoted passages were taken.

33 "Charges and Specifications Preferred Against All 3 Enrolment Board Members of 4th District," undated, "Fraud File."

34 Erhardt to Fry, Jan. 28, 1864, "Fraud File."

35 *Ibid.* Erhardt denied flatly that McFarland drank excessively or was ever drunk on duty, and produced half a dozen affidavits to document his opinion.

36 George W. Ernst to Major L. C. Turner, Sept. 19, 1863, "Fraud File."

37 "John Williams" to some unidentified person, Sept. 21, 1863; Brooks to Diven, Nov. 9, 1863, "Fraud File." Scroggs made mistakes, as the Larey Case (see above, p. 57) demonstrates, but they appear to have been honest errors of judgment.

38 Sitterly Affidavit, April 1, 1865, "Baker File."

39 Sitterly also stated that if his men were rejected at Owego he would have taken them to Norwich, headquarters for Gordon's 19th District. He had been told that his fellow brokers "had a sure thing at Norwich until the provost marshal at Utica wrote to the provost marshal at Norwich and spoiled it." *Ibid.* Again it should be noted that, although Gordon was under fire frequently, he was one of the eleven provost marshals who served the full term.

40 Parks to Stanton, Aug. 3, 1863; Hughes to Townsend, Aug. 19, 1863, "Fraud File." After the investigation was over Hughes wrote a peppery letter to Parks telling him to come to the provost marshal the next time he had a complaint to make and leave the Secretary of War alone. Hughes added that Parks' own exemption was under review and that he was to report back for another examination. If at that time his exemption should be revoked he would be treated as a deserter. Hughes to Parks, undated, *Ibid.*

41 L. C. Turner to Fry, March 29, 1865, "Fraud File." The details of Forsyth's system are related in a miscellaneous collection of documents which I will not bother to itemize.

42 *Ibid.*

43 Forsyth Case, "Fraud File"; PMG, *Final Report,* II, p. 137.

44 New York *Times,* Aug. 30, Oct. 8, Nov. 15, 17, 1863. The Fraud File," unfortunately, contains nothing on this interesting case.

45 Riley to Fry, Oct. 20, Nov. 12, 1864, "Fraud File."

46 *Ibid.*

47 *Ibid.* Hart, by the way, was elected to Congress in 1864, resigning as provost

marshal on Jan. 17, 1865. He served only one term, being defeated for reelection in 1866.

48 Diven to Fry, Nov. 23, 1864, "Fraud File."

49 *Ibid.* It might also be added in connection with Hart's running for Congress and Knapp's father engaging in the brokerage business, that there were no laws prohibiting such activity, so Diven could hardly be saddled with the responsibility for permitting it.

CHAPTER 9.

1 New York *Times,* April 16, 1864.

2 *Ibid.*

3 MM 1527. The Spinola court-martial packet contains the "Charges and Specifications," "Report of Special Committee on Volunteering," "Report of the Judge Advocate General on the Spinola Court-Martial" (hereafter called "Holt's Report), the "Trial Transcript," an important letter from Major Halpine to Dix, dated February 18, 1864, and a mass of exhibits.

4 "Trial Transcript." Although Halpine was referring to general conditions in the city, he also had Lafayette Hall specifically in mind.

5 New York *Times,* April 16, 1864.

6 "Charges and Specifications."

7 "Report of Special Committee on Volunteering"; "Trial Transcript." Blunt's plan is mentioned briefly above, p. 109.

8 "Report of Special Committee on Volunteering"; "Trial Transcript"; Halpine to Dix, Feb. 18, 1864.

9 "Trial Transcript"; "Holt's Report." See above, pp. 125-26, for an account of the unsuccessful attempts made at this time to develop a plan whereby the recruits would get their full bounty.

10 "Trial Transcript."

11 New York *Times,* April 16, 1864; "Trial Transcript."

12 *Ibid.*

13 *Ibid.* Throughout his entire testimony, Blunt hinted that all the trouble at Lafayette Hall was due to the government's officers and that the only improvements ever made there resulted from his own recommendations.

14 *Ibid.*

15 *Ibid.*; "Holt's Report."

16 New York *Times,* April 16, 1864; *Argus,* Jan. 14, 1864; "Trial Transcript"; Halpine to Dix; "Holt's Report."

17 New York *Times,* April 14, 1864; *Argus,* Jan. 14, 1864; Halpine to Dix.

18 "Trial Transcript."

19 *Ibid.*

20 *Ibid.*

21 *Ibid.*

22 *Ibid.*

23 Halpine to Dix.

24 "Holt's Report."

25 "Trial Transcript."

26 New York *Times,* April 16, 1864.

27 "Trial Transcript"; Halpine to Dix. John Lomas testified that Clapp worked closely with several brokers, Mose Monaghan, One Norton, Peter Reilly, Theodore Allen, and one or two others, but denied that Clapp "had done anything wrong at Lafayette Hall." "Trial Transcript." Clapp, on the other hand, insisted that he was not a broker, knew no brokers, and had no dealings with any brokers. *Ibid.* Clapp also accused Dix of trying to bribe him to give evidence against Spinola, something he refused to do. *Ibid.*

28 "Charges and Specifications."

29 "Holt's Report."

30 *Ibid.*

CHAPTER 10.

1 Roscoe Conkling served two terms in Congress, from 1859-1863; he was defeated for reelection in 1862, but ran successfully again in 1864.

2 Elmira *Daily Advertiser,* Dec. 13, 1864.

3 Syracuse *Standard,* Dec. 23, 1864; *OR,* IV, p. 920; Buffalo *Morning Express,* Dec. 16, 1864. Fry's account of Haddock's career was contained in his letter to Blaine, which was read before the House of Representatives on April 30, 1866 and was published in the *Congressional Globe,* 39 Cong., 1 Sess., pp. 2292-93, and reprinted in Fry, *The Conkling and Blaine-Fry Controversy,* pp. 188-94. This letter contributed importantly to the Blaine-Conkling dispute. The *Standard* reported that when Haddock was living in Watertown before the war, he figured in a balloon ascension in which the "aeronauts" were carried out over Lake Ontario, thought to be drowned, but landed safely in a Canadian forest. *Ibid.*

4 MM 2612. The Haddock court-martial packet contains the "Charges and Specifications," "Trial Transcript," "Conkling's Summation," the "Court's Findings," "Holt's Report," "Haddock's Appeal," and two important letters, "Crandall to Conkling" and "Munroe to Conkling."

5 "Trial Transcript."

6 "Trial Transcript"; "Conkling Summation." At the time of these letters, Crandall had not yet been appointed provost marshal of the 21st District; Colonel D. C. Poole held the post as an interim appointee. One week after Crandall officially assumed the office Haddock gave Richardson a similar letter addressed to him.

7 *Ibid.* One month after his arrest, Haddock sold the horse for two hundred and fifty dollars, half of its purchase price.

8 See above, pp. 88-89, Utica *Herald,* Jan. 6, 1865; *Argus,* Jan. 9, 1865; "Conk-

ling Summation." In Alfred R. Conkling's *Life and Letters of Roscoe Conkling* (New York, 1889), the author states that Richardson had come straight from Haddock to the Oneida supervisors with his offer. P. 220. This must be incorrect.

9 "Trial Transcript"; "Conkling Summation."

10 *Ibid.* On the same day he sold the horse, May 2, Haddock turned over the $2,000 to a government official.

11 *Ibid.* Haddock also tried to dun Richardson for another $2,250 by falsely asserting that it cost him seven hundred and fifty dollars a man to get Tracy to free the three recruits.

12 "Trial Transcript"; "Conkling Summation"; "Crandall Letter"; "Munroe Letter."

13 "Conkling Summation"; "Trial Transcript."

14 *Ibid.*

15 *Ibid.*; HR Report 93, pp. 45, 84-85, 100, 155-56; Utica *Herald*, March 14, 16, 1865.

16 "Munroe Letter."

17 *Ibid.*

18 *Ibid.*

19 HR Report 93, pp. 254-56; "Conkling Summation."

20 HR Report 93, *Ibid;* "Crandall Letter."

21 Commissioner Munroe wrote that "the many contradictory, conflicting, uncertain, and indefinite orders, letters, and communications of Major Haddock are matters which you ought to see and read, that you might better understand the embarrassing circumstances in which the Board of the 21st District have been placed since Major Haddock was appointed AAPMG." "Munroe Letter."

22 These papers, by the way, were all made out by Commander John C. Young at the Brooklyn Naval Rendezvous. See above, pp. 135-36.

23 "Crandall Letter."

24 HR Report 93, pp. 91-99.

25 *Ibid.*; Fry, *The Conkling and Blaine-Fry Controversey*, pp. 201-03.

26 Conkling, pp. 213-14; Fry, p. 191; HR Report 93, p. 156.

27 HR Report 93, pp. 155-56; Fry, pp. 196-99. The fact that Ludington went to Utica to investigate Conkling's appointee, Crandall, rather than to Elmira to investigate Fry's appointee, Haddock, might lend some color to Conkling's contention that Fry's investigation was more designed to embarrass Conkling than to get at the truth. Actually Ludington was ordered to both Elmira and Utica, but he appears to have been partial to the latter place.

28 Fry, p. 199; HR Report 93, pp. 45, 154-55; Conkling, pp. 216-17. In the Blaine-Fry v. Conkling controversy one of the big issues was whether Conkling solicited this appointment from Stanton in order to more effectively protect Crandall and prosecute Haddock. See Appendix C.

29 Conkling, pp. 218, 233-34.

30 "Charges and Specifications"; Conkling, pp. 235-36.

[31] "Conkling Summation."

[32] Conkling, pp. 237-39; "Conkling Summation."

[33] "Charges and Specifications."

[34] "Sentence"; "Holt's Opinion," also printed in HR Report 93, pp. 194-95; Conkling, p. 243-44.

[35] Syracuse *Journal*, Oct. 21, 25, 1865; Fry, pp. 191-92.

[36] "Haddock's Appeal."

Notes to the Appendices.

APPENDIX A.

[1] New York *Times*, March 18, 1864; Buffalo *Morning Express*, March 25, 1864; *Argus*, May 3, 1864; Utica *Herald*, Dec. 24, 1864.

[2] Syracuse *Journal*, Dec. 5, 1864; April 11, June 24, Dec. 26, 1865. See the New York *Times*, March 22, 24, 25, 31, April 1, 3, 1865, and Buffalo *Morning Express*, March 18, 20, 22, 23, 1865, for an account of ward meetings in those cities.

[3] Elliot G. Storke, *History of Cayuga County, New York* (Syracuse, 1879), pp. 136-37.

[4] This amount is incomplete because no final bounty figures from the 15th District were ever submitted to the Provost Marshal General.

[5] These and all subsequent figures on bounty expenditures are taken from PMG, *Final Report*, I, pp. 214-23.

[6] Table II was compiled from material found in PMG, *Final Report*, II, pp. 136-39.

[7] Table III was compiled from material found in PMG, *Final Report*, I, pp. 166, 171-72, 177, 181, 187, 193, 200-01, 205-06.

[8] Table IV was compiled from the same source as Table III.

APPENDIX B.

[1] Earnhart, 132-42.

[2] This study was based on the *OR*; PMG, *Final Report*; United States Census Office, *Population of the United States in 1860* (Wash., 1864), pp. 322-47; *Historical and Statistical Gazeteer of New York State* (Syracuse, 1860). Since the tables have been prepared from all of these sources, no attempt has been made to provide particular citations.

APPENDIX C.

[1] Donald Barr Chidsey, *The Gentleman From New York: A Life of Roscoe Conkling* (New Haven, 1935), p. 92.

2 Congressional *Globe*, 39 Cong., 1 Sess., pp. 141-42, 351-59, 376-89. Chidsey, pp. 68-72.

3 *Ibid.*, pp. 80-81.

4 *Globe*, p. 2151. Earlier, on December 5, 1865, Conkling made an oblique attack on Fry when he presented the following resolution: "That the Committee on Military Affairs be instructed to inquire whether the office of Provost Marshal General and offices subordinate thereto, cannot now advantageously be dispensed with and such business as remains at that Bureau be turned over to some necessary and permanent bureau of the War Department." The resolution was adopted. *Globe*, p. 9.

5 Fry, *Conkling and Blaine-Fry*, pp. 9-10.

6 As Chidsey points out, poor Grant as the most famous American of his day, frequently found his name invoked for and against various causes about which he knew or understood little. Pp. 410-11, fn.

7 *Globe*, pp. 2151-52.

8 *Globe*, pp. 2152-55. On the following day, April 25, Blaine accused Conkling of altering certain remarks he had made on the floor the previous day before they appeared in the *Globe*, so as to render somewhat senseless the unaltered rejoinders by Blaine. *Ibid.*, pp. 2180-81.

9 Fry, pp. 19-20. The text of the letter may be found in the *Globe*, pp. 2292-93 and in HR Report 93, pp. 35-39, and is reprinted in Fry, pp. 188-94.

10 *Globe*, pp. 2292-96. Fry transmitted a number of pertinent documents along with the letter, which are reprinted in Fry, pp. 188-203.

11 Edward Stanwood, *James Gillespie Blaine* (Boston, 1905), p. 71.

12 *Globe*, p. 2294.

13 *Ibid.*, p. 2297.

14 HR Report 93, pp. 1-34, *Globe*, pp. 3935-3942.

15 HR Report 93, pp. 2-5, 10-24.

16 *Ibid.*, pp. 5-10, 24-32.

17 *Ibid.*, pp. 10-11.

18 *Ibid.*, pp. 8-9.

19 *Globe*, pp. 3943-44, 3945, 3947.

20 Fry, pp. 5-15.

21 *Ibid.*, pp. 85-86, 94-97, 88-89.

22 *Ibid.*, pp. 112-14.

23 *Ibid.*, pp. 115-17.

24 *Globe*, pp. 2292.

25 Fry, pp. 57-58, 144-46.

Bibliographic Note.

Although I may be violating a union rule I am not going to list, in this bibliographic note, every book ever written on the Civil War and then casually observe that the list "is merely suggestive." In fact, I am barely going to mention any books at all; I pursue this policy simply because there have barely been any books written on the Civil War "bounty system." Certainly, the two principal volumes bearing on the subject—those by Fred A. Shannon and Jack F. Leach—have been helpful with problems of organization and have provided the broad background against which this specialized study was made. But the real meat of the text was gleaned from a careful study of daily and weekly newspapers in New York state.

Among the published documents, Provost Marshal General James B. Fry's *Final Report* is indispensable to any understanding of the bounty system. Next to it in importance are volumes III and IV of Series III of the *Official Records of the War of the Rebellion.* But more valuable than either of these published sources is the vast array of material on draft administration and recruiting frauds in Record Group 110 of the National Archives. This is virgin soil for the researcher and much work needs to be done there. I have relied most heavily on the "Historical Reports" of the district provost marshals and the investigations of corrupt practices in the "Fraud File" and the "Baker File." Since all monographic and secondary sources used are cited in the footnotes it would serve no purpose to list them again here. A number of works not mentioned in the footnotes were consulted for background and corroborative purposes.

Index.